West Indian
History and Literature

Frank Birbalsingh

First published in Great Britain by Hansib Publications in 2016

Hansib Publications Limited
P.O. Box 226, Hertford
Hertfordshire SG14 3WY UK

info@hansibpublications.com
www.hansibpublications.com

ISBN 978-1-910553-65-7

A CIP catalogue record for this book
is available from the British Library

Production by Hansib Publications Limited

Printed in Great Britain

To Norma

With thanks for a Lifetime of Support

EPIGRAPHS

1   "Nowhere [in Jamaica] was there a black hero depicted on a monument, only Nelson and Queen Victoria. Any book of history began with Columbus. How could history start at the moment of capture?" – Edna Manley.

Quoted in Rachel Manley, *Horses in her Hair: A Granddaughter's Story*, Toronto, Key Porter Books, Ltd., 2008, p. 111.

2   "Mr. Potter had no patrimony, for he did not own himself, he had no private thoughts… he had no thoughts about his past, his future and his present."

Jamaica Kincaid, *Mr. Potter*, New York, Farrar, Straus and Giroux, Ltd., 2002, p. 130.

3.   "To *Not* be Buried in One's Own Land. Now *that* is the Ultimate Insult!"

Caryl Phillips, *A Distant Shore*, London, Vintage, 2004, p.109.

4.   "The rot remains with us: The men are gone."

Derek Walcott, "Ruins of a Great House," *In a Green Night*, London, Jonathan Cape, Ltd., 1962, pp.19-20.

CONTENTS

CONTENTS

ACKNOWLEDGEMENTS

Grateful thanks are due to Harry Ramkhelawan, publisher of the Toronto bi-monthly Indo-Caribbean World, in which many of the chapters in West Indian History and Literature first appeared as book reviews; but the volume is also the result of collaboration with students and colleagues at York University, Toronto, Canada, over thirty-three years, a period during which "Commonwealth Literature" gradually gained world-wide recognition as Post-Colonial Literature. For technical assistance I am grateful to Christine Birbalsingh and Richard Carlson.

PREFACE

Unlike studies based on documentary sources or statistics, *West Indian History and Literature* relies on impressions of literary forms from fiction and poetry to history, biography or memoir. Edna Manley, for instance, wife of Norman Manley, one of the earliest political leaders from the Anglophone Caribbean, relied neither on research nor statistics when, according to her granddaughter Rachel Manley, she asked: "How could [Caribbean] history start at the moment of capture?" Although Edna's mother was a coloured (African-British) Jamaican, her father was British, and she was born in England where she grew up. It was after she married Norman in England and they settled in Jamaica, in 1922, that Edna observed with fresh (English) eyes, the superstitious glorification of British manners and culture, instilled in Jamaicans during their history as a British colony.

As the world knows, Columbus thought he had reached India on his first voyage, in 1492, when he made a mistaken landfall in Guanahini, the Bahamas. The mistake is poetically evoked by George Lamming in his novel *In the Castle of my Skin,* (1953) in the words of the character "Pa," an old man, who intones the sad fate of West Indians in a dirge that seems to issue spontaneously out of sleep, reverie or dream: "A sailor called Christopher followed his mistake...The only certainty these islands inherit is that sailor's mistake." (*In the Castle of my Skin.* (p. 211) Certainty persists, for example, in continuing usage of "West Indies" as an alternative for the Caribbean region, especially the Anglophone Caribbean.

In her novel *Mr. Potter* (2002), Jamaica Kincaid heightens the woe of this tale of: "the great [West Indian] cauldron of misery and small cup of joy that is all of life" (p. 101) by estimating her father's fate as an incoherent mix of mournful events, driven mainly by chance, guesswork or error, indelibly inscribed on his soul with the mark of Columbus, the Caribbean Cain. Addressed in the same pseudo-polite, wickedly mocking title of formal respect throughout the novel, "Mr. Potter" is first held in contempt by the midwife who delivered him. Then, at the age of seven, he is given away by his mother to a Ms. Shepherd before she (his mother) walks out forever into the sea.

We are also told that Mr. Potter was first to be named "Rodney" after one of Britain's naval heroes, described by Kincaid as: "the English maritime criminal George Brydges Rodney;" but instead, Kincaid's father is named "Roderick Nathaniel Potter," and although born in 1922, again according to Kincaid, begins his life in 1492. Later still, after fathering many children, Mr. Potter lives briefly with Kincaid's mother, Annie, who, after a quarrel with him, absconds with Mr. Potter's life savings, making sure he never again sees his daughter Elaine Potter Richardson, aka Jamaica Kincaid.

If incoherence and insignificance are most clearly seen in one individual, Mr. Potter, they become general emblems of West Indian history in Derek Walcott's poem "Ruins of a Great House" (*In a Green Night*, 1962) where they foreshadow themes of decline, decay and death. Standing on grounds of a long abandoned house that belonged to some official, the poem's persona discovers that the plantation grew limes which embitter his musings, and sour his descriptions of the Caribbean as a locale of "every ulcerous crime," "the leprosy of empire" and "the abuse / Of ignorance by Bible and by sword."

While Kincaid invokes the spiritual-psychological corruption of empire, Walcott confronts more physical horrors of slavery in the colonial period, as his persona wanders around ruins, and fears he may have trod on: "the bone/ Of some dead animal or human thing;" for plantation slavery blurs distinctions between animal and human life, and floods the poem with feelings of universal transience. Yet, like human handiwork everywhere, empire and colonialism came and went and, as Walcott's persona admits: "The rot remains with us, the men are gone;" that is to say, the rot of spiritual insignificance as in *Mr. Potter*, or dependence and mimicry as perceived by Edna Manley and George Lamming. And today, more than half a century after "Ruins of a Great House first appeared," Walcott's most recent volume of poems *White Egrets* (2010) updates his vision with fresh observation that newly constructed, twenty-first century, Caribbean shopping malls conceal structures of centuries-old, divisive, colonial plantations with their "rot" of economic exploitation and psychological mimicry.

The wonder is that in spite of these Naipaulian musings on dereliction and disorder, in largely island territories with few natural resources, and divisions of race, ethnicity, class and colour, *West Indian History and Literature* offers observations, opinions and reactions that prove defiant, sustaining, enduring and, in their own way, triumphant except that, as in Shakespeare's great tragedies, the argument here is less about the triumph of good over evil, than about a human capacity to endure trial and tribulation until evil exhausts itself.

INTRODUCTION

In 1655, during the Protectorate of Oliver Cromwell, Britain did not target Jamaica as a worthwhile prize: the island, then in Spanish hands, was only captured after a British force under Admiral William Penn and General Robert Venables, failed in their chief aim of seizing the larger, wealthier Spanish island of Santo Domingo, today, the Dominican Republic and Haiti. As a convenient after-thought to save face or redeem failure, rather than an object of deliberate design, the capture of Jamaica, a less adequately defended trophy, throws light on themes of incoherence, chance or improvisation that are today fixed features in Anglophone, Caribbean history and literature.

In the first chapter of *West Indian History and Literature* Matthew Parker's *The Sugar Barons, Family, Corruption, Empire and War* defines what may be regarded, if not as founding principles, at least as common attitudes and conditions in the colonization of West Indian territories. In Jamaica, for instance, in 1676, the government, judiciary and military were run by a few landowners, and Parker quotes an opinion of the island's governor as: "the openist atheist and most profest immoral liver in the world." Parker also identifies an important difference between British colonists, permanently settled on the American mainland, and British West Indian colonists who were largely absentee, plantation owners, intent on quick riches. American colonists valued: "a stable and rising population, family, long lives, religion," while Caribbean colonists floundered in: "money, alcohol, sex and death."

If the first literary representations of Anglophone Caribbean colonies came from British visitors such as Sir Walter Raleigh with his *The Discovery of Guiana* (1596), Henry Coleridge's *Six Months in the West Indies* (1825) or Anthony Trollope's *The West Indies and the Spanish Main*, (1859) the first novel by a native born author was *Creoleana* (1842) by Isaac Williamson Orderson, a white West Indian, who edited a local newspaper, the *Barbados Mercury*. In a region where African slavery had ended only four years before *Creoleana* appeared, a majority of the population consisted of descendants of slaves, together with a small number of mixed blood or coloured (brown) people and an even smaller élite of economically and culturally dominant Whites.

Post-slavery Caribbean society was rigidly differentiated along lines of race, colour and class inherited from slavery; and literature, institutions, economic structures, social customs and manners all continued to be dominated by race. Black servants continued to work for white masters or employers, and bigoted, racial attitudes prevailed, for example, in one episode of a play by Orderson that appears in the same volume as his novel, where an African prince, formerly enslaved in Barbados, re-visits his African homeland, and is re-united with his family. But such is the unnamed prince's unbounded admiration of white values in West Indian culture where his humanity is devalued by his colour, that he resolutely decides to return to Barbados, against the strongest possible protests and entreaties of his family in Africa.

Another novel *Busha's Mistress or Catherine the Fugitive: A Stirring Romance of the Days of Slavery in Jamaica* (1855) is again by a white author, Cyrus Francis Perkins, a Jamaican whose father was Canadian. The narrative of *Busha's Mistress* unfolds on a Jamaican plantation, Greenside, during slavery, when a coloured woman, Catherine Brown, concubine of a white overseer, is forced into hardship through passionate love and loyalty to her lover. The concrete circumstances of Catherine's saga are brilliantly evoked, even if claims of its "stirring romance" are less than convincing. Unlike Orderson, Perkins argues strongly against slavery as an institution. His argument may be inspired by genuine Christian belief, but what is more memorable are his realistic details about the inhumanity of slavery, for instance, the daily routine of flogging administered to slaves for mere laziness, or the greater horror of amputation of limbs inflicted on runaway slaves.

Novels by black, African or coloured authors began to appear in the mid-nineteenth century, for example, *Adolphus A Tale* which was printed in serial form in *The Trinidadian*, a newspaper in Trinidad, in 1853, and written anonymously probably by the paper's coloured editor, George Numa Dessources. *Adolphus* tells the story of Antonia, daughter of a well-to-do, free, black family, who is abducted by a mulatto/white reprobate Jean de Lopelle Pierre Paul De Guerignon, and rescued by the young black hero, Adolphus. Because of a false accusation, however, Adolphus is forced to seek refuge in Venezuela, although he later returns to Trinidad and is re-united with Antonia.

Perhaps the most memorable novel of this mid-nineteenth century period is *Emmanuel Appadocca or A Blighted Life: A Tale of Buccaneers* (1854) by another coloured Trinidadian, Maxwell Philip. Philip's father was white and his mother a slave. After elementary education in Trinidad, Philip was sent to Britain where he finished his education and trained as a lawyer before returning to Trinidad. Only after being appointed Acting Attorney General of Trinidad seven times does he realise that he would never be appointed in full as Attorney General, because of his colour. Bitterness from this disappointment, no doubt, is what inspires Philip to write, since his novel is driven by a seemingly inexhaustible thirst for revenge.

The novel's chief protagonist, Emmanuel Appadocca, is captain of a crew of blood thirsty pirates, who wreak wholesale slaughter and merciless acts of outrageous cruelty on victims captured at sea. Appadocca's chief discontent is that his father James Wilmington, a white man, neglected to care for him as a child because he (Appadocca) was born out of wedlock. In the novel, Wilmington is captured at sea by Appadocca and his fellow pirates, strapped to a cask, and set adrift to face certain death. Appadocca's revenge seems implacable. On the surface, he resents ill-treatment by his white father, but the unbending inflexibility of his revenge suggests a deeper core of discontent, namely, the historic crime of female, African slaves being regularly violated, with impunity, by white plantation owners and officials.

Jamaica in 1850 or the Effects of Sixteen Years of Freedom on a Slave Colony (1851) sheds unique light on immediate, post-Emancipation conditions in mid-nineteenth century Jamaica and the Anglophone Caribbean. As a citizen of the US which gained independence from Britain sixty-seven years earlier, the author, John Bigelow, has first hand knowledge of the struggle for freedom by former British colonists in the New World. Bigelow visited Jamaica in 1850, and his book is a collection of essays that he wrote for the *Saturday Evening Post*. What he sees convinces him that Jamaica is in a "decrepit condition" because it follows an Anglo-centric, colonial, economic model.

The model worked to the benefit of Britain during slavery, but it collapsed after Emancipation causing one hundred and fifty sugar plantations in Jamaica to be abandoned between 1834 and Bigelow's visit, sixteen years later. During the same period, Bigelow's facts and figures show a similarly sharp reduction in other Jamaican exports, and exports from other British Caribbean colonies as well. All this is strong evidence supporting his claim about the ill-effects of the Anglo-centric economic model, which he illustrates with a striking image:

"The heart [of the model] beats in London, the islanders [West Indians] have no more control of its actions than the finger nails have over the circulation of blood."

As the mere appendage of a larger, Eurocentric structure, Jamaica produces sugar and rum to satisfy the needs of people in Britain, rather than in Jamaica or the Caribbean. There is no incentive really for West Indians to produce rum and sugar or anything else just to supply the British market. The only reason Caribbean plantations flourished during slavery was because African slave labour was enforced by law. Although Bigelow does not mention it, an Anglo-centric economic model also had psycho-sociological effects that instilled and codified cultural imitativeness, subservience and habits of dependence in West Indians.

Not until the early twentieth century did the first West Indian writer, a coloured Jamaican, Herbert George DeLisser (1878-1944) produce a consistent body of work, chiefly journalism and fiction. DeLisser who was self-educated, became editor of Jamaica's leading newspaper *The Gleaner,* and published his first book of essays *In Cuba and Jamaica,* in 1909. In 1920 he also started an annual magazine *Planters Punch* in which many of his ten novels first appeared.

DeLisser is probably best remembered for his melodramatic novel *The White Witch of Rosehall* (1929) the story of an actual plantation mistress, Annie Palmer, reputed for dabbling in witchcraft which she used to dispatch her enemies. DeLisser looked white, was married to a white woman, and held deeply conservative views; but *Jane's Career* (1914) depicts the ground breaking career of a young, black heroine from the Jamaican countryside who shows unusual initiative in gaining work, as a domestic, with a coloured family in the city of Kingston. Dissatisfied with ill-treatment as a domestic, however, Jane musters further determination to secure another job in Kingston in pursuit of greater independence; she finally succeeds when she marries and settles down to family life.

In DeLisser's *Jane's Career* West Indian, post-slavery, social issues reveal an abundant literary source of drama and conflict, waiting to be mined. Such issues are eagerly taken up by a number of authors in Trinidad in the 1930s, for example, C.L.R. James, famous for his writing on cricket and politics, Albert Gomes, well known as a politician, editor and novelist, and Alfred Mendes and Ralph DeBoissière who excelled as writers of fiction. While James was black, Gomes and Mendes were Portuguese, and DeBoissière French creole. DeBoissière who was not of pure French creole or white descent, migrated to Australia where he died at the age of 101 years in 2008.

In his autobiography *Life on the Edge: the Autobiography of Ralph DeBoissière*, (2010) the author admits that social conditions in Trinidad were so divided in the 1920s and 30s that he had to take sides between the British colonial government, and working Trinidadians who included both Africans and Indians: "We [Trinidadians] were a mass. We had yet to be a people...Black or White they were all alike, promoters of a vile colonial system, ready to sing 'Rule Britannia' as often as required." DeBoissière fumed: "No great plot would arise out of the sycophancy of little colonial minds," but he later probably enjoyed the delicious irony of his comments when excellent West Indian authors emerged, including two Nobel prize winners, Derek Walcott in 1992 and V.S. Naipaul in 2001.

Although Alfred Mendes came from a wealthy, business family, his second novel *Black Fauns* (1935) surveys living conditions in a tenement yard with poor, mainly black residents in Port of Spain, Trinidad's capital city. Sexual relations seem flexible, and it is never certain whether female residents pay their own expenses or survive on gifts for sexual favours. Mamitz, a mature, coloured resident with good looks and a taste for dressing up, inspires envy and hostility, particularly in fellow resident Ethelrida, who suspects Mamitz of being a prostitute, and regularly refers to her as "de bitch". In a fierce, bare-fisted fight between these two women, keenly observed by fellow residents, equally divided in support of their chosen champion, no one is seriously injured; but Mamitz's dress is torn, and a court orders Ethelrida afterwards to replace the dress. The remaining impression of the novel is a brawling, bruising, elemental atmosphere of the yard, brilliantly and amusingly evoked by Mendes, and splendidly summed up in sage, hard-earned, practical advice from one resident to another, eager to recover an overpayment made to her lawyer: "Cock will get teeth before anybody get money back from lawyer."

The island of Antigua which first produced cotton and tobacco, turned to sugar cane cultivation in 1647. Samuel Smith (1877-1982) whose great-grand mother had arrived as a slave from Africa, worked on a sugar plantation in Antigua all his life, and by the age of fifty-seven, had fathered forty-three children. Based on interviews which he gave to his grandsons in *To Shoot Hard Labour: The Life and Times of Samuel Smith, An Antiguan Working Man (1877-1982),* one of Smith's stories is about a fellow worker, Henzel Weathered, whose extraordinary strength earned him the nickname "All Man Giant." In about 1890, Henzel agreed to help with preparations for a community harvest festival, but unwittingly ate bitter cassava the night before the event, and became too sick to attend. The next day, he was punished by estate authorities with a barbaric sentence of four months in jail, forty-eight lashes, twelve at the end of each month, plus a six-year ban from the estate; he was also locked to a seventy-five-pound metal ball, although his lashes were later reduced to twelve because of his hard work.

After he served his sentence, Henzel worked at another estate until he suddenly died, but Smith is sceptical about this end to his story: "the official talk was that he [Henzel] died of yellow fever. No coroner's inquest for black people in those days. When nega man dead, he done." Smith also speculates that Henzel may have been killed by a fellow black worker, out of envy or jealousy. What is most striking is blank, official indifference toward black workers, the cruel exploitation of their labour, and their humiliation and demoralization during the immediate, post-slavery, colonial period of Caribbean history.

In 1838, abolition of slavery may have promised change, but according to Cecil Foster's portrait of Barbados in his novel *Independence*, (2014) apart from superficial changes, the island had not greatly improved by 1966, the year of independence, when conditions of poverty and lack of opportunity drove many Bajan families to seek better opportunities in richer countries, abroad, particularly in Britain. As one character in *Independence* claims: "People so Br'ek. They Can't be Br'ek no More."

That Bajans should be in flight from Barbados which, a century and a half earlier, was a regional leader in news, culture and fashion, and was still the most orderly and best administered British Caribbean colony, surely displays decline rather than progress, at least, for a majority of Bajans! Rather it confirms Barbados as another appendage, part of an Anglo-centric, economic and cultural model that fulfils British rather than Caribbean aims or interests. But immigration itself is no bed of roses, and *Independence* outlines its human cost when the novel's young protagonist, Christopher Lucas, and his brothers are left in Barbados, under the fragile auspices of an ageing grandmother, waiting in vain for promised money to take them to join their immigrant parents in Britain.

If descendants of African slaves did not fare well in British Caribbean colonies, neither did descendants of indentured workers who were brought from India between 1838 and 1917. As the largest ethnic group among indentured workers, Indians who assumed plantation tasks formerly done by the freed Africans, remained on plantations after smaller ethnic groups like Portuguese and Chinese had moved into urban areas and, in time, became numerous enough to form about twenty percent of the Anglophone Caribbean population. Indians are sometimes credited with having saved the sugar industry, especially in Guyana and Trinidad, the two Anglophone Caribbean territories of largest, Indian settlement. It is why, until around independence in the 1960s, Indians were generally regarded as simple agriculturists or farmers.

One of the earliest fictional representations of indentured Indians in the Caribbean is found in DeLisser's novel *The Cup and the Lip* (1953) where Indian characters appear as an exotic minority, mere misfits, or cultural outsiders in the midst of an overwhelming majority of African-Jamaicans. Of the Indian characters, Ramsingh is timekeeper in a sugar factory, while his wife Marie is described chiefly in terms of animal imagery as having:" a kinship with the tigress of her ancestral India's jungles," or a body like: "that of a snake rearing itself to strike. "To one character: "Marie can spit and snarl and use her claws."

Similar unflattering terms appear in a novella by another Jamaican author, Olive Senior, in her volume *Arrival of the Snake-Woman and other Stories* (1989) which frankly describes the heroine in her novella "Arrival of the Snake Woman" as a "snake-woman," otherwise known as "Miss Coolie" or as "the heathen" or "witch," whose sari or Indian dress is considered a "Thin and sinful piece of cloth." No one could be more alien. For all that, by the end of the story, Miss Coolie's son Biya has become a lawyer and, through exceptional energy and initiative, Miss Coolie transforms herself into an entrepreneur, and a business tycoon with "dry goods, grocery, bar, butchershop" together with "her garden, her goats, her higglering."

Literary representations of Indian, indentured experience by Guyanese and Trinidadian authors tend to be different from those by Jamaican authors since they rely less on stereotypes. It is true that *Corentyne Thunder* (1941) by Guyanese Edgar Mittelholzer, one of the most gifted, Caribbean novelists, contains stereotypes of Indians as illiterate, money-grubbing peasants, but *The Shadow Bride* (1988) by Roy Heath, another African-Guyanese novelist, is a fictional study of Indian-Guyanese that is almost as finely detailed as V.S. Naipaul's portrait of his fellow Indian-Trinidadians in his celebrated novel *A House for Mr Biswas.* (1961)

Although it lacks the literary quality of novels by Heath or Naipaul, Clem Maharaj's *The Dispossessed* gives an unsparing description of conditions on Highlands sugar plantation, in Trinidad, around the 1950s. The Indian indentured workers are housed in huts, shacks or ramshackle barracks where their only "amenities" are smoking, drinking and gambling. Women workers suffer the most. Suraji, for instance, wallows in family problems and financial instability and declines into a common street woman, who is sexual prey to any man willing to buy her a drink. On the whole, the workers' spirit is broken at Highlands as we detect from a sense of finality in their lament: "We is cane people and notting else, and when the cane is done, we finish."

Golconda: Our Voices Our Lives (2009) collects comments and memories from villagers of Golconda, a former sugar estate in Trinidad. Villagers recall conditions not very different from those in *The Possessed*: "Sometimes I use to go to school without anything to eat and I drink water till I come home," and when another villager asserts: "They [indentured workers] worked as slaves but were never slaves," he puts his finger on a politically divisive issue in Guyana and Trinidad, where ethnic differences are inflamed by claims that one ethnic group suffered greater colonial victimization than the other, and therefore deserve greater entitlement to Caribbean space.

Since it is impossible to measure dimensions of suffering or victimization, the issue may never be fully resolved. Whereas Indians were indentured in the Caribbean for about seventy years, Africans were enslaved in Guyana for two centuries or more, which makes it likely that Africans were more liable to abuse partly because of their longer period of servitude, and partly because, as slaves, they were legal property which entailed more scope for abuse. Also, Africans retained little of their own languages or religions, whereas many Indians retained Islamic and Hindu religious beliefs, and even Indian languages. But now, fifty years after independence, when creole practices increasingly influence the language, religion and culture of both ethnic groups, argument about slavery or indenture conferring greater legitimacy to Caribbean space appears correspondingly less helpful or even relevant.

Increasing creole influence on Indians is seen in the poetry of Lelawattee Manoo-Rahming, an Indian-Trinidadian woman married to a white, Bahamian. For Manoo-Rahming, the evolving process of creolization is one of cultural adaptation not to a single synthetic, artificial culture, imposed by one politically dominant ethnic group, but to a more personal version of creole culture. In Manoo-Rahming's second volume of poems *Immortelle and Bhandaara Poems,* the persona requests services from Hindu goddesses Bhavani Durga and Shakti, as well as from an indigenous, Caribbean goddess, Coatrische, and the Greek queen of night Hecate. The title itself of Manoo-Rahming's second volume asserts a mixed, creole temper in her poetry, since the immortelle is a well known shade tree in Trinidad & Tobago, while "Bhandaaraa" borrows a Hindu, metaphysical structure in the poem.

This instinct for variety and mixing also appears in linguistic coinages such as "ovadotcom" and "planesforpeople," for mixing implies cultural unity as in a comparison of Trinidad's own Piparo Forest with the fabled forest in the Hindu sacred text the *Ramayana*. Similarly, the Hindu doctrine of predestination is invoked in "Mirror Glimpses" when discovery of a scorpion in a bag of cookies foretells the death of the persona's sister Sally. In Manoo-Rahming's poetry, the divisiveness of Caribbean history, embedded in a value system based on race, class and colour, the legacy of slavery/ indenture is either ignored or negated by unifying gestures of creole mixing.

Since independence, Caribbean writers and people in general have formed a diaspora particularly in Britain, Canada and the US. Caryl Phillips, for instance, was born in St. Kitts and taken as a baby to Britain where he established his reputation as a writer, not only of the Anglophone Caribbean diaspora, but of a wider, African diaspora now scattered in Britain, the Caribbean and the US. In his seventh novel, aptly named, *A Distant Shore*, Phillips probes the fate of African refugees in Britain, during the 1980s and 90s. Immigrants in this era have a more difficult time than those who struggled, in the 1950s and 60s, mainly with adjustment to new-fangled customs in a modern industrial metropolis. Now, in *A Distant Shore*, new arrivals are not even sure in which racial or ethnic category they are classified, whether "immigrant" "new migrant" or "newcomer."

The chief protagonist and narrator in Phillips's novel is Dorothy a fifty-five-year-old English school teacher in a small town in the North of England. Not only has Dorothy's husband walked out of their thirty-year marriage, but her sister has walked away from her male partner of twenty-five years after discovering her preference for a female partner, and Dorothy is spat upon by the wife of a Muslim, corner shop owner suspicious of Dorothy's sexual interest in her husband. Worst of all, Dorothy is forced into early retirement for harassing a supply teacher at her school who was her former lover.

Dorothy's views of events are twinned with those of a second narrator, Gabriel, known as Solomon Bartholomew after he arrived in Britain. Gabriel is a refugee from Africa where, as Major Hawk, he fought in his country's civil war under the command of Colonel Bloodshed. Only when he reflects on his tenuous position as an outsider in Britain, does Gabriel recall words from Bloodshed that are a perfect fit for his fluid, nondescript,, diasporic condition as refugee, immigrant, new migrant, or newcomer: "To *not* be buried in one's own land. Now *that* is the ultimate insult." The fact that Gabriel is later murdered by a gang of white youths and his body thrown into a canal, or that the account of his death may be a figment of Dorothy's unreliable memory, not only intensifies the truth of Colonel Bloodshed's pronouncement, but validates its insight into the spiritual pain and peril of diasporic homelessness.

Whether it is homelessness, or a sense of psychic disorientation, Inky, at the age of eighteen, the youngest of the protagonists in Guyanese Sharon Maas's novel *The Small Fortune of Dorothea Q*, (2015) was born and grew up in London, England, and knows nothing of Guyana, homeland of her parents. Reflecting on thoughts of her mother, Rika, who left her homeland of Guyana since she was sixteen, Inky wonders whether: "the texture of Guyana merged into her [Rika's] consciousness as London has in mine? Did she deny that sense of home…and if so, was she somehow damaged, stunted, broken? .Maybe deep down inside she missed that sense of home. And family." More to the point, Inky wonders about her own notion of home: "I grew nostalgic for a family, a home I'd never known." If Inky is right, a diasporic sense of homelessness can span generations. As Inky's grandmother Dorothea queries, with irresistible logic: "If you don't know where you come from, how you going know where you going?"

Cecil Foster's memoir *Island Wings* (1998) continues the story of his family started in his novel *Independence* in which the author and his brothers are left in Barbados, waiting to follow their parents who have joined an exodus of Barbadian immigrants to Britain. Weakening or fracture of family bonds is one of many testing aspects of diasporic experience. Paradoxically, the author and his brothers prevail against odds and start professional careers in Barbados, while their parents who reach the promised land of Britain are less fortunate. Their mother suffers serious illness, and their father Freddie, a talented musician and army veteran, is so shattered by disappointment and grievance against the British government, that he resorts to total seclusion, living away from everyone. As someone who began with talent, ambition and promise, Freddie may be contrasted with Joseph Conrad's Kurtz who, as a European emissary of light in the Congo, eventually encounters inner demons that illuminate darkness inside himself. On the other hand, like Jamaica Kincaid's Mr. Potter, Freddie discovers his own West Indian demons of incoherence, insignificance and confusion.

The poetry of Ian McDonald, a white West Indian, presents stronger Conradian parallels. McDonald is fond of saying he is Trinidadian by birth, Guyanese by adoption, and West Indian by conviction, a sort of proprietary claim no ordinary West Indian would dare to make, for McDonald is an emissary of light to West Indians, as Kurtz was to the Congolese. But having reached the age of 82, McDonald now considers themes of mortality and transience in *River Dancer*, his most recent collection of poems. When, in one poem, McDonald's persona argues that even if he were to give all his wealth to the poor it would not help them, like Kurtz, he confronts his own heart of darkness.

In *Harvey River: A Memoir for My Mother and Her People* (2007), the Jamaican author Lorna Goodison confronts demons too and gains illumination when she suggests that her mother's district, Harvey River in Jamaica, consists of remnants, bits and pieces, hypnotic social and cultural leftovers from the actions and experience of others, whether from Britain, Africa, Asia, or wherever, and that daily, human transactions are largely a matter of mixing memories and matching fragments, improvising, devising and creating in a continuing, daily, Caribbean effort to survive and endure. [For references to most quotations in the Introduction, see relevant chapters e.g. for references to Bigelow's book on p.9 of the Introduction see Chapter 12. The only exceptions are references to p. 123; p.147, and p. 69 of DeLisser's novel *The Cup and the Lip*, and p. 8 and p. 40 of Olive Senior's *Arrival of the Snake Woman* both of which appear in the Bibliography.]

"MONEY, ALCOHOL, SEX AND DEATH"

Matthew Parker
The Sugar Barons: Family, Corruption, Empire and War,
London, Hutchison, 2011, pp.446. ISBN 9780091925833

The Sugar Barons: Family, Corruption, Empire and War tells a story of British Caribbean colonies which extracted enormous wealth out of sugar cultivation and the labour of African slaves, from the early seventeenth century at least until 1838, when slavery was abolished in British territories. The author Matthew Parker relies on official records as well as personal letters and documents written by sugar planters, preachers and other correspondents, to create a captivating vision of European nations scrambling among themselves, mostly out of greed, four centuries ago, for possession of defenceless Caribbean islands and other territories.

Other crops were first tried - tobacco, cotton, indigo, ginger, cassava, sweet potatoes, plantains and other foodstuffs - but once sugar cane technology was mastered by the Spanish on the Canary Islands, and particularly by the Portuguese on offshore African islands like San Tome and Madeira and, in Brazil after 1500, the sugar industry spread like wildfire across the Caribbean.

Decline of Spanish power, by the end of the sixteenth century, opened sluice gates for other European nations, chiefly France, England and Holland, but also Prussia, Denmark and Sweden, to join in. What Parker bluntly regards as a coldly calculating and cynical enterprise of piracy and plunder cannot reassure modern-day apologists of empire: "from the earliest days of the Spanish empire, the Caribbean was a constant theatre of violence and war, declared or not – infested by privateers, pirates, corsairs, call them what you will. It was a lawless space, a paradise for thieves, smugglers and murderers." (p. 18) During the early seventeenth century, inspired by a fresh sense of anti-Catholic and anti-Spanish nationalism, English cut-throat slave traders and adventurers like Drake and Hawkins joined in the gory game, as they saw it, of Protestantism and profit.

Sir Thomas Warner first landed settlers in St. Kitts, in 1623, and a few years later another British colony was established in Barbados with white workers drawn from poorer classes of people, religious dissenters or the politically disaffected who indentured themselves in return for free passage to the colony, subsistence and wages. In 1630, the population of Barbados was 2,000; in 1636 about 10, 000; and, according to Parker, Barbados would become: "the cradle of the British West Indian sugar empire;" (p. 171) for Barbados established a prototype for sugar monoculture in the Caribbean and, by 1645, sugar accounted for forty percent of its agricultural acreage, and the island no longer produced its own food.

By 1700, Barbados was the wealthiest colony in the world, with more than 20,000 African slaves, and by the late eighteenth century, sugar accounted for ninety-three percent of Barbadian exports. Such was the economic prestige of slavery that a slave-trading company, the Royal Adventurers into Africa, attracted investors such as King Charles the Second and, for a time, even the philosopher John Locke, while planters (sugar barons) like James Drax acquired enough legendary wealth from sugar to give currency to a new phrase "rich as a West Indian." Starting with only three hundred pounds in Barbados, Drax could soon afterwards buy an estate in England worth ten thousand pounds.

In "The Grandees" the second section of *The Sugar Barons*, Parker expatiates on the prosperity of men like Drax who returned in triumph to England where he was knighted and became influential in politics. But such ostentatious prosperity did not convey the full reality of West Indian conditions. In Jamaica, for instance, where the sugar industry began to flourish around 1676, a handful of land owners also ran the government, judiciary and military, and the Governor Sir Thomas Modyford is described by a contemporary as: "the openist atheist and most profest immoral liver in the world," (p. 140) while the epigraph to Chapter Fifteen of *The Sugar Barons* quotes from a Baptist minister, James Phillipo, who describes West Indian colonies as: "one revolting scene of infamy, bloodshed and unmitigated woe, of insecure peace and open disturbance, of the abuse of power, and of the reaction of misery against oppression." (p. 180)

Wealth gained from slavery and oppression was the dilemma behind the long drawn out controversy over the ending of the slave trade in 1807, and outright abolition of slavery itself about thirty years later. Decline and decadence inevitably set in through a variety of factors, from soil exhaustion caused by intensive agriculture to widespread corruption of managers, merchants, money lenders, crooked governors, frequent wars between Britain and other European nations, occasional outbreaks of disease and natural disasters, American Independence which cut valuable trading links between the Caribbean and former American colonies, competition from new sugar producers in Java and Madagascar that lowered the price of sugar, and growth of the beet sugar industry in Europe.

Parker puts his finger on the central problem of the colonial Caribbean: "the exercise of almost unlimited authority over a turbulent community." (p. 190). When, for instance, the Governor of Barbados, Christopher Codrington attempted to improve conditions for African slaves, Parker comments: "he [Codrington] came to understand the brutal realities of the garrison society that slavery had created, where violence and fear were crucial weapons to protect the numerically inferior planters." (p. 201) Codrington belonged to one of the richest plantation families in Barbados, and his Christian benevolence in "treating enslaved Africans as people rather than property" not only "undermined the whole foundation of their society and prosperity," but contradicted "the system on which his family had built their fortune." (p. 206)

Perhaps the most valuable discovery in *The Sugar Barons* comes from analysis of links between British Caribbean and mainland American colonies. While the latter were regarded as places of permanent settlement, Caribbean colonies were seen merely as temporary residences for absentee, plantation owners intent on quick riches. In Parker's view, Caribbean colonists lacked the persevering spirit of American colonists, not to mention: "a stable and rising population, family, long lives, religion. Instead [in Caribbean colonies] there was money, alcohol, sex and death." (p. 294)

HISTORICAL FICTION OR FICTIONALISED HISTORY?

Ron Ramdin
The Griot's Tale Victoria, Canada, Trafford Publishing, 2009,
pp.480. ISBN 978-1-4251-8406-3.

Born in Trinidad, biographer, editor, historian and novelist Ron
Ramdin lives in the United Kingdom. His first novel *Rama's
Voyage* (2004) dramatises the experience of Indians who went to
the Caribbean as indentured workers mainly in the second half
of the nineteenth century, while his second novel *The Griot's Tale*
explores efforts to abolish African slavery, and observe severe
living conditions endured by freed Africans in England, during
the late eighteenth and early nineteenth century.

The narrator of *The Griot's Tale,* Adamah, is a freed African
who lives in a poor district of London where he acquires
notoriety as a "rabble-rouser, radical, passion-charged moralist,
persuasive speaker and preacher" (p. 359) among fellow "Black-
birds" as people of colour were derisively known, around 1807,
when the African slave trade was abolished in England. Adamah
composes *The Griot's Tale* while awaiting the verdict of his trial
for murder which he later loses; but he wishes his story to be seen
as: "a faithful record of the truth of my life and times, a story
that I'd like to be passed on not only among those who live now
but also to those yet unborn." (p. 316)

By his account, Adamah's mother Mina was only sixteen
when she was kidnapped in her West African homeland, and
taken as a slave on a ship sailing to an unnamed Caribbean

island. After being raped by her English owner, Mina gives birth to Adamah, and is later beaten for having a child when she lands. Adamah has nothing but praise for his mother whom he fondly remembers for teaching him about her African oral tradition, a priceless repository of learning and wisdom, out of respect for which he is named Adamah, "the Griot" or story teller. By the age of eleven, Adamah learns to speak English, converts to Christianity, and is taken to England where he is given freedom. At the time, English ladies of fashion fancied black boys as trophies, and after joining the household of Lady Candida, Adamah writes: "I'd graduated from being a plantation slave and servant in the island 'Big House' to a human pet" (p. 99) [in London.]

He eventually settles in a poor neighbourhood populated mainly by: "mendicants, missionaries, beggars, boxers, writers and preachers of all kinds from different lands," (p.289) around Sugar Loaf Lane, where most of the action of *The Griot's Tale* is enacted, as Adamah becomes Minister of Flagstaff Square Church, and conducts a vigorous programme of speaking, writing and agitating against slavery and the slave trade. He also marries an English woman Rachele, and endures much grief when they lose their first child.

Once, during brisk and vigorous agitation, when he produces essays such as "Our common Rights" and "Religion, Hypocrisy and Slavery," and often criticises white Abolitionists for parading insincere humanitarian motives, Adamah agrees, along with "'brothers' and fellow-pleaders of our 'Cause,'" (p. 408) to visit the home of Sir Henry Meadows, a Government Minister, for a discussion of local issues of unemployment and poverty. Upon gaining entry to the Minister's home, however, Adamah and his three "friends" are confronted by Sir Henry's butler, and in the ensuing fracas, one "friend" stabs the butler with a pike which he then gives to Adamah before he and his mates escape, leaving Adamah holding the murder weapon that eventually leads to his arrest. Only afterwards does it dawn on Adamah that one of his "friends" was a police informer.

In a narrative crowded with dozens of characters, copious descriptions of people, places and issues, including names of streets, buildings, and titles of books, pamphlets and newspapers, Ramdin deserves credit for formidable research in dramatising actual events and re-creating historical personalities like Mr. Malleson, a Member of Parliament, probably based on William Wilberforce, the British MP who helped to pilot the Abolition bill through the British House of Commons in 1834. Like the historical Thomas Clarkson who wrote a major anti-slavery text, Ramdin's character Mr. Bizbee is also indefatigable in collecting evidence of the manifold injustices of slavery. Fictional names also appear in the *Griot's Tale* for historical African authors who help to expose abuses of slavery.

Like other writers of historical fiction, Ramdin steers as dexterously as he can between history and fiction, without slipping completely into either. Richly textured details and graceful, fluent writing emphasise the historical value of his version of late eighteenth and early nineteenth century London, and the day-to-day activities of Abolitionists; but they also tend to give *The Griot's Tale* the impression of a largely journalistic guide to the Abolition saga within a stark, Hogarthian context of gin drinking, boxing, and misery of Blacks and other jobless, starving people in London. This impression is supported by devotion of the final one third of the novel to an interrogation of the narrator by the Reverend William Bragg, and a protracted discussion of moral and philosophical issues arising out of African slavery.

It is strange how revelations both about Reverend Bragg and the narrator, during their discussion, stimulate feelings of surprise, suspense, even shock that greatly enhance the appeal of the narrative, purely as fiction, considering the presence of numerous minor characters, and the superabundant, mainly polemical interest of multifarious discussions. Yet on the whole, despite its bravura exhibition of scholarship, the fictional integrity of *The Griot's Tale* is further enhanced by the irony of the narrator's unjust hanging for a murder he did not commit, and his turbulent family relationships, firstly with Rachele, then with their daughter Elizabeth who writes a moving Epilogue about her subsequent connection with Reverend Bragg.

WEST INDIAN DNA

Jamaica Kincaid
Mr. Potter, New York, Farrar, Straus and Giroux, 2002,
pp. 195. ISBN 0-374-21494-8

While enchanting portraits of the author's mother Annie
Victoria Richardson appear in earlier novels such as *Annie
John,* (1985) *The Autobiography of my Mother,* (1996) and *My
Brother* (1997) the last of which focuses on her brother Devon
who died of AIDS in 1996, Jamaica Kincaid's *Mr. Potter,* the
fifth volume of the family's fictional saga, scans the life of her
father Mr. Potter who was born in 1922, in Antigua, when
the island was still a British colony. The author's first-person-
narrator technique in her previous novels works as brilliantly
in *Mr. Potter* for which she probably deserves extra credit, since
the novel creates events that her illiterate father could neither
have understood nor recorded for himself.

No doubt the focus of her first person technique on family
affairs, in so many texts, may arouse suspicion of incestuousness
or narrowness, for Kincaid's mother is never far away, not even
in *Lucy (*1991), her second novel which surveys the author's early
experience in the US, while still registering the brooding effect
of Annie Richardson in distant Antigua. It only goes to show
the bewitching appeal of Kincaid's first person family narratives,
and the supreme success of their confessional intensity.

Mr. Potter takes the author's style to its ultimate limit since
it holds us spellbound by a dirge-like, meditative chant in

which the speaker/narrator, daughter of Mr. Potter, dutifully intones what might be taken for a benediction on her father's pitiful life, perhaps more elegy than benediction, lamenting the woeful predicament not only of the author's father, but of her family, community and nation, all West Indians, descended mostly from Africans brought during previous centuries as slaves to the Caribbean, where today they survive in a condition unflinchingly appraised by George Lamming as one of "sprawling dereliction" in his classic novel *In the Castle of my Skin* (1953). Look, for instance, at the narrator's estimate of her father as someone: "not unfamiliar with upheavals and displacements and murder and terror; his very existence in the world in which he lived had been made possible by such things;" (p. 7) or Mr. Potter: "did not curse the day on which he was born, he only cursed the day when each and every one of his ancestors was born." (p. 58)

Referred to as "Mr. Potter" throughout the novel, until his death at the age of seventy, the narrator's father was the last child of Nathaniel Potter, a fisherman who was: "the father of eleven children with eight altogether different mothers." (p. 36) At his birth, we are told, Mr. Potter was held in contempt by the local midwife who delivered him, then his mother Elfrida Robinson turns out as someone whose life at sixteen: "was already shrivelled and pinched," (p. 64) before, at the age of twenty-three, when her son was seven years old, she: "grew tired of him and gave him away to a woman named Mrs. Shepherd, and then she walked into the sea," (p. 70) and drowned herself.

Such rooted and endemic personal tragedy is not the result of some exotic or psychotic excrescence, but insidious proof of intimate, umbilical connection between the Anglophone Caribbean and British colonialism; for Mr. Potter's mother first considers naming him "Rodney" after "the English maritime criminal George Brydges Rodney," (p. 64) although she eventually settles for "Roderick Nathaniel Potter" because:

"she wanted a name that had no meaning at all for her;" (p. 64) and we are later told: "Mr. Potter's lifetime began in the year fourteen hundred and ninety-two but he had been born on the seventh day of January, nineteen hundred and twenty-two," (p. 177) reminding us of deep-seated dubiety in the very DNA of West Indians, since 1492 is the year when Columbus is CREDITED with DISCOVERY of the Caribbean.

The rest of the narrative follows this false, shifting colonial trajectory: after he is taught to drive by Mr. Shepherd, his foster father, Mr. Potter becomes a taxi driver employed by a foreigner, the Lebanese businessman Mr. Shoul. It was unusual for Mr. Shepherd, as a black Antiguan, to acquire a car: "he had not expected ever to own a motor car." (p. 91) Like his father before him, Mr. Potter fathers several children by different women before he meets the narrator's mother Annie Richardson, who works as an assistant in the office of Dr. Weizenger, a Jewish dentist who had fled from Czechoslovakia during World War Two. Mr. Potter and Annie live together briefly, and Annie has four abortions until she is seven months pregnant with the narrator, and has a bitter quarrel with Mr. Potter. Annie then: "took all of Mr. Potter's savings money he had stored in a crocus bag under their bed," (p. 142) and leaves so that Mr. Potter never sees their baby, named "Elaine Potter Richardson," partly after a daughter of Mr. Shoul for whom Annie also works.

As hinted above, the real triumph of *Mr.Potter* is a style that repeats phrases with a kind of choric, incantatory regularity that sounds hypnotic, mesmerising, while it increases both the poetic intensity and moral depth of Kincaid's inspired and sombre exploration of the DNA of West Indian civilisation, for example, through comments on the collective lives of her characters: "the small, irregular stumble that their existence had made in the vast smoothness that was the turning of the earth on its axis was no more and was not celebrated or even regretted by anyone or anything;" (p. 55) such withering insignificance springs not simply from awareness of our common insignificance as hapless human beings within a mysterious, celestial universe, but from Kincaid's deeply tormented consciousness of the additional, man-made or colonial origin of dereliction and despair in the Caribbean where: "Mr. Potter had no patrimony for he did not own himself, he had no private thoughts...he had no thoughts about his past, his future and his present." (p. 130)

"INDIFFERENCE AS COLD AND AS ICY AS DEATH"

Maxwell Philip
Emmanuel Appadocca; or A Blighted Life: A Tale of the Boucaneers, Amherst, University of Massachusetts Press, 1997, pp. 275. ISBN 1-55849-076-0

Edward Appadocca; or A Blighted Life: A Tale of the Boucaneers, first written in 1854 by African-Trinidadian, Michael Maxwell Philip (1829-1888), is edited by Selwyn Cudjoe who also contributes "Afterword: *Emmanuel Appadocca* the first Anglo-Caribbean Novel," to this re-publication of Philip's novel. Cudjoe correctly claims that critics had placed the origin of the Anglophone Caribbean novel around the start of the twentieth century but, in addition to *Emmanuel Appadoca*, another novel, *Adolphus A Tale,* appeared anonymously in a Trinidadian newspaper in 1853, and tells a similar story of a mixed blood (African-European) Trinidadian.

Maxwell Philip who was the son of an African slave and a white father from the planter class, was born in South Naparima, Trinidad, and after elementary school in the town of San Fernando, received secondary education in Britain, where he also trained as a lawyer. Later, in Trinidad, he held several government positions, for example, as mayor of Port of Spain; but after serving as acting attorney general seven times, he realised he was being denied the highest position of attorney general of Trinidad because of his mixed race.

Brief epigraphs from almost the entire canon of Shakespeare's plays appear at the beginning of each chapter of Philips's novel. Not only that, Philips displays a comprehensive knowledge of Victorian novels of mystery, romance and adventure, historical novels of Sir Walter Scott, fiction of Dickens, the Bronte sisters, Thackeray and American writers such as Harriet Beecher Stowe, famous for *Uncle Tom's Cabin* (1852). For a West Indian, in 1854, to imbibe elements of narrative style from such a wide range of the best known mid-nineteenth century writers in Britain and the US, and blend them into a realistic Caribbean milieu and atmosphere, together with his own creole subject matter, speech and manners is a remarkable and inspired feat of literary innovation and original creativity!

The balance, rhythm and fluency of Philip's writing, together with the colourful imagery of his Caribbean scenes, whether on land or sea, reflect not only acute powers of observation and literary versatility, but an ingrown, patriotic connection to his homeland, as seen in a single sentence of his magnificent description of the Gulf of Paria: "Above these are seen the blossoming coral-trees with their scarlet flowers, that chequer the densely wooded hills, and stand amidst the dense foliage that surrounds them, marked and conspicuous like thousands of growing wreaths, that administering nymphs eternally offer to tropical nature in gratitude for her marvellous and beautiful works." (p. 35) Hypnotic language summons up an almost fairy tale atmosphere. Perhaps *Emmanuel Appadocca* could be dismissed as an unrealistic fantasy if lavish devotion to tropical Caribbean splendour were all, but like so much else in Caribbean literature, the region's Edenic surroundings become blighted in Philip's novel, and serve as a theatre of grisly cruelty and human degradation.

From its opening scene, *Emmanuel Appadocca* is steeped in alarming violence with cut-throat pirates seizing a vessel by force and, after wholesale slaughter, showing the unnamed pirate captain strutting on deck, brazenly dividing the spoils among his blood thirsty comrades. An old sailor, for instance, relates the gross exploit of a commodore who: "took his sword, opened [a captive's] breast, tore out his heart and bit it." (p. 28) Only later is the pirate captain revealed as Emmanuel Appadocca, and one of his captives as James Wilmington, his white father who neglected to care for Emmanuel as a child because he was born out of wedlock. Emmanuel then straps Wilmington to a cask and sets him adrift to face certain death at sea to satisfy the implacable thirst for revenge which is at the core of his novel, and drives him to seek retribution for the historic crime of white Caribbean, plantation owners in regularly violating African slave women with impunity. As Emmanuel admits: "an offended mother... [is] the only – friend that I had in this bitter, bitter world." (p. 228) Miraculously, however, Wilmington survives and reaches the island of St Thomas where Emmanuel is arrested for piracy and setting Wilmington adrift.

The rest of the novel then meanders through many melodramatic twists and turns, typical of lesser works of nineteenth century English fiction, as Emmanuel encounters grave dangers and thrilling adventures, through all of which he passes safely, until he is reunited with his faithful friends Lorenzo and Jack Jimmy, and regains control of his pirate schooner. Emmanuel's creed of piracy is nourished by: "indifference, as cold and as icy as death, indifference, such as nature can admit but only when every fibre of feeling is burnt into hard callousness by the searing iron of some deep unpardonable offence." (p. 70)

If this creed sounds exaggerated or over-indulgent, consider the amoral universe of Caribbean slavery in which white power is not only supreme but impregnable, and all that black slaves could do, for example, through exploits like those of the West African trickster figure Anansi, was to harass or harm, and stir up ructions, but never destroy the perverse but dominant, white superstructure. Emmanuel's ironic role may thus be seen to commit wrong (piracy) against Whites which seems right, and inflict evil (revenge) against racism which appears good; and when his Venezuelan lover Feliciana begs him to renounce revenge, we may better understand the solemn confession that his only salvation will be, at the moment of his death: "to shut my eyes and say, 'mankind, you have among you nothing that is dear to me.'"(p. 181) Within terms of romantic melodrama, Emmanuel's bewildering gesture of self-sacrifice is exactly what raises him to the stature of a tragic hero, and *Emmanuel Appadocca* to the first major work of fiction by a black West Indian.

BIGOTRY OF A WHITE RULING CLASS

J.W. Orderson
Creoleana and *The Fair Barbadian and Faithful Black*,
Oxford, Macmillan Education, 2002, pp. 264.
ISBN 0 333 776062

Creoleana, a novel written in 1842 by J.W. Orderson, is
announced by John Gilmore, editor of *Creoleana* and *The
Fair Barbadian and Faithful Black* as: "the first novel of
the Anglophone Caribbean to be written by somebody
demonstrably a native of the region." (p. 2) As editor of a series
of Caribbean texts first published before the twentieth century,
Gilmore also includes a play by the same author - *The Fair
Barbadian and Faithful Black*.

Born Isaac Williamson Orderson in Barbados, in 1767,
the author worked on his father's newspaper the *Barbados
Mercury*, becoming editor in 1787 and, in 1795, sole
proprietor, a position he did not relinquish until 1810. Editing
a Barbadian newspaper gave Orderson unique insight into
the workings both of the economic and social structure of
a model, British Caribbean, island colony at the time; but
events in his novel which occur in the 1780s and 90s, elicit
feelings of nostalgia for his youth in someone writing only
five years before his death in 1847. This may explain why
Barbados seems somewhat idealised in *Creolana* as a Utopia
of peace, happiness and order, as well as generosity, kindness,
hospitality, benevolence and more.

The truth is that, as a slave colony in 1816, only two decades after events in *Creoleana*, Barbados witnessed a major slave uprising, Bussa's rebellion; but nothing could be more remote from Orderson's narrative than the brutal, British colonial practices that sparked rebellion. Instead, *Creoleana* delights in the opinion of a strongly paternalistic and intensely loyal monarchist whose narrow, Anglo-centric attitudes bubble up constantly, for example, when French Revolutionary forces threaten the nearby French colony of Martinique, and English soldiers based in Barbados successfully relieve the Martiniquans from: "the pernicious spirit of republicanism" (p. 138). For Orderson this intervention which is all the more laudable for being led by Prince William, later Duke of Kent, exemplifies the: "magnanimous humanity so characteristic of British officers." (p. 138) His jingoistic complacency betrays his world view: "England and France now dwell in neighbourly amity and peace; and long, long may their united arms be the safeguard of Europe and of the world." (p. 142)

Fiction, rather than historical or statistical commentaries, often capture human attitudes and relationships in their most life-like dimensions from one era to the next; and Orderson's depiction of his main characters, English-descended Barbadian plantation owners, or their social acquaintances from an equally Anglo-centric world of commerce or the military, preserves much valuable, historical information. The two main families, the Fairfields and Goldacres, become more closely linked when Jack Goldacre marries Caroline Fairfield. Dramatic interaction between their individual attitudes, personalities and family relationships during the period of their courtship is illuminating. Remote, stilted or pretentious as they may now appear, these are the very attitudes, values and conventions, reflecting deeply-rooted reliance on British or foreign institutions and manners, that have left enduring marks on Anglophone Caribbean culture.

Like *Creoleana,* Orderson's play *the Fair Barbadian and Faithful Black* tells a simple love story about Judge Errington's daughter Emily who, obeying her father's wishes, gets engaged to her cousin Tom Appleby, a wild and thoughtless libertine. Emily is also courted by a military officer, Captain Carlove, and after much discussion between the principal characters, including Emily's aunt Alice, and Hampshire, her father's confidential black servant, she finally marries Captain Carlove. Perhaps this is to be expected. What is less expected is the evidence used to reject Tom Appleby which comes from none other than the slave Hampshire. That Judge Errington should base a crucial decision about his daughter's future on the word of a mere slave is astonishing if not bizarre, and intended to draw whatever venom of cruelty or inhumanity historical evidence imputes to slavery.

Since African slavery provided the labour for plantations that were the lifeblood of Barbados in the eighteenth century, its importance in *Creoleana* and *The Fair Barbadian and Faithful Black* is not surprising. More surprising, indeed preposterous, at least for twenty-first century readers, is the notion of slavery as not merely benign, but positively civilising. In the play, for example, we are told about an African prince who is taken back to Africa after being enslaved in Barbados, and when entreated by his father, a Dahomey chief, to remain in his homeland, insists on returning to Barbados because: "he liked the white people ways and their victuals and dress." (p. 92)

Similarly, Judge Errington claims that although a slave may sometimes suffer abuse: "he is by no means habitually ill used or systematically oppressed; but his labour is rather as a copartner with his owner." (p.174) In addition, when Judge Errington offers Hampshire his freedom, he flatly rejects the offer: "Wha I want with free?... You gee me free – who den gee me cloths – who gee me victuals – who gee me money? ...Massa! if you will part wid Hampshire, gee he to Miss Emily! ... No gee he free!" (p. 206)

Both Errington's bigotry and Hampshire's dependency are typical of slave society, just as some Afrikaners, in apartheid South Africa, could afford to show limited kindness toward their black countrymen so long as they retained political and economic control over them. Through an insider's dramatisation of such attitudes in context of the informal, social relations of his chief characters, their ready, open-air spontaneity, hypocritical, allegedly bible-based ethics, and pervasive reliance on British cultural models, Orderson's rendition of formative aspects of Anglophone Caribbean culture explains a great deal about the true history of West Indian social development.

"FRIGID TRUTHS ... DRESSED IN GARMENTS OF ROMANCE"

Cyrus Francis Perkins
Busha's Mistress or Catherine the Fugitive: A Stirring Romance of the Days of Slavery in Jamaica, Kingston, Jamaica, Ian Randle Publishers, 2003, ISBN 976-673-044-3, pp.173. & Princeton, New Jersey, Markus Wiener Publishers, 2003.

Like most fictional accounts of Caribbean slavery that focus on sensational or exotic feats of action, adventure, romance and derring do, *Busha's Mistress or Catherine the fugitive: A Stirring Romance of the Days of Slavery in Jamaica* offers a factual account of day-to-day life during slavery. The author, Cyrus Francis Perkins (1813-1867) was a white Jamaican, and son of a Canadian who wrote the novel in 1854-1855 while he was visiting relatives in Canada (Upper Canada, as Ontario was known before Confederation in 1867). The text of his novel is reconstructed from three earlier versions: the original manuscript, a version that appeared in two Jamaican newspapers, and copies of yet another manuscript. Credit for such radical reconstruction goes to Paul Lovejoy, Verene Shepherd and David Trotman, historians all, who not only edited the text, but included an erudite introduction, magisterial foot notes, a map and pictures of Jamaica, and some of the author's poems.

Most of the action of *Busha's Mistress* is enacted in Greenside, a sugar estate near the town of Falmouth on the North-Western coast of Jamaica. Catherine Brown, mistress or slave concubine of overseer Jackson (also known as the Busha), is driven by jealousy to escape from her lover, after she discovers his attempt to seduce Mary Ann Peach, another brown woman like herself. With the help of white friends, Catherine and her child travel to England where she learns to spell and read; but after a few years she returns to Jamaica and, realising that she still loves Jackson, seeks him out in the city of Kingston where he: "has fallen into very indigent circumstances." (p. 119) Catherine's predicament is then resolved by the somewhat expedient means of a bequest from her deceased mistress, Mrs Christy, which enables her to buy her freedom and marry Jackson.

Because of this somewhat unconvincing, sensational ending, the crises and changes in Catherine's story deliver less drama than they promise. In addition, the narrative of Catherine's career is interrupted by lengthy gaps or leaps that break continuity by introducing more seductive information about slavery. Her story thus tends to become secondary, and the structure of the novel too fragmented to register the full emotional upheaval or dramatic appeal expected from a "stirring romance."

But editors of *Busha's Mistress* have not laboured in vain. As someone committed to the Christian, reformist Wesleyan movement of his time, Perkins's achievement is similar to that of the American author, Harriet Beecher Stowe, who exposes evils of slavery in her frankly propagandistic novel *Uncle Tom's Cabin* (1852), for example, through discussions on slavery between characters in *Busha's Mistress*, and superbly detailed, historical illustrations of actual working conditions, social and religious practices, and acts of resistance of slaves in Jamaica, together with depictions of the perverted practice of levying, or buying and selling slaves.

Perkins conclusively exposes the inherent iniquity of a system, in which offences such as insubordination to drivers, or mere laziness are punished by a daily routine of flogging, and victims, including women, are: "stretched on the ground and held in that position by four men and a driver placed on either side" (p.48) to administer alternate lashes. Judicial sentences for the offence of running away, may include amputation of limbs and cutting off of ears, in addition to flogging; and since slave evidence is inadmissible in court, masters who murder slaves escape punishment for lack of evidence.

In one instance, at least, *Busha's Mistress* measures the pain and suffering of slaves, in lifelike dimensions, normally achieved only by fiction or imaginative writing. Historical or strictly documentary accounts of slavery do not generally match the dramatic power found, for example, in the scene in Perkins's novel where Catherine defiantly intervenes to stop a fight between Jackson and an estate colleague.

For a woman to fight like a tigress to rescue the very man who sexually exploits and turns her into a virtual prostitute, is at least ironic, if not almost incredible! At the same time, the drunken brawling of Jackson and his colleague depicts two white masters in the same degraded light as slaves whom they regard as uncivilised. The charged and condensed ambiguity of the scene illustrates the dramatic or artistic potential of the novel, even if it may not be fully realised in Perkins's doctored and perfunctory format.

Busha's Mistress falls between two stools: a serious, polemical literary genre that strikes a blow for human equality, and a more popular genre of sensational story telling that was mentioned earlier. In his Preface, the author virtually admits this when he confesses to "frigid truths [about slavery] dressed in garments of romance" in his novel. As the editors correctly claim, *Busha's Mistress* advocates true equality between white and black less than it does a form of benign paternalism formerly embraced, for instance, by some liberal whites in apartheid South Africa.

Perkins's undoubtedly sincere moral revulsion against slavery, like that of Harriet Beecher Stowe, is not matched by due political awareness of its equally repugnant social and economic injustice, and the real value of his novel which is more historical than artistic, remains its emphasis on documentary aspects of slavery, achieved through a factual, eye-witness record of day-to-day dealings between slaves and masters, black and white, in Jamaica and the wider Caribbean, plantation society.

"THE MAN IS MINE TO DO WITH AS I WILL"

Kevyn Alan Arthur
The View From Belmont, Leeds, Peepal Tree Press, First
published 1997. Reprinted 2008. pp.200.
ISBN 13:9781900715027.

For its historical record alone of social events and routine,
business activities, during the early 1820s, when Trinidad was a
British colony, bedecked with coffee and cocoa plantations that
relied chiefly on African slave labour, *The View From Belmont*
strongly recommends both itself and its author, Kevyn Arthur,
who was born in Barbados, grew up in Barbados and Trinidad,
and now lives in the US.

Arthur's narrative of letters from Clara Bayley, English
mistress of a Trinidadian coffee and cocoa plantation, to
her friend Alice in England, between December, 1822 and
January, 1824, revels in racy revelations about social, cultural
and economic conditions in Trinidad, not long after British
acquisition of the island in 1797. What distinguished Trinidad
from most other British Caribbean colonies, at the time,
was the large number of settlers from the French-speaking
West Indies who had flocked to the island in response to two
population declarations, "Cedula de Poblacion," issued by the
former Spanish colonial Government of Trinidad, in 1763 and
1783, to attract Catholic immigrants who were not Spanish.

French creole immigrants, who then formed some eighty
percent of the population of Trinidad, consisted of Whites as

well as mulattoes, free Africans and their African or mulatto slaves who, according to Clara, felt ill-treated by their new British rulers. Coloured immigrants, in particular, resented the British Order-in-Council: "which they see as the final abrogation of that equality under the law which had been their privilege under the [former] Spanish administration [in Trinidad]." (p. 86) Clara indicts her (English) countrymen in Trinidad for being: "a bigoted and supercilious lot. The French and even the Irish are more humanitarian in their outlook," (p. 188) while she cites as "the extreme example" (p. 188) of English bigotry, the actions of Governor Sir Ralph Woodford, ironically honoured today by Woodford Square, in Port of Spain, Trinidad's capital city.

Racial bigotry, a universally accepted belief in the superiority of Europeans over all other peoples and cultures, frequently appears in Clara's letters referring to the: "savage blood" (p. 47) of Africans, or: "the natural inferiority of the negro and the deleterious nature of negro blood;" (p. 95) and Clara regularly sneers at claims of African humanity or equality by William Wilberforce and Thomas Buxton, on behalf of the anti-slavery movement, then at its height in England; for her belief that alleged (black) savagery can be redeemed by contact with (white) civilisation is no different from Sir Ralph's own creed of a struggle by white blood in mixed race people: "to antidote and disenvenom the 'vile contagion' [of their black blood.]" (p. 94)

Bigotry sustains stereotypes of Whites as intelligent, civilised, rich and powerful, and Blacks as childish, simple minded, cunning, deceptive, thieving and inefficient, even if it breeds multiple contradictions and anomalies, for example, Bellah, an intelligent, enterprising and efficient female slave who runs a huckstering business, prosperous enough to enable her to lend money to her mistress Clara, who needs it because of uncertainty in her crops and plantation finances.

The novel's most spectacular exposure of African slavery as "an execrable villainy," an expression first applied by the evangelist John Wesley, is Clara's own hypocrisy when, as an English (white) female plantation owner, responsible for running her plantation following the untimely death of her husband, she depends principally on help from her French creole manager, Pierre Pinchet, whose proposal of marriage she rejects, before loneliness draws her into more intimate sexual encounters with lieutenant Thorpe, an Englishman, and Andre des Vignes, a French creole mulatto and plantation proprietor.

More hypocritical still is Clara's seduction of her (African) slave, Kano, who is also her cook. Recognising Kano's culinary and artistic abilities, Clara relies on him: "for his assistance in the management of my household affairs," (p. 83) and regards him as: "a wise and resourceful man." (p. 91) She also recognises her legal power: "he [Kano] is in fact my chattel, my property! The man is mine to do with as I will." (p. 91) There's the rub: Clara exercises her "droit de Madame" over Kano, in the same way that, for centuries, white slave masters exercised their "droit du Seigneur" over black, female slaves.

But Clara's story is only part of the narrative of *The View From Belmont*. After a house is demolished, her letters, accidentally discovered in an "old dutty clay jar" (p. 14) are read by the novel's unnamed narrator and his friends, contemporary Trinidadians who, about the time of Abu Bakr's failed Muslimeen coup in 1990, discuss Clara's private, epistolary confessions while sharing comments among themselves in their own racy, raffish and raunchy, Trinidadian idiom. These comments should not be dismissed simply as adventitious, coarse or bawdy drollery: they also function like the chorus in Greek drama reflecting larger implications, in this case, feminist motives in Clara's predatory, erotic manoeuvres even if they may seem anachronistic in the 1820s Caribbean.

True enough, Clara writes privately to confess her most intimate secrets to a correspondent who is a trusted female friend, presumably of her own age; but her letters depicting Kano as a mere object, are also displayed to a twentieth or twenty-first century audience; and a male author's depiction of his heroine's erotic exploits, within a system that permits legal domination of one individual by another may risk being considered pornographic whatever its historical or artistic value.

PATERNALISM NOT EQUALITY

Lise Winer, Ed.
Adolphus, A Tale (Anonymous) & *The Slave Son* (Mrs.
William Noy Wilkins), Mona, Jamaica, The University of
the West Indies Press, 2001, pp. 364. ISBN: 976 640 133-0

Adolphus, A Tale by an anonymous author and *The Slave Son*
by Mrs. William Noy Wilkins are mid-nineteenth century
Trinidadian works of fiction republished in the second
volume of the Caribbean Heritage Series of "historically
significant works" of West Indian fiction edited by Professor
Lise Winer, with annotations and an introduction by herself
and Bridget Brereton, Rhonda Cobham, Mary Rimmer and
Karen Sanchez-Eppler. *Adolphus* first appeared in serial form,
in 1853, in a newspaper, *The Trinidadian,* owned and edited by
George Numa Dessources, a Trinidadian of mixed (African/
European) blood.

By the end of slavery in 1838, and especially during
the Spanish colonial administration in Trinidad, from the
time of Columbus until the British take over in 1797, many
among Dessources's ethnic group had emerged as affluent
and educated, free Coloureds or free Blacks; but after 1797,
restrictions to their freedom appeared, and both *Adolphus,* no
more than a novella of seventy-five pages, and *Slave Son,* a full
fledged novel, lament these restrictions.

The author of *Slave Son* is believed to be Dessources himself
or one of his free coloured or black associates, who tells the

story of an orphaned child of escaped slaves, Adolphus, during the first decade of the nineteenth century, when he is raised in Trinidad as an educated, free Black by a Catholic priest Padre Gonsalez. Adolphus falls in love with Antonia, daughter of a free, well-to-do black family, the Romelias, but when she is abducted by a mulatto/white reprobate, Jean de Lopelle Pierre Paul De Guerignon who attempts to rape her and she resists, he simply taunts her with: "it is all money – money can make the stiff laws to bend – and make you love me too." (p. 38)

Although DeGuerignon's dark designs are foiled by Antonia's stubborn resistance and quick wit, as well as the bravery of Adolphus who rescues her, so pernicious are laws of class and colour that Mr. Romelia, Antonia's father, is arrested on the basis of false evidence and dies in prison, while an equally false accusation for robbery against Adolphus forces him to take refuge in Venezuela. Only through the help of friends is De Guerignon later punished, and Adolphus able to return to Trinidad.

In *Slave Son*, the hero Belfond is the son of a white, plantation owner St. Hilaire Cardon and a female slave. As a mulatto who enjoys freedom with restricted rights in Trinidad, Belfond feels bitter about his divided existence, both racially and socially: "sneered at by my mother's people – hunted like a wildcat by my father's." (p. 224) Worse still, when he is sent to Europe for education, he is turned off by the harshness of European culture, their: "avarice, their hardness of heart, their inhospitality." (p. 259) It all encourages him to alienate himself from his father, and find refuge among maroons (slave rebels) who, by the end of the novel, launch an insurrection in which his father is killed. Through all this turmoil, Belfond finds satisfaction only in his love for a young coloured woman Laurine, who is also free and with whom, at the end of *Slave Son*, like Adolphus in the previous novella, he escapes to Venezuela.

For all their high drama, the stories in *Adolphus* and *Slave Son* provide mere scaffolding to hang details of slave society in Trinidad, shortly before full Emancipation in 1838. There are rules that: "Negroes or coloured people ... are never permitted to eat or be seated in the presence of the higher race;" (p. 136) and one group of people, Africans, are considered beasts of burden, while Whites, exercise power virtually of life and death over the former. But *Slave Son* does not simply expose hardship and injustice or disclose dates, facts and statistics: as an imaginative, true-to-life rendering of actual individuals in regular, day-to-day relationships with each other, the novella 's characters engage us like people in our own lives, and make us feel the effects of slavery in personal terms.

We shrink when we hear slaves being loudly addressed in animalistic terms like: "good for nothing old raccoon" (p. 193), "shrivelled bat" (p. 194), "crooked ape" (p. 215), or "black monkey" (p. 230); or learn that Cardon is considered "merciful" when, instead of execution, he orders a slave: "to be bound and flogged till not an atom of flesh on his back remained whole." (p. 198) It is one thing to learn about such inhuman abuse from the reported account of a documentary narrative, quite another to visualise it enacted, before our eyes, on individuals with whose relationships and activities we are imaginatively engaged.

If *Adolphus* is the work of a native Trinidadian, the author of *Slave Son* (1854) was born Marcella Fanny Nugent in Ireland, in 1816, and probably lived and married in the West Indies. Her novel is one of several fictional works, by expatriate or creole Whites, about early periods of West Indian history, only recently unearthed and republished, for example, *Creoleana* a novel about Barbados written by J.W. Orderson in 1842.

In a society rigidly structured on race, class and colour, for instance, Mrs. Wilkins sees similarities between restrictions against free Coloureds in the West Indies, and laws against

Catholics, in Ireland, in the seventeenth century. However, if her support of Coloureds is based on: "the grafting of the European intellect on the warm strong feelings of Africa," (p. 132) it appears more as a species of liberal paternalism, rather than genuine belief in racial equality.

A WORM GOING AGAINST A NEST OF ANTS

Keithlyn B. Smith, Fernando C. Smith
To Shoot Hard Labour: The Life and Times of Samuel Smith,
An Antiguan Workingman (1877-1982), Toronto, Edan's
Publishers, pp.171. ISBN 0-921073-00-3

To Shoot Hard Labour: The Life and Times of Samuel Smith, An
Antiguan Workingman (1887-1982) is an autobiography based
on taped interviews by Samuel Smith's grandsons, Keithlyn
and Fernando, in the 1970s. Smith's death on 6th December,
1982, barely twenty-six days short of his one hundred and
sixth birthday, ends a career of bare survival, as an African-
Antiguan, facing unspeakable hardships of indigence and
injustice, like most working people in the Caribbean, during
slavery or a century and more after full emancipation in 1838.

Antigua was first settled as a plantation colony by
British owners who grew cotton and tobacco before, in 1647,
concentrating on sugar and the labour of African slaves. Freed
Africans continued working on these plantations until 1981,
when the island became independent, and Smith recollects
commonplace incidents during much of this time. Although
his recollection may lack statistical rigour, it wins conviction
partly because of his candour and the conversational
informality of its first person narrative. As Carl James writes
in his "Foreword": "history is not only forged by battles and
treaties; it is also, and more importantly, made by the everyday
lives of the people." (p. 12)

Smith's great grandmother "Mother Rachael," arrived as an African slave, in Antigua, in 1800., and her daughter Countis, the first post-slavery baby, supplied Smith with much of his information about slavery; not that the difference in living conditions between the slavery and post-slavery periods was all that noticeable, as Smith often confesses. A typical anecdote in his meandering narrative of episodes, sketches and reflections is about a fellow black worker, Henzel Weathered, who lived on Jonas estate where his extraordinary physical strength caused him to be regarded as "All Man Giant," and earned him "respect" even from planters who reserved their most difficult tasks for him.

In one instance, in 1889 or 1890, when Henzel was set important tasks at a harvest festival, he failed to turn up because he had unknowingly eaten bitter cassava that made him ill. The next day, Massa Arthur rejected Henzel's excuse of illness, and had him beaten by two white militiamen. Henzel was also charged with being absent from duty and stealing molasses, and was sentenced to four months in jail, forty-eight lashes, twelve at the end of each month, and a ban of six years from Jonas estate. His punishment included being locked to a seventy-five-pound ball in jail; but hard work eventually earned him a pardon of only twelve lashes, and after jail he worked at another estate for some years until he suddenly died in 1908.

Smith does not conceal his scepticism: "The official talk was that he [Henzel] dead from yellow fever. No coroner's inquest for poor people in them days. When nega man dead he done." (pp. 50-51) There was also a rumour that Henzel was poisoned. Doubt and uncertainty are themes found in many of Smith's reflections confirming the deeply demoralising effect of slavery on its victims, not only before the Emancipation bill in 1834, but for generations afterwards. Smith speculates, for instance, that Henzel could have been killed by his fellow

Blacks: "I think maybe Henzel's job breed grudge among his own people and maybe they just decide to wipe him out. One of our own "down fall" (sic) is that some of the people get envious over one another for nothing. Life was so hard that one nega man hate to see another do well." (p. 51) Total oppression breeds fear and suspicion and saps the will of its victims.

Oppression in Caribbean slave society is illustrated in other incidents and chapter headings of *To Shoot Hard Labour,* for example, "Massa Was King and King Do No Wrong," or "Nega Even Though Them Right, Them Wrong" or again "Field and Factory: It Was Work Like a Bull." The title of the book also creates an atmosphere of hard, brutally enforced labour: "Both the workers at the mills and the ones in the fields had to shoot hard labour." (p. 45) Resistance was not possible: "No way for us to fight back – it was like a worm going against a nest of ants," (p. 46) and abject powerlessness breeds inner disintegration and an instinct for self-harm among Antiguans.

But within this oppressive system, it is strange how enlightened leadership can make a difference, as it did briefly during the régime of Governor Sir Eustace Fiennes who, between 1921 and 1929, introduced measures such as increased water supply, piped water, enhanced tourist facilities in St. Johns, the capital city, improved public health through new laws, setting up a Home for poor people, and even inducing employers to raise rates of pay for their workers.

Although successors to Governor Fiennes were less enlightened, Governor Gordon Lethem, twenty years later, enacted a law to form a trade union; and, in 1951, the Antigua Trades and Labour Union was born, giving, in Smith's own words: "a very clear sign that it was just a matter of time before massa have to go back home to England." (p. 150) But such good fortune proves illusory, and Smith's description of sustained colonial exploitation in *To Shoot Labour* leaves an impression of almost no respite from unrelieved, subhuman conditions in Antigua where, by the age of fifty-seven, he had fathered altogether forty-three children, in circumstances from which they could expect no better than bare survival.

NOBLESSE OBLIGE

A.N. Nichols
"Diary of a Trip through the Grenadines, May 2 - June 18, 1891", Unpublished.

Even if the main purpose of Dr. A.N. Nichols's trip through Grenada, St. Vincent and the Grenadines, during May/June 1891, was to study the prevalence of yaws, his unpublished diary/report, released by his daughter Maggie in 1950, discloses wider information about British Caribbean colonies generally. Henry Alfred Alford Nichols (1851-1926) a British medical doctor, migrated to Dominica as Assistant Medical Officer shortly after his graduation, in London, in 1875, after which he married a Dominican, Marion Crompton, with whom he had ten children. Nichols became Chief Medical Officer in 1904, was knighted by King George V, and retired in 1925. Not only is he credited with expanding Dominica's health service, and discovering "Boiling Lake" on the island; but he had a mountain and a parrot named after him, was known as "The Uncrowned King of Dominica," and became grandfather of Phyllis Shand Allfrey (1908-1986), author, and Minister of Labour and Social Affairs in the short-lived West Indian Federation.

Dr. Nichols's trip starts in Tobago, after which he stops briefly in Trinidad before arriving in Grenada on 8th May. Travelling by steam boat, the entire trip lasts forty-seven days and, after Grenada, he makes further stops in St. Vincent,

Carriacou, Bequia, Union Island, Cannouan and other smaller islands. The arrangements are striking: every stop overflows with lavish hospitality, sometimes accompanied by champagne, music or dancing and always by good food, convivial company, and after-dinner pipe smoking, all in surroundings of pristine tropical scenery, white sand and blue sea.

Unmistakably, there is a distinct aura of privilege, security, service and serenity around Dr. Nichols as a high ranking member of a ruling, British, colonial élite whose every wish is a command to locals. Upon reaching Grenada, for instance, the Governor's Private Secretary informs Dr. Nichols that a police boat will take him ashore, and a carriage drive him to the Governor's residence where he is a guest of Sir Walter Holy Hutchinson and his wife. Customs and immigration formalities are naturally waived. Baggage is handled by Seignet (sometimes spelt Sigonet), presumably a servant. When Dr. Nichols is to leave Carriacou at 9.00 a.m. for Grenada, another British official suggests that the steamer will wait to allow him extra time for sight seeing, and upon his return he is informed he needn't have hurried because the captain would have waited longer, if necessary.

If Dr. Nichols enjoys privileged hospitality, and writes with relish about ladies who catch his eye, he does not shirk work. Almost daily he tracks down yaws patients, sometimes in isolated communities accessible only by horseback, interviews people, keeps up with correspondence on yaws and other topics, and maintains a record of his work in the form of a diary/report more than four thousand words long. His diary is a brilliant piece of autobiographical/travel writing that pays handsome homage to the tropical beauty of a landscape in which he was not born, but chose to make his home. Besides its historical and scientific value, his diary also provides a guided tour of islands whose history, economy and administrative structure are sketched with authority, and embellished with instructive descriptions of the feudalistic "metayer" system of agriculture, [in which a farmer receives only a share of the yield] the farming of nutmeg and cotton, the process of growing and marketing arrowroot and cacao, the treatment of yaws and much else. In addition, paragraph after paragraph of the diary consists of lists of plants recorded in their Latin names, perhaps not unexpected from someone known for his interest in botany and a textbook on tropical agriculture.

Dr. Nichols was also an avid collector of artefacts left by Caribs, and collects items such as Carib stone implements and a stone stool, while admiring two sacrificial stones, one as much as twelve feet broad and twenty feet high. Equally interesting are his comments on small communities of Caribs whom he meets. As he explains, the so called black Caribs, those mixed with African blood, did not oppose British colonisers, and enjoyed a better rate of survival, while other Caribs who were defeated were removed to a rocky island where many died of starvation and exposure. It is a brutal history, but merely fifty years after the end of African slavery, Dr Nichols feels saddened by abandoned sugar estates: "once the scene of busy industry" (p. 23) which now: "strike a cord (sic) of sadness or raise feelings of regret." (p. 23) Although these estates were maintained by slave labour, he feels nostalgia for the adventure, dash and glamour of an imaginary incident long ago when a pirate schooner threatened: "cold blooded butchery and fierce rapine." (p. 105)

But rather than expose Dr. Nichols as an admirer of crude or authoritarian, colonial practices, his diary presents him as a Victorian whose prestige and privilege are accepted perquisites of British colonialism, so that when he attends a lecture in Grenada, for instance, and the editor of "a radical newspaper" asks a question intended to discredit the government, Dr. Nichols merely reports: "as Mr. D. [the editor] was persistent the Governor had to order him to sit down."(p. 10) Dr. Nichols also writes about the Grenadian village of Marquis: "the people themselves appeared to be low down in the field of civilization," (p. 23) hinting that his zealous devotion to duty implies a sense of "noblesse oblige", paternalism, that could not contrast more sharply with the later, more democratic outlook of his grand daughter Phyllis Shand Allfrey. For all that, his diary remains a rare and valuable item of West Indian literature, not only because yaws is believed to be caused by the same bacteria responsible for syphilis.

"EVERY BLACK MAN ... EXPECTS TO SEE ENGLAND SOME DAY"

Stephen N. Cobham
Rupert Gray: A Tale in Black and White; Ed. Lise Winer, Annotations and Introduction by Bridget Brereton, Rhonda Cobham, Mary Rimmer and Lise Winer; Jamaica, The University of the West Indies Press, 2006, pp.171. ISBN 976-640-182-9.

Rupert Gray: A Tale in Black and White, one of the earliest full-length works of fiction by a West Indian-born author, first appeared in Port of Spain, Trinidad, in 1907, and was reprinted in 2006 with a forty-one-page Introduction and zealous annotations or end notes, forty-four pages in length, prepared by editor Lise Winer and Bridget Brereton, Rhonda Cobham and Mary Rimmer. As the fourth volume in a series of re-published, previously unavailable texts, mainly by nineteenth century West Indian authors, the re-appearance of *Rupert Gray* boosts a long-needed service in West Indian cultural and literary retrieval.

Biographical details about Stephen Cobham are sketchy: he was born probably around the 1860s or 70s in Trinidad, where he first worked as a school teacher before turning to law. In 1908, he moved to British Guiana, and later the Virgin Islands without, apparently, returning to Trinidad. *Rupert Gray* was inspired by Cobham's mixed (African-European) ancestry, and specifically by struggles against the injustice of Crown Colony government, which incited strong feelings of dissatisfaction and retaliation, among middle class African-Trinidadians during Cobham's lifetime, notably Henry Sylvester Williams, whose retaliatory pan-Africanist activism probably plays a role in *Rupert Gray*.

Although Rupert is black, he is highly esteemed as chief clerk and accountant in Serle and Murchison, a white creole firm that owns cocoa estates and maintains their head office in Port of Spain. Gwendoline Serle, the twenty-year old daughter of the firm's senior partner, Mr. Primrose Serle, returns from studies in Europe and England and, after taking short hand lessons with Rupert, falls in love with him. This is the crux of the matter; for, according to the author: "Her [Gwendoline's] ethics clashed with the social rules of her caste," (p. 39) which forbids marriage of a white woman to a black man as violation of an unwritten, racist social code in British Caribbean colonies.

It is ironic that Serle who holds Gray in high enough esteem to offer him a partnership in his firm after he dies, should so strictly observe the colonial social code: he claims, for instance: "the West Indian negro barely stands within the threshold of culture," (p. 58) and allows for only: "a European lady marrying a black. It [inter-racial marriage] may obtain in Europe where the black man is not known. It is not fashionable out here in the black man's home." (p. 58) The irony is that while Serle admits to believing in racial equality, he does not believe in black men mixing: "in the company of our wives and wanting to marry our daughters." (p. 58) His view, apparently, one of gradualist development of black people in the professions, government service and commerce, but not socially, is well expressed by the title of one chapter, "Thus Far and no Farther." It is the West Indian version of apartheid: racial prejudice that is not legally institutionalised as it was in South Africa during the second half of the twentieth century; but morally just as repugnant.

Inevitably, Serle's view clashes with his daughter's and their conflict comes to a head when he shoots and wounds

Gray in an incident that also nearly causes Gwendoline's death from drowning. Gray and Gwendoline are only saved by quick and fortuitous action from Gwendoline's friend Dr. Florence Badenock, after which Serle takes to drink, and his daughter pines, withers and dies. In time, Serle himself dies. But such melodramatic tragedy is not all: an equally bizarre subplot has Rupert helping an old school friend, Jacob Clarke, who later writes an anonymous letter to the Linnaean Society in London making damaging but false accusations against Rupert. The Society is then forced to withdraw both their membership from Rupert and the award of one thousand pounds they had previously granted him. Even more unconvincing is the final resolution of a happy ending contrived through a character who supposedly dies and later, it seems, mainly to satisfy needs of the plot, turns out to be alive.

Such techniques include thinly drawn characters who are either completely good or bad, coincidence, frequent exclamations, flowery diction, and sententious maxims and precepts that betray Cobham's influence by literary forms, cultural assumptions and values, prevailing among popular writers in Victorian Britain, for example, Gothic contrivances, long orations, Gunga Din loyalty to empire, and adulation of imperial grandeur accompanied by attitudes of colonial subservience and respectful genuflection: "Every black man in the West Indies expects to see England some day," (p. 98) or "Play in England and live, dreams the average Trinidad batsman." (p. 51) None of this, however, takes away from the pioneering value of Cobham's novel as a dramatisation of the economic structure of Caribbean, colonial society, based on criteria of race, class and colour, and as a fore runner of more skilful, Trinidadian novelists, for example, C.L R. James, Alfred Mendes and Ralph DeBoissière, soon to appear after Cobham.

ANGLO-CENTRIC COLONIAL ECONOMIC MODEL

John Bigelow
Jamaica in 1850 or the Effects of Sixteen Years of Freedom in a Slave Colony, Westport, Connecticut, Negro Universities Press, 1970, (First published George Putnam, New York, 1851).

In addition to being an American lawyer, soldier and editor, John Bigelow served as US ambassador to France during the Civil War (1861-65), and worked as a journalist on articles collected in *Jamaica in 1850 or the Effects of Sixteen Years of Freedom in a Slave Colony.* How surprising that Bigelow's articles for the *New York Evening Post*, in 1850, should still interest contemporary West Indians! West Indians would probably be equally drawn to any report on a British Caribbean colony with a majority African population freshly emerging from slavery; moreso if, like *Jamaica in 1850*, the report was written by someone who himself grew up in former British colonies alongside enslaved Africans. As an American citizen, Bigelow was against slavery and, shortly after 1850, saw action in the American Civil War, fighting against the pro-slavery Confederacy.

He is struck by the "decrepit condition" (p. 38) of early post-slavery Jamaica which he attributes partly to the island's Legislative Assembly whose members are chosen mainly because they meet a high property qualification not accessible to most Jamaicans: "The result is the poor are utterly excluded from all participation in its [the Assembly's] privileges and responsibilities." (p. 39) Another problem is the island's economic system which is based on a model of promoting: "the growth and sale of [only] sugar and rum" (p. 39) industries that serve economic needs of Britain, not Jamaica. Contemporary West Indians are also interested in Bigelow's views of 1850 Jamaica, partly because they expose an Anglo-centric, colonial, economic model which, not only flourished in most British Caribbean colonies until West Indian independence in the 1960s, but contrasted sharply with American economic policy geared to benefit citizens themselves of newly independent American states.

As Bigelow notes, the Jamaican Legislative Assembly and Executive Council may create a semblance of authority by levying taxes, maintaining highways and paying police and other officers, but their authority is deceptive since it is subject to approval from the British monarch and parliament through their local representative, the Governor of Jamaica. Jamaica's colonial relationship to Britain is described through a telling image: "The heart which gives it [Jamaica's colonial relationship] life, beats in London; the islanders have no more control over its action than the finger nails have over the circulation of the blood." (p. 41) Without resorting to sensational images of subjugation or exploitation, Bigelow's image aptly catches the essence of the British colonial system, in which Jamaica serves merely as a marginal appendage, whose function is to sustain Britain at the centre of an Anglo-centric universe.

Bigelow is not short of figures and statistics to back up his claims: of 653 sugar plantations that flourished in Jamaica, in 1834, at the time of Emancipation, 150 lay abandoned by 1850, while 200,000 acres of land had gone out of cultivation. Similarly, the volume of Jamaican exports in rum, sugar, ginger, coffee, molasses and pimento had fallen sharply. And Jamaica was not alone. With phrases such as "ruined and helpless" (p. 58), and "desolation and decay" (p. 59) the author detects bleak desolation and decline in most British Caribbean colonies at the time.

In British Guiana, for instance, between 1838 and 1850, out of 258 estates, 71 were abandoned and 111 "sold under execution," (p. 58) while on the Courantyne coast of the county of Berbice, "magnificent estates" (p. 59) "wealthy proprietors" (p. 59) and "a peasantry beyond all compare, the most happy and prosperous in the world," (p. 59) were replaced by "impoverished proprietors," (p. 59) and "a peasantry relapsing...into a state of greater barbarism than at any former period." (p.59) Many reasons are given for post-Emancipation decline: freed Africans from some colonies refused to continue as plantation labourers, while others, for instance, in British Guiana, bought abandoned plantations, but found their efforts deliberately compromised by inadequate drainage and irrigation still controlled by owners of the plantations they had vacated.

Bigelow mentions other (psychological) causes of decline as well: "the degrading estimate [first noticed in Ireland] placed upon every species of agricultural labor by the white population... [and] its pernicious effects upon the "blacks". (p. 75) If Caribbean plantations flourished before 1834, it was because they relied on the enforced labour of African slaves. When, after 1834, labour was no longer enforced, the plantations collapsed. Part of the problem was that labour operated within a rambling economic structure, in the Caribbean, based on absentee owners living mostly in Britain.

As Bigelow writes: "The blighting influence of absenteeism [first noticed in Ireland]" existed in Jamaica where the plantation was managed by a resident attorney who reported to the absent owner. The attorney, meanwhile, hired an overseer who, in turn, hired from one to three bookkeepers. Bigelow concludes: "These different agents have to be paid for services made necessary by the absence of the proprietor from the island." (p. 81) While a plantation that flourished on slave labour could afford such elaborate and wasteful expenses, a less productive, post-slavery plantation employing free labour could not.

Jamaica in 1850 is quite polemical and conducts interesting debates on slavery, and the issue of absentee ownership of Caribbean plantations. Perhaps the author's sharpest perception is of waste inherent in the slave-plantation structure itself, and: "the carelessness, the improvidence, and corruption of these middlemen [attorney/overseer/bookkeeper] in whose hands was the control of most of the real estate of the island [Jamaica]." (p. 87) Is it really so difficult to identify the waste and corruption of contemporary Caribbean governments as a direct inheritance of plantation practices and ethics outlined here by Bigelow?

"I GOT TO LIVE AND I'LL SCAB THROUGH HELL TO LIVE"

Claude McKay
Home to Harlem, Boston, Northeastern University Press, 1987, pp.340. ISBN 1-55553-023-0. First Published 1928.

Home to Harlem is the first of three novels by Claude McKay (1889-1948) poet, fiction writer, and one of the first West Indian authors to win fame abroad. A black Jamaican from a farming community, McKay first encountered British literary classics in the library of his older brother, a school teacher, and was encouraged by Walter Jekyll, a British folklorist, to take the revolutionary step of infusing Jamaican creole speech idioms into his writing, for example, in his first two volumes of poems *Songs of Jamaica* (1912) and *Constabulary Ballads* (1912). In 1912 McKay left Jamaica for the US where he became embroiled in the struggle against American racism and, like prominent African-Americans such as Richard Wright and Paul Robeson, armed himself with socialism or communism.

Home to Harlem opens during World War One when Jake (Jacob Brown), an African-American soldier, deserts his army in France and, after a brief stop in England, returns home to Harlem. Jake sleeps with a prostitute one night, but fails to find her the next day when he takes up with a woman nick-named Congo Rose. As a black enclave during Prohibition, in 1916, when liquor could not be legally sold in the US, and Blacks were denied elementary human rights, ill-treated, and in certain areas lynched, Harlem was in the opinion of a female denizen named Suzy: "a bloody ungodly place where niggers nevah go to bed. All night running around speakeasies [shebeens where illicit liquor was sold] and cabarets, where bad, hell-bent nigger womens am giving up themselves to open sin." (p.79)

In an atmosphere of wild licentiousness, Jake soon detaches from Rose and leaves Harlem for work on the railway where he meets Ray, a Haitian with unusual intellectual/literary interests. Much of the novel then turns to discussions between Jake and Ray about moral (rather than political) issues that arise out of racial injustice inflicted on Blacks, the world over. Ray then settles down with his friend Agatha who is less typical of Harlem than Rose or Susy and, in true Harlem fashion, Jake re-connects with Felice the woman who abandoned him at the start of the novel.

In a Harlem bar, when Felice struggles in vain to escape from Zeddy, an unscrupulous gambler armed with a razor, she is released only after a violent confrontation with Jake who pulls a gun on Zeddy. Just as Jake casually becomes reunited with Felice, he carries a gun simply because he happened to receive it from a friend without asking for it. Since things might have turned out very differently without the gun, we realise that pure chance or living on a knife edge, without forethought or expectation, remains a governing principle in McKay's Harlem. Coincidence is all or, as Jake admits when Felice confesses she never liked Zeddy and just happened to meet him: "Oh, you don't have to explain me nothing. I know it's jest connexidence." (p. 330)

The neologism "connexidence" suggests that the lifestyle of nondescript wretches: "waiters, cooks, chauffeurs, sailors, porters, guides, ushers, hod-carriers and factory hands" (p. 225) in *Home to Harlem* is less random than it seems. When Ray admonishes Jake to adopt a less: "kind of free life" (p. 207) Jake replies: "Ise lak a sailor that don't know nothing about using a compass, but him always hits a safe port." (p. 206) There are reasons for this seemingly rampant coincidence of events in Jake's life which are neither entirely haphazard nor a result of mere chance. For instance, Ray perceives a contrast between white, European and black or African civilizations when he admires: "the white citizen of a nation that can say bold, challenging things like a strong man," but this is: "Something very different from the keen ecstatic joy a man feels in the romance of being black." (p. 154)

Ray's perception seems influenced by négritudinist ideas which circulated in McKay's time and, in the 1930s, were incorporated in writing mainly by francophone African and black, Caribbean authors. No wonder négritudinist ideas in the novel are supplied by Ray, a francophone West Indian. Not that *Home to Harlem* is overtly négritudinist; but deep within themselves, seemingly despairing and desperate characters nurse an enduring will to live with militant pride. These characters may not recommend themselves, in social or political terms, which is why *Home to Harlem* was denounced by eminent African-Americans like W.E.B. Du Bois and Richard Wright; but the novel's triumph is its sturdy and defiant resistance against racism embedded in the linguistic virtuosity of McKay's wonderfully improvised, and freshly creative African-American coinages, idioms, rhythms and diction.

Here, for example, is Zeddy's reaction to Jake when he is accused of strike-breaking: "One thing I know is niggers am made foh life. And I want to live, boh, and feel plenty o' the juice o' life in mah blood. I wanta live and I wanta love. And niggers am got to work hard foh that... I loves life and I got to live and I'll scab through hell to live." (p. 49) Zeddy's raw, conversational, vernacular idiom rings true and expresses conviction, resolve and zest simply in being alive. In particular, this conviction and zest find their match in *Their Eyes Were Watching God* (1937) an extraordinary novel by Zora Neal Hurston, a black

American anthropologist who, like McKay, explored African folklore in America and the Caribbean. Readers who condemn *Home to Harlem* for demeaning African-Americans perhaps miss the essential humanity of characters, trapped in crippling conditions of injustice, which they may endure but not escape, at least, not in their own historical milieu or era.

A RAINBOW WORLD

Ralph DeBoissière
Call of the Rainbow, Melbourne, Australia, L. A. Browne, 2007. (360pp.)

Call of the Rainbow, last in a quartet of novels by Ralph DeBoissière, mostly about Trinidad where he was born in 1907, was published in the author's one hundredth year, in Australia, where he had settled since 1948, and where he died in 2008. *Rainbow* summons up thoughts of mystery, intrigue, adventure, wanderlust, tenacity and zest for life in DeBoissière as a true adventurer and literary pioneer who, along with Herbert DeLisser and Claude McKay of Jamaica, fellow Trinidadians Alfred Mendes and C.L.R. James, and Guyanese Edgar Mittelholzer, planted seemingly fresh seeds of modern West Indian literature in the first half of the twentieth century. DeBoissière knew Mendes, James and Mittelholzer; but did not follow James and Mittelholzer to London where, in the 1950s, West Indian literature sprouted, as never before, in the hands of Roger Mais, George Lamming, Samuel Selvon, V.S. Naipaul, Mittelholzer and others.

The action in *Rainbow* deploys in Trinidad in the 1930s and 40s when the British colony squirmed with social disturbances and strikes heralding anti-colonial struggle that would sweep Trinidad & Tobago to independence in 1962. Action is driven by passion for social, economic and political justice, every bit as fierce as in the author's first novel *Crown Jewel* published fifty-five years earlier; for *Crown Jewel* considers an identical situation in Trinidad, and includes characters who carry some of the same names as those in the author's fifth novel, for example, the businessman Joe Elias, trade union leader Ben Le Maitre, the author's friend Alfred Mendes, and Aurelia Henriques a seamstress whose mixed, ethnic, middle class identity matches that of Antonia Reyes of *Rainbow.*

These similarities confirm the unbroken integrity of DeBoissière's single-minded political vision, inspired partly by anti-colonial conviction, and partly by an indelible imprint on his very soul of Trinidad's history, culture, language and motley population of Europeans, Africans, Indians, French creoles, Portuguese, Lebanese and Chinese. While the political aspect of DeBoissière's vision is also behind his fourth novel *No Saddles for Kangaroos* which deals with economic injustice suffered by white, factory workers in Melbourne, Australia, it does not compare with the intensity of impact and political conviction of his native land with its matchless mix of race, class, colour, language, slavery and indenture.

If there were second thoughts about structure in the author's earlier novels which consist of episodes that tend to go on and on like those in Thackeray's *Vanity Fair, Call of the Rainbow* arouses few such worries. There are still a great many characters in this fourth novel, but their doings share a central focus on the fate of the People's Party, led by celebrated historian Peter Burman, whose aim is to achieve political liberation for all Trinidadians. Extensive biographical details of Burman's academic success, political activities and struggle with corruption in his party, not to mention his family problems, all cooperate to build a tense climax including a military revolt, and risk of national chaos and collapse. But Burman's successful handling of this national crisis is expertly linked to reconciliation with his own family that smoothly resolves tension and settles matters.

A sombre note of political drama rises out of scenes of economic hardship, exploitation and struggle that appear side by side with episodes of racy Trinidadian speech, barbed outbursts of picong, and incidents of rib-tickling humour as, for instance, in this excerpt from a description of revellers during Carnival, the most popular street festival in Trinidad: "one who had daubed his naked body with soot; another, without pants, in top hat and tails; a buxom woman in an old-time bustle; a youth with a fake sausage as a penis; and all singing a bawdy calypso then popular." (p. 242) Evocation of Trinidadian local colour is DeBoissière's real forte with its improbable mixture of bizarre and absurd elements, and combination of boisterous ebullience with effervescent ribaldry reflecting core aspects of a uniquely Trinidadian culture.

After more than half a century's residence in Australia, it is a *tour de force* for DeBoissière to reproduce as pure and pristine a fictional evocation of Trinidad as in *Call of the Rainbow*! Equally extraordinary is the sturdy fervour of his Marxist rhetoric, the lure of a rainbow world free of exploitation, inequality and injustice, which neither wilted nor waned over a similar period. Thanks to this fervour, young West Indians whose only access to important events in their history lay in often dreary academic commentaries, can now witness these events through familiar, everyday speech, and lively scenes with flesh and blood characters such as Peter Burman (Dr. Eric Williams) and Joe Elias (Albert Gomes).

The portrait of Burman, for example, struggling with nuances of his own reaction to political change, is subtle and moving. In one scene when he fears that his youthful political dreams are in danger of being crushed by harsh reality, Burman observes the crushed wing of a butterfly: "Ideals..." he thought, and his expression grew dark and distant." (p. 255) This is political self-examination like we used to get from novels of Doris Lessing in her early, Communist Party days.

No wonder, in his essay "On Writing a Novel", DeBoissière recalls the influence of nineteenth century Russian writers on his fiction; for Lessing too, in *Going Home,* (1957) notices the similarity between societies in British colonies and those in Tsarist Russia which were riddled with feudal inequalities. DeBoissière confesses in his essay just quoted: "Taking a side can hardly be escaped." This is perhaps why, in *Call of the Rainbow,* DeBoissière handles taking sides, in fictional terms, better than he has ever done. It is a fitting finale to a fully-lived career!

"NOT TAKING SIDES WAS IMPOSSIBLE"

Ralph DeBoissière
Life on the Edge: The Autobiography of Ralph DeBoissière,
Caroni, Lexicon Trinidad Limited, 2010, pp.295.
ISBN 978-976-631-055-4.

Life on the Edge: the Autobiography of Ralph DeBoissière is both
a family record, and a kaleidoscope of Caribbean development
during the twentieth century, when English-speaking
territories not only gained political independence from
Britain, but won international recognition for their literature.
Ralph DeBoissière was born, in Trinidad, in 1907, and after
school, worked and devoted himself to a literary career by wide
reading and association with other local writers. He also got
married and, in 1947, left for the US where he did a course
in motor mechanics, before migrating to Australia the same
year. Ralph was later joined by his wife and two daughters and,
with the help of friends in Australia, finally got his writing
published. Apart from two brief visits abroad, one to China
and the U.S.S.R. in 1958, and another to his homeland in 1976,
he remained in Australia until his death in 2008.

As his surname suggests, DeBoissière was of French creole
stock, a descendant of French planters who flocked to Trinidad
from other Caribbean islands, at the end of the eighteenth
century, after African slaves had overthrown French rule in
Haiti. Despite this aristocratic ancestral link, the DeBoissière
branch of the family was of mixed (African/European) blood

which, in the colour/ethnic dispensation of the time, assigned him to a lower social and economic class than his pure-blood relatives. He writes simply: "I was not pure. My wife [Ivy] was even less pure." (p. 118) And "she [Ivy] went to what the children called 'little convent' where the blacks, the coloureds and the illegitimate were schooled by black teachers under white nuns. It was close to the 'big convent' which accepted only whites." (p. 87)

If the handicap of ethnicity was bad enough in Trinidad, during the 1920s and 30s, politics was worse. So polarised was the political situation in his British Caribbean colony that DeBoissière was left with no choice: "I began to see that in the [colonial] world I knew the decision was a political one. Not to take sides was impossible." (p. 104) The two sides were the British colonial government on one hand, and Trinidadian working people [mostly Blacks and Indians] on the other; and as DeBoissière saw it: "We [Trinidadians] were a mass. We had yet to be a people...Black or white they [Trinidadians] were all alike, promoters of a vile colonial system, ready to sing 'Rule Britannia' as often as required." (p. 104) In June 1937 though, colonial inequality and exploitation provoked riots from striking oilfield workers. To the author's middle class relations and office colleagues who supported the government, the workers were: "a body of cowardly, ignorant people stirred up by a few hooligans who needed the whip." (p. 105) But, as he realised: "Our working people were not united, they were confused and ignorant;" (p. 105) and they were quickly defeated. It taught him an important lesson: that his first novel *Crown Jewel* on which he was then working had to be re-written so that: "This time the point of view would fundamentally be that of working folk." (p. 105)

Solidarity with the working class then became a guiding light to DeBoissière, and a mainspring of inspiration in his five novels: *Crown Jewel* (1952); *Rum and Coca Cola* (1956);

Homeless in Paradise (Unpublished); *No Saddles for Kangaroos* later renamed *Waiting for the Dawnlight* (1964); and *Call of the Rainbow* (2007). A musical play "Calypso Play" was also produced in Melbourne in 1955, although several other plays still remain unpublished. DeBoissière's circumstances of writing and publication, along with his social relationships and his experience in Australia are fully fleshed out in the second half of *Life on the Edge*. On his visit to Trinidad in 1976, he admits he had left his homeland for good: "Despite Trinidad's haunting presence in our lives ever after, Australia had claimed us." (p. 266) His older daughter Jacqueline did return to live in Trinidad, but her younger sister Marcelle remained in Australia which is also where Ivy died in 1984. Perhaps Ralph's strongest connection to Australia then followed after he married Annie Greet, an Australian, with whom he spent his final years.

As already mentioned, DeBoissière is one of several early twentieth century authors who helped to inaugurate modern West Indian literature, for example, George Lamming of Barbados, Edgar Mittelholzer of Guyana, and Ralph's countrymen C.L.R. James, Alfred Mendes and Albert Gomes who had founded the innovative literary magazine "Beacon" during the 1930s. These authors also fostered a sense of national consciousness that sparked a movement for Independence by the 1950s and 60s. This is the main achievement of *Life on the Edge*: it illuminates the process by which an author who originally foresaw only limited literary prospects in his homeland lived long enough to see the blossoming of a rich and thriving literary tradition take root and prosper.

The achievement of *Life on the Edge* is greatly enhanced by Professor Kenneth Ramchand's editorial expertise, comprehensive Introduction, detailed endnotes, wonderful photos and exhaustive information about the DeBoissière family. But literary history is one thing: *Life on the Edge* also contains an authentic, sociological survey of colonial Trinidad, glorious evocation of the island's tropical landscape, original commentary on the impact of American troops, in Trinidad, during World War Two, sensitive exploration of the impulse for Caribbean diasporic disintegration, and best of all: an endearing love story between Ralph and Ivy, related by an author at the top of his game.

THE PRICE OF CONSCIENCE

Brinsley Samaroo
The Price of Conscience: Howard Noel Nankivell and Labour Unrest in the British Caribbean in 1937 and 1938, Hansib, Hertford, United Kingdom, 2015, pp.117.
ISBN 978-1-910553-04-6

Brinsley Samaroo's *The Price of Conscience: Howard Noel Nankivell and Labour Unrest in the British Caribbean in 1937 and 1938* tells the dramatic story of a British Colonial administrator, Howard Nankivell, (1893-1938) who was born in Jamaica of British/American parentage, and attended Christ's Hospital school in Britain. In 1911, after school, Nankivell returned to Jamaica where he joined the British Colonial service as Assistant Clerk. In 1916, he enlisted in World War One and won medals in the Royal Flying Corps. He also met his first wife Sybil during the war, but the marriage was short-lived. After the war, Nankivell continued working in Jamaica. In 1925, he was promoted to First Class Clerk, and five years later to Principal Clerk. In April 1928, he rose to the rank of Assistant Colonial Secretary, but was transferred to Port of Spain, Trinidad & Tobago.

Nankivell's career is best understood within the context of economic hardship in British Caribbean colonies generally, following the Great Depression and: "decline of the European market for West Indian sugar" (p. 12) in the 1930s, "unrest among the sugar workers in Central Trinidad in 1934," and "uprisings in St. Kitts, British Guiana, St. Vincent, St. Lucia, Barbados, Jamaica and Trinidad & Tobago" (p. 11) especially in 1937 and 1938. This gives an impression of imperial neglect in the Anglophone Caribbean, during the century after the abolition of slavery in the 1830s; and the impression is reinforced by W.M. MacMillan's book *Warning from the West Indies A Tract for the Empire*: (1936) mentioned by Professor Samaroo. A review of this book by P.G. appears on page 350 of *The Labour Monthly* in June, 1936: "The West Indies, like Newfoundland, have been sucked dry by the absent landlords and imperialist landholders. Misery, starvation, squalid conditions and death is the lot of the population."

While still in Jamaica, in 1925, Nankivell had first-hand experience of West Indian unrest when striking Kingston Corporation workers clashed with police in a dispute over pay, and three people were killed, and others wounded. Upon arrival in Port of Spain in April, 1929, he threw himself into a flurry of activity granting oil leases to British, American and Canadian investors, and mediating between Government and the East Indian community in Trinidad. He was also Secretary to an inter-colonial conference on trade relations with Canada, and often acted as Colonial Secretary, and served as the Governor's Deputy, for instance, in 1932 and 1934. But the most interesting aspect of the work of both Nankivell and his second wife, a Dutch woman, Florence Muysken, whom he met in Trinidad, was their: "concern for ordinary people ...and the socio-economic situation of the working class." (p. 37)

Such concern was not exactly in the job description of British colonial officials in the early twentieth century. It was conspicuously absent in colonies visited by British writers, notably George Orwell who worked as a policeman in Burma and depicts British rule in Burma, negatively, in his novel *Burmese Days*. Another British writer, James Pope-Hennessy, who worked briefly as aide-de-camp to the Trinidad Governor, shortly after the Nankivells left Trinidad in 1938, came to a similar conclusion in his memoir *West Indian Summer: A Retrospect*: "everything that could be done to keep them [West Indian colonies] poverty-stricken and neglected, to make them sullen and disloyal had been done by the colonial office." (p. 79) Speaking about John Gorrie, former Chief Justice of Trinidad & Tobago, Professor Samaroo's colleague Bridget Brereton, is quoted in *The Price of Conscience*: "the entire structure of the empire worked against his [Gorrie's] efforts to protect the humbler subjects of Her Majesty in Mauritius, Fiji and the Caribbean." (p. 13)

As a couple, the Nankivells adopted the rare and grossly neglected, civilising mission aspect of the imperial creed, and Florence, a pianist, gave recitals to raise funds for needy causes, or made speeches recommending improvement in housing and living conditions, which were later adopted in the Moyne Report of the West India Royal Commission that was sent out to investigate unrest in British Caribbean colonies in 1937/38. In his chapter "Nankivell in Action" where the author outlines the conflict between élite merchants, planters and oil magnates against workers' representatives such as Tubal Uriah Buzz Butler (1897-1977) and Adrian Cola Rienzi (1905-1972), Nankivell does not conceal which side he is on when he speaks of the Government : "collecting large revenues, " (p. 64) and the oil companies "paying big dividends" (p. 64) and "Government, the oil industry and the sugar industry being able to pay a fair wage to provide decent conditions for labour." (p. 64)

According to the author, these remarks "were to seal his [Nankivell's] fate," (p. 64) when the Foster Commission of Enquiry was later set up to report on the unrest: despite support for Nankivell from Governor Sir Murchison Fletcher, fierce lobbying of colonial officials by the usual suspects of vested interests representing oil, sugar, shipping, cocoa and the asphalt industry forced the Governor to resign on grounds of ill health, and Nankivell to be demoted and transferred to Cyprus as Colonial Treasurer. Florence then took the couple's two children to London, and Nankivell travelled to Cyprus in September 1938.

If this was the end of his drama, Nankivell might be considered fortunate; but he worked in Cyprus for twelve weeks before taking sick leave and setting out again on 15th December, 1938. On 21st December, while *en route* to England through France, he fell from his train into the path of an oncoming train, and was killed. Despite a verdict of accidental death, Professor Samaroo claims: "Howard Nankivell committed suicide" (p. 88) due to: "intense depression caused by the injustice of a system over which he had no control." (p. 88) Although proof of suicide may now be impossible, *The Price of Conscience* suggests it is entirely plausible.

"TRAINING A NATION OF CLERKS TO THE EXCLUSION OF THE VITAL RESOURCES OF THE ISLAND"

Vncent Tothill,
Trinidad's Doctor's Office: The Amusing Diary of a Scottish Physician in Trinidad in the 1920s, Cascade, Trinidad, Paria Publishing Company Limited, 2009, pp.208.
ISBN 978-976-8054-76-0.

Trinidad's Doctor's Office: The Amusing Diary of a Scottish Physician in Trinidad in the 1920s was first published under the title *Doctor's Office*, in 1939, in Glasgow, Scotland. The diary records the author's experience as a medical doctor working firstly for the oil company, Trinidad Leaseholds, and later for himself as an independent General Practitioner in San Fernando, South Trinidad, from 1921 to 1937. Dr. Tothill writes authoritatively both about medical matters such as the diet and diseases of his patients, and the Trinidadian system of health care, or lack of it. He also comments on Trinidad's mixture of races and culture, its education, religion, architecture, sport and general prospects.

Dr. Tothill latches on to similarities and differences between the island's two major ethnic groups, indentured Indians and descendants of African slaves whom he calls "Negroes," following usage at the time: "The Negro is happy-go-lucky, the Indian contemplative and calculating. "(p. 126) This may be amateur ethnography without support of research; but it also includes a scathing description of barracks for indentured Indians which the author observed in 1937: "They [the barracks] were filthy, verminous, full of rats, leaking and very dark. No water was laid on. The people were really no better off than the rats who lived with them" (p. 132)

Even without further research, the author's personal witness of this hell hole is enough: in spite of exhausting agricultural labour and wages of merely two shillings a day Indians survived chiefly on boiled rice, and although they suffered from vitamin deficiency, hookworm and malaria, never lost their: "innate habit of hoarding money." (p. 133) Dr. Tothill suggests, more with wondering detachment than disdain: "It is astonishing how out of these meagre wages Indians will amass comparative wealth at the expense of the necessities of life." (p. 133)

By contrast, Africans are not only physically robust, but they are born musicians and actors skilled in the art of make believe. Unlike Indians, Africans are thriftless, sexually promiscuous and subject to venereal disease as well as malaria; but they make expert carpenters and joiners, love the cinema and rum, and are excellent cricketers. The African loves: "talking for the pleasure of hearing his own voice," (p. 170) is fond of the high sounding importance of names like "Melchisedek" taken from the bible, and is keen on funerals. As Dr. Tothill describes it, an African wake is: "one of the great social festivities of the West Indies." (p. 117); but: "the real tragedy of the West Indies" is that: "deep down they [Africans] long to be white, or high brown, or have straight hair or clear skin, in fact, anything that is not entirely black." (p. 135).

So far, Dr. Tothill trades mainly in familiar and rather obvious stereotypes, but he is more convincing on the subject of religion. He is: "definitely biased against" Christian missions," (p. 168) condemns them for regarding West Indians as heathens, and argues for equal respect to be given to Hinduism and Islam as Christianity which, he claims, is inspired: "by the predatory habits of the white man." (p. 171) He compares the healing powers of "La Divina Pastora" a Catholic statuette in the South Trinidadian district of Siparia, with those of our Lady of Lourdes, and approves of the syncretism of "La Divina Pastora" being: "adopted by the local, uneducated Hindus as a sort of additional patron saint or goddess alongside their Pantheon of gods from the *Mahabharata* and *Ramayana*." (p. 173)

Dr. Tothill is more convincing on education and politics, for example: "The trend of education in Trinidad is toward training a nation of clerks to the exclusion of the vital resources of the island, which are oil and agriculture." (p. 177) Writing long before the University of the West Indies was established in 1948, Dr. Tothill could have taken the words right out of the mouth of Lloyd Best, the Trinidadian economist, who inveighed vehemently against the "stupidness" of the curriculum of the University of the West Indies until his death a few years ago. Dr. Tothill would also have been very disappointed with the curriculum of an institution whose very formation he advocated more than a decade before it was established. He pleads, for instance, for scientific agriculture when most cocoa growers: "are extremely ignorant of all science pertaining to agriculture," (p. 178) and the rice industry is: "run by hopelessly ignorant and out of date methods. (p. 178)

Doctor's Office is less an historical treatise than an informal blend of memoir, autobiography and travel literature. Nor does its humorous assertion of personal opinion, and free wheeling, full blooded zest and candour entirely deprive it of historical value when we recall how much early West Indian social history, up to about World War Two, first came to us from foreign, chiefly British travellers whose point of view was often less free of bias or stereotypes than Dr. Tothill's.

Although he is not a spokesman of empire, Dr. Tothill implicitly acknowledges the seemingly foreordained, worldwide, dominance of European power and culture which sometimes betrays a patronising tone, for example, when he writes that Christian missions: "served a useful purpose in giving white representation to coloured races," (p. 168) or when he claims that, without Christian discipline, Africans would: "relapse towards voodoo." (p. 169) This claim betrays a belief in the civilising mission of empire even if Dr. Tothill's notion that the prospect of Federation was hampered by the: "petty jealousy of individual islands" (p. 179) later proves to be prescient, practical and pertinent.

"SEXLESS, CREEDLESS, CLASSLESS, FREE"

Eliot Bliss
Luminous Isle, London, Virago, 1984, pp.372. First published,
London,1934.

In her excellent Introduction to Eliot Bliss's second novel
Luminous Isle, Virago editor Alexandra Pringle considers
both *Luminous Isle* and Bliss's first novel *Saraband* as
"extraordinary," despite what looks like the author's
negligible literary reputation. Pringle attributes this
seeming contradiction to Bliss's personal problems, and
her *oeuvre* of only two novels; but whether Bliss's neglect is
justified or not, her description of Jamaica during the World
War One era, in her second novel, deserves attention for
reminding us of Caribbean, colonial customs and attitudes
from a vanished past.

The author/narrator Em (Emmeline) of *Luminous Isle* was
born in 1903, in Jamaica, where her father Captain Hibbert was
stationed as an army officer; but after early, local schooling, she
was sent to stay with relatives in England. Although episodes
of recollection and flashback fill in details of the author's life
up to 1925, they mainly cover a period from 1923 to 1925
when Em returns from England for a brief visit to Jamaica,
and assiduously documents life in colonial Jamaica from the
point of view of her white, British ruling caste.

In Em's view, Jamaica is typical of British Caribbean
colonies in the early twentieth century, with the feudal

structure of a small group of affluent Whites (Europeans), an overwhelming majority of impoverished Blacks (Africans), and another small group of brown, mixed European/Africans in between. Built on African slavery (and also indenture of other ethnic groups), this structure was maintained by military force, represented in Jamaica by Captain Hibbert and his Garrison. What catches our eye is that Em bucks the trend by opposing a conventional view of her ethnic group who believe they endure beastly conditions of tropical heat, social and cultural hardship and worse, in Jamaica, for the sake of improving the lives of benighted, black savages, whereas Em is: "frustrated and stifled by ... their [white] sexual attitudes, their endless trivial gossip and pursuits, their golf, their tennis, their bridge, their vocabulary and lack of it, their social code with its hypocrisy and hidden indecencies." (p. 119)

In her Introduction, Alexandra Pringle claims that Harold Nicholson compared *Luminous Isle* to E. M. Forster's novels, and there are certain similarities between Em's version of Anglo-Jamaican society and the shallowness and hypocrisy of Anglo-Indians in Forster's *A Passage to India,* (1924) or exploitation of Burmese by Anglo-Indians in *Burmese Days,* (1934) George Orwell's novel about colonial Burma. Even stronger similarities exist between *Luminous Isle* and the fiction of Jean Rhys who grew up as the daughter of a Welsh doctor in Dominica, and later enjoyed a close friendship with Bliss in London.

Much of Rhys's fiction, especially her novel *Wide Sargasso Sea* (1966) and her story "Let Them Call It Jazz," (1962) expose inhibited or hypocritical English cultural attitudes. One of Em's earliest memories is of being severely whipped by her mother when, as a child, she lifts up her dress to exhibit her petticoat to boys with whom she is playing. Sarie Hibbert's excessively cruel punishment for a mere, childish prank, illustrates puritanical and hypocritical inhibitions every bit as crippling as the (psychological and physical) confinement of Antoinette Cosway, the West Indian bride of Mr. Rochester in *Wide Sargasso Sea*.

Em's perceptions also imply differences with the fiction of Forster, Orwell or Rhys. Her criticism of social conventions around her, for example, is partially prompted by her unusually tender (lesbian) feelings for women which fly directly in the face of early twentieth century, social convention, especially when they are accompanied by hostile feelings towards men as "Intolerable egoists" who "thought the world was for them." (p. 84) Neither is marriage exactly considered as an option for Em: although she gets engaged, chances are that her engagement will not last. To Em: "The stream of life to which she belonged simply refused to be circumscribed or cornered … She was not a wife; not even altogether a woman." (p. 356) Her aim: "to be sexless, creedless, classless, free" shows how different and impractical she is so far as conventional, Anglo-Jamaican society is concerned.

Two aspects of Em's character betray her impracticality: her perception of the "magical significance" (p. 134) of the Jamaican landscape, and her instinctive love for black Jamaicans. *Luminous Isle* abounds in passages celebrating the rich tropical variety, colour and splendour of the Caribbean, and in a novel where the "N" word is used explicitly and shockingly, both in dialogue and narrative, it is not at all unusual for Em's mother to describe black Jamaicans as: "an indolent, lazy lot…Can't treat them as if they were whites" (p. 144) Here again, Em goes against the grain with her: "strong instinctive sympathy felt since childhood for the black people." (p. 88)

The historical value of *Luminous Isle*'s record of racism is enhanced by a feminist critique which, like the early novels of Jean Rhys, presage a worldwide feminist movement soon to emerge. The "flowing delicacy" of the novel's prose is identified in the Introduction. This is generally true, except in some scenes, events and characters, not always directly relevant to Em's story. It is doubtful too, whether Bliss's novel is "extraordinary" in a literary sense, partly because of its bloated plot, and because its exposure of racism is bolstered by perceptions of black people: "as part of the landscape," when they are swimming in water, (p. 250) or by comments delighting in the: "inexplicable fascination of the black and coloured 'people.' (p. 262) Such comments sound somewhat patronising and paternalistic, since they are not supported by a credible critique of the oppressive political system that sustains the racism to which the narrator so strenuously objects.

RABID RACISTS EXPERT ONLY IN SMALL TALK"

Michele Levy, Ed.
The Autobiography of Alfred H Mendes 1897-1991, Kingston,
Jamaica, University of the West Indies Press, 2002, pp.192.
ISBN 976-640-117-9

Known mostly for his two novels, *Pitch Lake* (1934) and *Black
Fauns* (1935), together with ninety-nine stories, some of which
appeared in Albert Gomes's *Beacon,* and others in scripts still
not located, Alfred Hubert Mendes, a descendant of Madeiran
Portuguese who settled as indentured immigrants in Trinidad
since the 1840s, started composing his autobiography in 1975,
and covered events up to 1940 before giving up on the volume;
but he later updated it to 1975. Now the volume has been edited
by Michele Levy who revised Mendes's "Conclusion," and
supplied useful appendices, footnotes and information about
his poetry, family and friends.

Mendes's *The Autobiography of Alfred H Mendes 1897-
1991* outlines the experience of Portuguese-Caribbeans, one
of the smaller indentured groups or ethnic communities, like
Chinese, who settled in the Caribbean after the abolition of
African slavery in the 1830s. In 1846, the British government
permitted importation of Portuguese immigrant workers from
Madeira to Trinidad: "on condition that the immigrants were
to be employed on cocoa estates only where the conditions
of work were infinitely more suitable for Europeans than the
sugar fields that lay wide open to the debilitating heat of the

sun's direct rays." (p. 4) West Indians also were doubtful about the Europeanness of Madeirans as confirmed by Mendes: "Basque, Frank, Goth, Celt, Greek, Arab, Phoenician had been meeting and clashing in the Iberian peninsula ... and all had commingled to produce a mixed people." (p. 18)

As with most Madeiran immigrants, Mendes's grandparents - Mendes on his father's side, and Jardims on his mother's - did not stay long in plantation work, and soon set themselves up as shopkeepers, in the case of Mendes's grandfather, selling assorted goods such as Madeira wickerwork chairs and tables, onions, salted fish and Madeira wine. Considering that Portuguese-Caribbeans are generally well known as staunch Roman Catholics, what is unusual about the Mendes family, at least on his father's side, is that they were converted by a Scottish Presbyterian missionary in Madeira, and immigrated to Trinidad fleeing from persecution as Presbyterians.

After elementary education in Trinidad, Mendes was sent to a private secondary school in England, in 1912, but was summoned home by his father in 1915, soon after the outbreak of World War One. Keen to see military action, however, Mendes enlisted after he got back to Trinidad. Here, in a portrait that roughly reflects on white Trinidadians generally, Mendes describes two other white Trinidadians who accompanied him to war: "both [were] devout Roman Catholics and arrogant over the infallibility of their church, rabid racists, and expert only in small talk." (p. 43) Mendes later reports on the horror and frustration of trench-fighting in France, with the same unsparing detail as in his main narrative of domestic life, and experience as a Portuguese-Trinidadian during peacetime. Upon his return to Trinidad in 1919, he married Jessie Rodriguez the same year, but Jessie died two years later, and Mendes married for a second time. He also began writing poems and stories and, like his father, was active in the Portuguese Club.

While Mendes's main narrative offers revealing glimpses into the fate of the Portuguese-Trinidadian community, a more enthralling aspect consists of views and opinions about the pre-World- War-Two development of West Indian literature in which he played a pioneering role. His revelations create an impression of Trinidad, in literary terms, as the most creative of the Anglophone Caribbean territories, and four out of the ten chapters (Chapters 6 to 9) of his autobiography are devoted entirely to his writing, either in Trinidad between 1919 and 1933, or while he was in New York between 1933 and 1940.

In 1929, Mendes and C. L. R. James edited and published a magazine called *Trinidad*; and they brought out a second issue in 1930. Although the second issue did not carry James's name, Mendes is careful to add: "this did not preclude his [James's] putting as much work into the second [issue] as he did into the first." (p. 76) The magazine included fiction from Ralph DeBoissière, and some of its stories were re-printed in *E.J. O'Brien's Best Stories* for both 1929 and 1930. *Trinidad* was also praised by Aldous Huxley who visited the Caribbean and wrote an introduction to Mendes's novel *Pitch Lake*.

Mendes continued to work on his novels and publish stories locally as well as abroad. His stories were so true-to-life that one of them "Sweetman" provoked a libel suit brought by the individual on whom the story was based. Mendes lost the case and his angry father had to pay up. Around the same time, another member of the *Trinidad* group – Tony DeBoissière - cousin of Ralph, published two periodicals "Callaloo" and "Picong" which lasted a few years. Best of all, between 1931 and 1933, as mentioned above, another Portuguese-Trinidadian, Albert Gomes, initiated the *Beacon* which Mendes regards as: "the most advanced, influential and revolutionary magazine Trinidad, if not the British Caribbean, has ever known." (p. 85)

During his time in New York, 1933-1940, Mendes met many famous writers, including Malcolm Lowry and William

Saroyan; he also had sexual adventures, and married Ellen Perachini in 1938. Before returning with Ellen to Trinidad in 1940, always agonising over his writing, he set fire to seven of his unpublished novels in a fit of despair. Decades later, in 1974, he and Ellen finally settled in Barbados where Ellen died in February, 1991 and Mendes in August the same year. In 1972, his crucial contribution to West Indian literature was recognised through an Honorary Ph.D., awarded by the University of the West Indies.

"SELLING RUM AND CIGARETTES TO COMMON NIGGERS AND COOLIES"

Alfred Mendes
Pitch Lake: A Story of Trinidad, London, New Beacon Books, 1980. pp.352 (First Published in 1934) ISBN 901241 38 5

Alfred Mendes's novel *Pitch Lake: A Story of Trinidad* provides the most complete fictional account that we so far have, of the Portuguese minority in English-speaking, Caribbean society. Drawing probably on personal experience, the author describes events, around the 1920s and 30s, in the family of Antonio da Costa, an indentured Portuguese immigrant shopkeeper in San Fernando, South Trinidad. Antonio may be considered successful since his wife and daughters can afford to live in New York and, toward the end of the novel, he can sell his shop and leave Trinidad to join them.

But economic success is not all, since it sows division between creole Portuguese (those born in Trinidad) and Madeirenses or more recently-arrived immigrants from Madeira when, for example, it opens a rift between members of the Portuguese Club by creating one club for socially established Portuguese creoles, and another for Madeirenses: "the creoles felt they should not be associating themselves with the [newly-arrived] shopkeeping class," (p. 60) which leads the creole club to form a committee to: "black-ball any undesirable, so that the better-class [of Portuguese] is protected." (p. 60)

The trouble is that division between Portuguese immigrants occurs within a longer-established social context of deeply ingrained division on the basis of race, colour and class in Trinidad and the wider Caribbean: "The Portuguese, of all the white communities on the island, were the most despised: they made themselves too cheap by running the shops on the island and coming into contact with the common coloured people."(pp. 14-15)   Further division among Portuguese simply increases an already entrenched instinct for social fragmentation.

Pitch Lake is less social history than a dramatic study of perverse divisiveness in the mind and spirit of the chief character, Antonio's younger son Joe, whose six years of labour in his father's shop inflict a deep sense of hurt and humiliation in him. Having joined his father's shop immediately after leaving school, Joe felt he had: "wasted so many years of his life in selling rum and cigarettes to common niggers and coolies who were not fit even to tie his shoe laces." (p. 14) Joe's application of racially derogatory terms to Africans and Indians betrays the depth of socially engineered humiliation common at the time.

After his father sells the shop, Joe collects eight hundred dollars of his savings and heads out to the capital city, Port of Spain, where he lives with his reticent brother Henry and his live-wire wife Myra. Henry tries to get Joe a job, while Myra organises his relationship and eventual engagement to Cora Goveia, a resourceful but unconventional, young Portuguese woman. This fresh opportunity, alas, is blunted by rooted feelings of isolation and alienation in Joe. At a party: "he [Joe]was out of his element, as a fish must be when he is out of water; or better still, as a worm must be when it is taken from its earth-hole and deposited on the clean table of the scientist:" (p. 119) it simply increases his tension and anxiety.

What heightens this inner drama is that Joe has two relationships, one with Maria a young black woman in San Fernando, and another with Myra's Indian maid, Stella, in Port of Spain. BeforeJoee leaves San Fernando, Maria's mother suggests a more permanent relationship between him and Maria that causes him to erupt: "You've got a blasted cheek asking me to marry your daughter. What do you take me for? Go and ask one of those little coloured boy friends of hers to marry her, not a white man." (p. 45) This is followed by an even more embarrassing confrontation with Maria's mother which is only settled after Joe pays Maria twenty dollars. Still, Joe has sexual relations with Maria one more time before she migrates to Venezuela, and: "his [Joe's] conscience smote him with hammer-like blows. He felt unclean in every part of his body and mind." (p. 298)

The affair with Stella is more troubling since, by this time, Joe has a job as salesman in a large firm, and forms a relationship that is approaching marriage with Cora, a young woman of his own class. Joe considers his options by reflecting on advice from a fellow sales clerk on how to treat customers: "They [customers] lie to you about prices they can buy at outside, so you have to lie too. Here it's two negatives making a positive, not two wrongs making a right." (p. 284) Similarly, Joe learns that his married colleague Wrigglesworth has extramarital relationships: "'If,' he [Joe] thought, 'Wrigglesworth, who is a married man, can go to other women, why can't I, who am not married, have another woman [Stella]?" (p. 300)

To justify himself Joe reasons: "Damn it, Stella was a lucky girl! He had actually done her a favour, yes a favour! For him to be noticing a girl of her colour, her class." (pp. 254-255) Suddenly, events spin out of control when Stella becomes pregnant, and Joe's desperate attempt to arrange an abortion ends in tragedy. The constant churning of pitch black asphalt in the bowels of Trinidad's pitch lake, the world's largest natural deposit of asphalt, links Joe firmly to his homeland, and serves as a perfect symbol of the deep distress and anguish that he inherits from perverse and twisted colonial, social values in Trinidad & Tobago.

"COCK WILL GET TEETH BEFORE ANYBODY GET MONEY BACK FROM LAWYER"

Alfred Mendes
Black Fauns, London, New Beacon Books, 1984, pp. 328.
(First Published, Duckworth, London, 1935)

Black Fauns, Alfred Mendes's second novel comes out of a period when authors like Mendes and C.L.R. James (*Minty Alley*, 1936) sprang up with novels almost out of the blue, and other Trinidadians like Albert Gomes, Ralph de Boissière and his cousin Tony either contributed stories, or edited magazines such as "The Beacon", "Callaloo" and "Picong" that created a sense of literary awakening in Trinidad & Tobago, in the 1930s. Perhaps, most interestingly, all of these writers were middle class and all, except James, were white or coloured.

Mendes himself came from a Madeiran, Portuguese, business family who were wealthy enough to afford sending him to high school in Britain from 1912 to 1915: but the action of *Black Fauns* takes place entirely in a common tenement yard, in the city of Port of Spain, in the 1930s, with mainly black characters, mostly women, living in a society structured on typical Caribbean, colonial values of race and colour. No wonder, in an interview, the author admits that, in preparation for his novel, he lived for about six months in a similar tenement yard, in an attempt to catch the right atmosphere, and study the local, creole vernacular spoken by his characters.

The first strand of narrative in *Black Fauns* is the biography of an old, black, tenement yard resident, Ma Christine, who acts as spiritual leader and presiding priestess, largely because of her seniority through age, not to mention her expertise in obeah or the occult. Ma Christine knows everyone's business, and relishes every opportunity to proffer advice, often by quoting apophthegms from her dead "husband" Jordan Wellington which confirm the ultimate seal of her authority. Another mark of prestige is the "success" of her son Snakey in immigrating to New York and, largely to build suspense, we are reminded of Snakey's imminent return to Trinidad for a visit, at strategic stages of the story.

Ma Christine's tenement yard existence is one of hand-to-mouth survival. She was never married; she and her "husband" lived as partners/lovers just like other women in the yard. According to Miriam, another resident: "Marriage is made for white people, not for nigger people like all we." (p. 134) Except for the money they receive from their men, for instance, it is never clear how the women can pay their living expenses. Poverty is so dire it drives Estelle to deny the very existence of God when she rhetorically asks her friend Martha: "Can you worship that kind of god if he make you like you say he make you – an' then leave you to starve?" (p. 147)

Another episode is about Mamitz, a mature, mixed blood woman whose good looks and stylish dressing inspire everything from envy to fierce hostility among fellow residents, one of whom Ethelrida (Etel'rida) dubs Mamitz "de bitch" and never ceases to apply that epithet, from a safe distance, to every sighting of her. Ethelrida suspects that Mamitz is nothing but a prostitute, and it is not long before she and Mamitz come to blows in a ding dong, bare-fisted spectacle, witnessed by the entire yard. Mamitz's dress is torn, and support for Mamitz or Ethelrida is evenly divided among residents, while their trial ends with Ethelrida being ordered merely to replace Mamitz's dress.

In other episodes, Martha and Estelle are first seen in a very intimate relationship during which Martha steals money from Ethelrida which she gives to Estelle; but in steaming, hothouse surroundings where so many women live cheek by jowl, often sharing communal facilities, conflicts are rife; and at a later stage, after they fall out, Martha attacks Estelle with a knife. Constable Bartholomew cannot press charges because no one is willing to testify they saw the knife, betraying, with a nice sense of paradox, like honour among thieves, a genuine feeling of community that still survives among yard dwellers despite disagreements, disputes and seeming degradation.

As expected, Snakey's arrival, halfway through the novel, sparks further trouble. While Ma Christine is ecstatic to be reunited with her son, who brings hard cash as well as trappings of speech and dress that advertise his American prosperity, the combination of money and sex that follows proves too potent a mix even for the yard. Through deft masterstrokes interweaving strands of plot, Mendes contrives a dénouement where the money earlier stolen from Elfrida changes hands, and ends up in Snakey's pocket. Tension rises sharply; everything becomes not only confused, but dangerous; and Martha launches an attack with a penknife on Mamitz who dies later in hospital. As the author writes at the end: "Miss Etel'rida in jail, Miss Estelle in jail...Mannie in jail, Seppy dead, Snakey gone," (p. 326) Imagine the skill to deploy so many characters implicated in so many interlocking events that draw them all into such an explosive and ill-fated climax!

Despite confusion and bleakness, however, the action of *Black Fauns* is relieved by spirited dialogue, whether in anger or sorrow, that implies a tough and resilient capacity for endurance through pervasive humour among yard residents. Here is Miss Aggie's description of her fellow resident Christophine: "Christophine carry tale, she lie, she lie till she was more blacker in the face, an' bam! everybody was enemy...

She small like mouse, but she got ears more quick than mouse." (p. 47) Similar dialogue, throughout *Black Fauns* proves that, impoverished and downtrodden as they might be, residents of the yard remain profoundly realistic and self-reliant, entirely free from self pity or fear like Ethelfrida who, although realising she deserves to get back money already paid to her lawyer, calmly accepts the practical wisdom of Miriam's sage counsel: "Cock will get teeth before anybody get money back from lawyer." (p. 303)

"ONENESS FOR THE WORLD'S HUMANITY"

Alison Donnell Ed.
Una Marson: Selected Poems, Leeds, Peepal TreePress Ltd.,
2011, pp.184 ISBN 13: 9781845231682

In *Una Marson: Selected Poems*, Alison Donnnell, Reader in
the Department of Language and Literature at the University
of Reading, selects seventy-three poems from four volumes by
Una Marson (1905-1965): *Tropic Reveries* (1930) *Heights and
Depths* (1931) *The Moth and the Star* (1937) and *Towards the
Stars* (1945). To make up a total of eighty in the volume, two
poems are included from *Keys,* the journal of the League of
Coloured Peoples, together with five more that were previously
unpublished. Revival of interest at least in Marson's poetry
helps to redeem neglect of her trail blazing effort in promoting
West Indian culture, well before West Indian literature gained
international recognition by the 1960s.

Daughter of a Baptist minister, and born in Jamaica, Marson
won a scholarship in 1915 to Hampton, a prestigious local high
school and, by 1928, became Jamaica's first woman editor/
publisher with her magazine *The Cosmopolitan*, described as "A
Monthly magazine for the Business Youth of Jamaica and the
Official Organ of the Stenographers Association." Her work on
periodicals like *Cosmopolitan, Keys* and *Public Opinion*, organ
of Norman Manley's People's National Party, together with
speeches to "progressive" audiences, illustrate the originality
and independence of Marson's activism in West Indian social,

cultural and political development. She also wrote plays like "At What a Price" (1931), "Pocomania" (1937), and broadcast on the B.B.C. with "London Calling" (1938). In 1945, she started a new programme "Calling the West Indies" which was re-named "Caribbean Voices" and aired stories and poems by authors later regarded as pioneers of modern West Indian literature, for instance, Edgar Mittelholzer, George Lamming, Samuel Selvon, V.S. Naipaul and many others.

Since Marson's activism appears in the World War Two era when West Indians were beginning to envision positive political and social change from their status as colonised people, her poems examine colonial issues about racial discrimination, social justice and equal rights for women. Several poems consider the psychology of white domination through imposed stereotypes of black inferiority. The persona in "Little Boys," for instance, complains about racial abuse from white school friends because he is black, and "Cinema Eyes" illustrates Hollywood-type images of white superiority that breed self-hatred in black people: "But I know that black folk/Fed on movie lore/ Lose pride of race." (p. 141)

To Marson, white domination and black self-hatred collaborate to inflict intolerable and irremovable aggravation in Jamaicans. Forced by dominant European notions of beauty to press her hair and bleach her skin, although she resents it, the young black persona of "Kinky Hair Blues" reluctantly decides to do so purely to win a male admirer; and, as its title implies, "Black Burden" laments the psychological burden of inferiority generally placed on black people by Whites.

Other poems peddle the commercialised, tourist's view of Jamaica as a tropical paradise of sun, sand and sea, even if poems like "Home Thoughts" rely on more realistic documentation of Jamaica's botanical features and tropical riches. But "In Jamaica," records a less complimentary assessment of the island as: "a dreary life for the beggars," a rough life in slums, and a place where dark-skinned children are "facing a stiff fight," (p. 78) by a patriot, none other than an old soldier who fought in foreign wars (no doubt with the Jamaican Regiment) and returned to Jamaica where "All it hab is poverty/ But noting more." (p. 155) The soldier's sadly succinct conclusion: "Foreign is nice but here it hard" (p. 155) balances the more starry-eyed, tourist view of Jamaica.

There are also more personal issues in Marson's poems. In England she had fallen in love with a younger Jamaican, who married someone else, which meant that she did not get married until she was sixty, living in the US, and apparently suffering from depression or mental illness. Some of her love poems betray touches of sentimentality, while others summon enough intellectual rigour to redeem uncontrolled emotion and reflect genuine pain from unrequited love. If her best poems about race expose ingrained inequality without hysterics, so does the female persona in "Reasoning" stoically accept her lover's rejection with equally controlled resignation. In "Love Songs" too, the persona's firm assertion: "I sing of love/ Because I am a woman" (p. 114) projects a considered, actively womanist point of view rather than weak-kneed submission to male domination, or merely token, (feminist) assertion of gender equality.

As for the stilted romantic diction in some of Marson's poems, for instance, Wordsworthian rhythms and rhymes, or influence by Blake's theology about white representing evil and black good, they simply reflect influence of the author's British-Caribbean-colonial schooling in the 1920s and 30s. Nor does this detract from her musical gifts or versatility, for example, when she uses the Shakespearean sonnet form in her poem "Winifred Holtby" or the Petrarchan form in her sonnet for the International Alliance of Women for Suffrage and Equal Citizenship.

Marson's pioneering mastery of Jamaican creole speech not only catches the flavour of thought, speech and action in the religious spirit worship of a poem like "Gettin de Spirit," or the authentic drama of a Jamaican labourer's despairing wish for divine rescue from human misery in "The Stonebreakers:" it also truthfully documents the experience of people who, despite distortion and disablement by colonialism, somehow, retain faith in a Christian vision: "Of oneness for the world's humanity," as we see in "There will Come a Time." (p. 81)

A BAJAN MAGIC POTION

Austin Clarke
The Polished Hoe, Toronto, Thomas Allen, 2002, pp.462.
ISBN-0-88762-110-4

No wonder *The Polished Hoe,* Austin Clarke's tenth novel,
was garlanded with the Commonwealth Writer's Prize and
the Giller, Canada's richest literary award, for it not only goes
further than any of Clarke's novels or stories that grapple either
with racial discrimination in Canada, or political turmoil in
the Caribbean, but it extols characters with an instinct for
bristling speech and humour, despite a sorry history of social
depredation and economic distress. In *The Polished Hoe* this
instinct distils memories from the author's "Bajan" (Barbadian)
homeland into a veritable magic potion brewed in the deepest
recesses of his Bajan-West Indian soul.

A crucial element, especially in his short stories, is Clarke's
use of a West Indian oral tradition, inherited largely from
West African slaves on West Indian sugar plantations, and
consisting mainly of myths, legends, songs and folktales, or
riddles, sayings, aphorisms, proverbs and jokes that hugely
influence the basic speech habits and practices of most West
Indians. These habits appear in profusion in a formal, twenty-
four-hour statement to Sargeant, a policeman, by a black,
plantation worker, Mary Gertrude Mathilda, who is suspected
of the murder of Mr. Bellfeels, a white, plantation manager, and
former lover of Mary.

Far from regarding herself as a character in a common detective or mystery story, however, Mary speaks of the murder weapon, her well polished hoe, almost with reverence, as first belonging to her mother, and becoming an almost sacred tool or weapon, not so much of vengeance as of retribution for long-festering, deep-seated, ancestral wrong, what Derek Walcott calls an "ulcerous crime" visited upon black West Indians, during centuries of enslavement and colonialism. Mary confesses: "I am talking about more than one act. I am talking about history," (p. 102) which is exactly what we get as the novel launches Mary on a marathon saga of stories and anecdotes, half remembered facts, fragments, casual reminiscences and recollections that amount to nothing less than a history of Bimshire, vernacular for Barbados, where her story takes place, in Flagstaff village, about the time of World War Two.

That Mary, an unlettered, fifty-four-year-old, black, agricultural, field worker should furnish a general history of her native island is surprising enough; that she should do so through a continuous narrative that she instinctively recalls, apparently without preparation, is truly remarkable; that her account reveals more than we are likely to get from any academic inquiry, however doctored with dates, documents, references, records, notes and statistics is perhaps the most astonishing of all! For Mary's use of local, informal, Bajan speech supersedes results of formal scholarship, because it penetrates into hidden depths of narrative to uncover the truth of victims like herself, whose only weapon in resisting colonial domination in Bimshire, is her gift of memory and language.

Mary's account is based on her felt experience of issues, events and people whom she knows at first hand, having seen, touched and heard them, or lived with them all her life. Flagstaff village, like Bimshire itself, is small, and whether it is Reverend Dowd the minister, Manny Biscombe the rum shop owner, Waldrond the cabinet maker, constable Sargeant, Mr

Bellfeels, or any of the women characters, Mary knows them all from the inside. Not only that: their destinies are intertwined; Wilberforce, Mary's son by Bellfeels is Sargeant's doctor, and Sargeant himself was once romantically linked with Mary; not to mention that Mary's own mother served as Bellfeels's mistress before Mary.

In a socially incestuous community like Bimshire, feudal values bind master to slave, and workers to relationships between people of different race, colour or gender, one glaring example being the anonymous English Governor who visits his Bajan mistress at her home, while her husband is sent outside to the yard, and forced to salute whenever the Governor's carriage passes him in the street. Mary who remembers this story because the Governor's mistress is eventually prompted by her humiliation to poison her lover, is herself prompted to compare Barbadian victims of colonialism to little fishes swimming in a large oil drum of barracudas: the fishes, she believes, would have been better off in the sea surrounded by sharks, because sharks, at least, eat only when they are hungry, whereas: "a barracuda would eat you just for spite". (p. 245)

Coming out of a consciousness so intimately linked to everyone around her, rich or poor, high or low, white or black, Mary's bitter experience merges smoothly with that of her class, island and region. From her own bitter experience, she notes with simple but comprehensive candour: "The rich people, and the Plantation-people have land and trees, pigs and cows and money ...But all we possess to hand-down is love. And bitterness. And blood. And anger. And all four wrap up in one narrative" (p. 355) But for all its comprehensive sweep, this narrative would be nothing without Clarke's practised mastery of Bajan speech idioms such as: "best not to get involve in chicken fight if you is cockroach" (p. 72).

This is the pithy Bajan vernacular, at once humorous and serious, poignant and pitiful, that combines with oral structures of his novel, to meditate on historic bitterness, deeply embedded in the Caribbean soul, with such winning warmth and wry wisdom. *The Polished Hoe* is not only Clarke's crowning, artistic achievement: it stands shoulder to shoulder with the best West Indian novels, most of all, the evergreen, *In the Castle of my Skin* (1953) of George Lamming.

A WHITE WEST INDIAN'S PLACE IN THE CARIBBEAN

Lizabeth Paravisini-Gebert, Ed.
It Falls into Place: The Stories of Phyllis Shand Allfrey, London
and Roseau, Dominica, Papillote Press, 2004, pp.138.
ISBN: 09532224 1 1.

The nine stories in *It Falls into Place: The stories of Phyllis Shand Allfrey* are a mere fraction of her fictional output that includes about twenty stories, *The Orchid House* (1953), her novel and *magnum opus*, and three unpublished novels. Allfrey also wrote poems and worked lifelong as a journalist; and Professor Lizabeth Paravisini-Gebert's retrieval of the author's stories from forgotten journals and newspapers is an inestimable literary and cultural service.

Phyllis Shand Allfrey (1908-1986) belongs to an English family who lived in Dominica for three hundred and fifty years. Born Phyllis Byam Shand, she lived in Dominica until she was nineteen, then married Robert Allfrey, on a visit to England, in 1927. During the World War Two period, she was active as a Fabian socialist, associating with members of the British Labour Party, and working both with socialist author Naomi Mitchison, and the Parliamentary Committee for West Indian Affairs in London; but, in 1954, she returned to Dominica where she founded the Dominica Labour Party. After winning a seat in elections of the newly formed West Indian Federation, she became Minister of Labour and Social Affairs; but the sudden collapse of the Federation, in 1962, started a downward spiral in her political career: she was forced out of the party she had founded, and stubbornly struggled against all odds to maintain her own newspaper, *The Dominica Star,* until 1982.

"O Stay and Hear" the first story in *It Falls into Place* studies relations between a white couple and their brown maids in the Caribbean. The white mistress's exotic name, "Madame-la," gives away the story's lightness of touch since her only reaction when she sees one of her maids straightening her hair is to casually mention to her husband: "I can't think... why they [the maids] should want to have hair as straight as ours, when they mock at us so." (p. 21) The irony is neither critical nor snobbish, merely light, delicate, playfully mischievous, even elusive.

Similar irony again appears in "Breeze" the story of a fourteen-year-old, delinquent Dominican girl, a known ruffian and jailbird who had: "hit a policeman, sent him to hospital for weeks, kicked the matron, jumped the prison wall and disappeared into the hills." (p. 28) The affluent ten-year-old, white narrator is relaxing in her secluded back garden lawn, when Breeze suddenly drops out of a mango tree and threatens to bite her, unless she gives up her golden bracelet which Breeze snatches, then escapes. Throughout her frightening ordeal, the narrator is "huddled petrified;" (p. 27) yet, she is also "fascinated" (p. 27), and thinks of Breeze "with fond partisanship." (p. 28)

The only clue we are given for this curiously ambivalent reaction is: "perhaps ... my loyalty to her [Breeze's] enviable freedom." (p. 28) There is similar ambivalence in Madame-la's reaction in the previous story and we remember *Wide Sargasso Sea*, by Jean Rhys, another white Dominican, whose white West Indian heroine, Antoinette, reflects similarly divided loyalties by calling out instinctively to her black, childhood friend, Tia, in Dominica as she is about to succumb, in a fiery holocaust, in far away England, in Charlotte Bronte's *Jane Eyre.*

In "Parks" the scene shifts to New York where Minta Farrar, a mixed blood, West Indian woman who passes for white and is married to a white American, instinctively dresses in: "the costume of a native West Indian belle" (p. 37) one night while her husband is away, and goes to the Trinidad Nightclub where she happily mingles with fellow (black) West Indians, and dances all night with a Barbadian before she gives him some money and leaves. The escapade relieves her "torpor" which was "dangerous" and threatened her "like a sense of doom." (p. 37) Allfrey compares Minta to the heroine in Tennyson's poem "The Lady of Shalott," who was doomed by a mysterious curse to look at life only through a mirror, and dies one day when she looks out of a window. Minta too is apparently cursed with guilt over her confinement by whiteness; for while her status as a white West Indian assigns her affluence, it also separates her from her fellow West Indians a majority of whom are black.

Most stories in the volume tend to dramatise incidents from the author's family experience. "Uncle Rufus" for instance, is based on the author's Uncle Ralph who violated his white, caste taboo against marriage to non-Whites by marrying a coloured or mixed blood woman and having 'outside' children. Some stories like "A Real Person" or "A time of Loving" relate domestic incidents touched by gentle irony or whimsy, and "A Talk of China" introduces a young woman with a passion for socialist ideology very similar to Allfrey's.

In the title story the narrator, Philip, researches the life of a fictional poet Chrysotome, based on Dr. Daniel Thaly, a real-life Dominican physician and poet who was in love with one of Allfrey's 'outside' cousins. Like Thaly, Chrysotome achieves fame in France although he came from the same Caribbean island in which Philip was born, and which he now regards as a: "barely civilised colony." (p. 122) Philip's Aunt Caroline knew Chrysotome, and Philip remembers her reading George

Meredith's novel *Diana of the Crossways* in which the heroine Diana Warwick, a strong willed woman trapped in an unhappy marriage, is inspired by Caroline Norton, an early Victorian pioneer in the fight for women's rights. The elusive aspect of Philip's story is the result of an unresolved struggle of white West Indians, perhaps like Allfrey, with radical/romantic views, to fall into place with change from inherited, feudal ethics in their society.

TRANSCENDENT REVELATION

Joyce Gladwell
Brown Face, Big Master, Oxford, Macmillan, 2003, 180 pp.
ISBN 0 333 97430 1

Brown Face, Big Master, the autobiography of Jamaican author Joyce Gladwell (mother of Malcolm Gladwell), first appeared in 1969, then quickly sank into obscurity, supporting claims of the book's "suppression" made by Sandra Courtman, editor of the re-issued volume. Gladwell, the author, also reports objections to her book's "presentation of a racially mixed marriage" (p. 17), and its account of a "sexual encounter" which "was considered pornographic." (p. 17) Such bigotry is probably due to *Brown Face* being first published as early as in 1969 when sexual ethics were more traditional especially in an evangelical, religious readership like the Inter-Varsity Christian Fellowship.

The current edition of *Brown Face* is re-published: "in the light of feminist and post-colonial enquiry" (p. 38), and "as an important existential tract which explores notions of authentic agency and resistance to dogma." (p. 38) While the re-issue of an autobiographical work of such pioneering value is a great service to West Indian literature, the single-minded, almost revolutionary zeal used to justify its re-publication seems unnecessary. The book undoubtedly has special appeal for women and/or Christian readers, who may readily identify with its moving record of a young West Indian woman's deepest feelings and spiritual reflections and longings. But the appeal is not limited only to Christian fundamentalists or feminist ideologues. Nor does Gladwell reject Christian dogma in *Brown Face*: if Jamaican social history is taken into account, she rather struggles to reconcile her Christian belief in a benevolent God - the Big Master - to the seemingly contradictory evidence of her own, lived experience.

Joyce Gladwell, née Nation, and her twin sister Faith were born, in 1931, to parents who were both teachers in Mandeville, Jamaica. Joyce and Faith attended a primary school of which their father was headmaster, before winning scholarships to St. Hilary's, a Church of England secondary school in Harewood, Jamaica. In 1948, after graduating from St. Hilary's, and failing to win a further scholarship, like her sister, to attend university in England, Joyce remains briefly in Jamaica, before joining Faith as a student, in 1950, at London University. On her voyage to England, in 1950, the dreaded "sexual encounter" occurs, when the ship's doctor attempts to seduce the author, and only relents because: "it was an unsuitable time of the month." (p. 114)

In 1953, the author graduates from London University with a degree in psychology. As her book gives a report of eye-opening, sociological and religious discoveries during her time at St. Hilary's, it also reports on the author's experience in England, and her marriage to a fellow student, an Englishman, Graham Gladwell, who was President of the Christian Union in her first year at university. Later, we hear of Gladwell's role as mother and housewife, and of her family's travels to Jamaica and the US before they settle, in 1963, in Southampton, England.

So far as her spiritual odyssey is concerned, Gladwell inherits typically deep, Christian faith from her Jamaican childhood, but complains that: "God did not give peace as I expected." (p. 66) She accuses St. Hilary's of "a surfeit of religion" (p. 89) "moral tyranny" (p. 84), and a "strident voice of repressive discipline" (p. 93), all of which culminate in feelings of self-condemnation and guilt. Gladwell also suffers the first of several bouts of depression that last for thirteen years. Her wavering faith is further tested at St. Hilary's when she reads about "the intellectual inferiority of the Negro race" (p. 101) in the *Encyclopaedia Britannica,* and her confusion increases when she later becomes a victim of racial prejudice in several incidents, in England, one of them being reported in the final episode of *Brown Face* when the author is called "Nigger" by an English boy. The trauma shakes Gladwell's Christian faith to its foundations until, after meditating on Francis Thompson's poem "The Hound of Heaven" she accepts the possibility of a transcendent, liberating vision of peace if she submits herself fully to God.

But religious introspection is only half the story in *Brown Face.* What clinches the volume's pioneering value is its bold investigation of society and culture in a British Caribbean colony, around the time of World War Two. Seldom before, in West Indian literature, had the primacy of race, colour and class, been so clinically diagnosed from a personal point of view: "My father might have passed for white in England, though not in Jamaica. My mother's skin was smooth chocolate. My sister and I were in between." (p. 68) Her lighter skin colour prescribes a higher social class for Gladwell than for Jamaicans of darker colour. The British-dominated educational system is also part and parcel of this race-based, feudal structure: "Our books and our poems were from England, often about England, often illustrated by English scenes and faces." (p. 58) Only through agonising, self-abasing candour does Gladwell come to realise that her inherited, Jamaican social privileges derive from "false attitudes" (p. 88), and only then is she able to achieve spiritual liberation.

In England, similar candour enables the author to perceive cold, social relations that: "produced a death inside. I was part dead in a world of walking dead." (p. 153) Brief as they are, such quotations reflect searing simplicity in the author's language, and confessional insight into both her sociological observation and religious introspection, all of which seeps into a narrative of transcendent revelation, reminiscent of *Songs of Innocence and Experience* by the English poet-mystic, William Blake. Gladwell's book conveys a Blakean sense of innocent, childlike confession that inspires enlightening, inward illumination. As a West Indian woman pursuing higher education in the 1950s, Gladwell's career definitely has gender or feminist implications; but it is religious and sociological introspection rather than feminist ideology that transforms *Brown Face, Big Master* into a minor West Indian, literary classic.

"FOBBED OFF WITH TINNED SCOTTISH SONGS"

James Pope-Hennessy
West Indian Summer: Retrospect, London, B.T. Batsford Ltd.,
1943, pp.117

West Indian Summer: Retrospect, by British author James
Pope-Hennessy, (1916-1974) is a memoir of his brief stint,
in 1939, as aide-de-camp to Sir Hubert Young, Governor
of Trinidad & Tobago. The volume also: "sets out to tell
again the published experiences of nine English visitors to
the West Indies." (p. v). Pope-Hennessy's liberal sympathies
may stem from his pedigree as grandson of Irish-Catholic
Sir John Pope-Hennessy, (1834-1891) who condemned
the ill-treatment of Barbadian labourers when he was
Governor of the Windward Islands in the 1870s. In *West
Indian Summer,* Pope-Hennessy speaks through the device
of a fictional character, Cashel, a name adopted from an
Irish town that asserts the author's (revolutionary) Irish
ancestry, while adding a greater semblance of objectivity
to his narrative.

The first two British travellers discussed are Robert Dudley
(1532–1588), illegitimate son of the Earl of Leicester and close
friend of Queen Elizabeth the First; and Sir Walter Raleigh
(1552-1618) famous as an explorer and author who was lured
to the Caribbean by the legend of El Dorado and Manoa, city
of gold, which supposedly existed on the Venezuela/Guyanese
border. Raleigh's account in "Discovery of Guiana" (1596) is

one of the earliest descriptions of territory a part of which is today named "Guyana."

Reactions of the novelist Anthony Trollope in his 1859 travelogue, *The West Indies and the Spanish Main,* seem typical of an educated, Anglo-centric, Victorian gentleman who expects to see English customs and manners in overseas Anglophone countries. Pope-Hennessy contrasts Trollope with an English lady who visits St. Vincent expecting fresh tropical fruits like guavas, pineapples and pawpaws, only to be disappointed when she is served preserved English raspberries: In Trollope's view: "Nothing ... was of value in the West Indies that did not come from 'home.'" (p. 9) In Pope-Hennessy's opinion also, Trollope did not trust negroes, and felt that the future of the West Indies belonged to: "the coloured [mixed-blood] people." (p. 12)

The author of *Six Months in the West Indies* (1825), Henry Nelson Coleridge (1798-1843) was a barrister who, through marriage to Sara, daughter of Samuel Taylor Coleridge, the Romantic poet, became both the poet's son-in-law as well as his nephew. Pope-Hennessy does not much like *Six Months,* and considers Henry Coleridge "detestable." (p. 35) But even if Coleridge's comments in *Six Months* imply innate racism, he is not alone among nineteenth century British travellers. What is more, Coleridge displays some perception in recognising: "the vigorous precocity of life which is so common in the West Indies;" (p. 130) he is also generous and/or has a sharp eye for female beauty when he confesses: "I think for gait, gesture, shape or air, the finest women in the world may be seen on a Sunday in Port of Spain." (p. 142)

James Anthony Froude's *The Bow of Ulysses: The English in the West Indies* (1889) is especially interesting because of its provocatively prejudiced comments that drew a response from John Jacob Thomas, a black Trinidadian, who, in *Froudacity: West Indian Fables by James Anthony Froude* (1889) attempted to refute Froude's negative opinions and generalisations about ethnic disunity and futility among West Indians. Not that Pope-Hennessy completely agrees with Thomas. Indeed, he supported Froude's claim of West Indian futility; but did not believe it was the fault of West Indians. Instead, as already mentioned, he argues that: "everything that could be done to keep these [West Indian] colonies poverty-stricken and neglected, to make them sullen and disloyal, had been done by the colonial office: their prospects need not have been, but indubitably were, quite hopeless." (p. 79)

To Pope-Hennessy British Caribbean colonial policy is, fundamentally, one of exploitation rather than cooperation; it was capitalism in its most naked form: investment purely for profit without much concern for workers or their conditions. Observing the curriculum in a Trinidadian school, for instance, Pope-Hennessy writes: "By the same custom that sends tinned mutton, tinned peas, and tinned English potatoes to these islands, West Indian youth is fobbed off with tinned Scottish songs... boys seemed to have been writing an essay upon the constitutional crises of the reign of Charles the First...it might have been as interesting to teach these young negroes some West Indian history instead." (p. 93) Here Pope-Hennessy puts his finger on culture and education as essential allies of economic exploitation in British Caribbean colonies.

Pope-Hennessy's comments on naval surgeon John Waller, the Duchess of Albemarle, or Charles Kingsley, priest and novelist, may be passed over in favour of his remarks on *Domestic Manners of the White, Coloured, and Negro Population of the West Indies* (1834) by Mrs. A.C. Carmichael which throws light on African slavery, one of the most formative aspects of Caribbean plantation society. Mrs. Carmichael and her husband managed a sugar plantation in Trinidad in the early 1830s, but their paternalistic attitude blinded them to the real, underlying horror of slavery: "She [Mrs. Carmichael] never saw a flogging [on her estate] ... but had she observed other estates...she would have seen the long hide thong of the driver, and the bleeding wounds that its cruel and constant application left." (p. 93)

The integrity of Pope-Hennessy's insight into British Caribbean colonialism is matched by his factual, erudite, and elegant writing seen, for example, in his description of a sugar estate: "It was a swaying Elysian landscape. Beneath a sky of powder-blue the acres of cane trembled in the wind, scarlet and yellow birds dipped over the pastures; purple butterflies fluttered in the sunshine; at the rural stations stood hedges of pink and cream-coloured flowers like the enamelled toys of Fabergé [and further on] the white houses of the proprietor, the long negro barracks, the slender chimneys of the usines that form the heart of each big estate." (p. 84) Where else can one find a more pastoral evocation of a Caribbean sugar plantation, with the sheer horror of hell lurking behind its ornate, deceptive, Elysian façade!

"THE LONG STRUGGLE OF THE DARK FOLK OF THE EARTH"

Peter Abrahams
The Coyaba Chronicles: Reflections on the Black Experience in the Twentieth Century, Kingston, Jamaica, Ian Randle Publishers, 2000, pp.415. ISBN 976-637-014-1.

In *The Coyaba Chronicles: Reflections on the Black Experience in the Twentieth Century* Peter Abrahams, who was born in 1919, in Vrededorp, South Africa of an Ethiopian father and coloured mother, considers issues of race and colour following the collapse of old, European empires during World War Two, and emergence of new non-white nations in Asia, Africa, the Pacific, South America and the Caribbean. Abrahams migrated to England in 1940 and, in 1956, under influence from Norman Manley, moved to Jamaica where he settled in Coyaba, a district: "high up in the hills of West Rural St. Andrew." (p. 23)

For Abrahams *The Coyaba Chronicles* consists of: "remembrances and reflections on events and people who helped to shape and influence my life and outlook over these past eighty years." (p. 410) The first section of his book re-creates the author's upbringing, early career and relationships with other writers or activists, for example, African-Americans like Richard Wright, Langston Hughes and James Baldwin, Africans such as Jomo Kenyatta of Kenya and Kwame Nkrumah of Ghana, and West Indians like George Padmore and Norman

Manley, some of whom became politicians who helped liberate their native countries from British colonial rule. Abrahams assesses post-independence, African leaders with admirable tact: "Somewhere along the road to freedom, the leaders of our freedom struggles had become like those they had fought against." (p. 130) Only someone with his prestige of decades of reporting from the frontline of a universal, black freedom movement, could get away with this subtle rebuke of erstwhile black heroes.

In the second section of his memoir, Abrahams analyses Jamaican political history with inside knowledge and shrewd perception into the personalities of the first few Prime Ministers, Norman Manley, Alexander Bustamante, Michael Manley and Edward Seaga. He sympathises with their policies geared to Cold War exigencies, but laments the tenacious grip of West Indian slavery on the mind and soul of Jamaicans. Norman Manley's People's National Party (PNP) came to power in 1955 following two consecutive victories by Bustamante's Jamaica Labour Party (JLP); and Abrahams who served as editor of the PNP paper *Public Opinion,* makes no bones about his preference: "Manley's Jamaica, for me, was an example of how poor, Third-World countries should set about working their troubles away." (p. 200) Nor does he conceal his dislike of Manley's rival: "Busta was a shrewd and smarter political manipulator of situations than Manley," (p. 208) or: "Busta's government did not disturb the relatively enlightened colonial policies or dominant position of the local white establishment." (p. 208)

The final section of *The Coyaba Chronicles,* completes the author's commentary on Jamaica's decline into violence, random killing, and so-called "ethnic cleansing," based more on class than ethnicity, when whole black neighbourhoods in Kingston, the capital city, are forcibly dispossessed because of their political affiliation, real or imagined. Reasons for violence may be complex, but Abrahams gets to the heart of the matter: "Nowhere in Africa have I found the same deep-seated contempt for their blackness that I found among Jamaicans." (p. 299) The perilous psychological legacy of Atlantic slavery is also recognised by black American thinkers like W.E.B. DuBois who speaks of the "two-ness" of African-Americans: "a Negro, two souls, two thoughts, two unreconciled strivings, two warring ideals in one dark body," (p. 14) and Jamaican Marcus Garvey who defies: "the whole superstructure on which the notion of the inferiority of black folk was based." (p. 22)

The Coyaba Chronicles includes a vast compendium of theories of race and colour, Jamaican Rastafarians, Black Power, reverse racism in Jamaica, or the more mundane effects of hurricane Gilbert, in Jamaica, in 1988. Nothing is missed whether Cold War politics of the US in destabilising Michael Manley's government in the 1970s, or praise for Mikhail Gorbachev's role in ending the Cold War. Throughout, Abrahams gives the impression both of not taking sides, and being concerned only with accuracy. Despite his strong admiration of Norman Manley, when: "Forbes Burnham shamelessly manipulated Guyana's electoral system to keep Cheddi Jagan in the political wilderness," (p. 229) and Manley and other West Indian leaders kept quiet, Abrahams writes: "This is the one thing on which both Norman Manley, and later his son, Michael, disappointed me." (p. 229)

Abrahams's wide sympathies and rare integrity as a journalist are only part of his achievement: *Mine Boy* (1946) is a classic of African literature, the first of eight novels, not to mention documentary works, stories and poems, and another classic, *Tell Freedom*, his first and much loved autobiography, written as long ago as 1954. If *Mine Boy* exposes the calculated injustice of South African, apartheid colonialism, Abrahams's remaining books launch an unrelenting search for antidotes to the poison of colonial exploitation, and a noble meditation on: "the long struggle of the dark folk of the earth to be, and be seen... to be acknowledged as capable of running their own affairs with honour and integrity." (p. 336)

"REBELLIOUS SLAVES...DICTATED THE NECESSITY FOR EMANCIPATION"

Richard Hart
From Occupation to Independence: A Short History of the Peoples of the English-Speaking Caribbean Region, London, Pluto Press, 1998, pp. 189. ISBN 0 7453 1377-9

As solicitor, politician and author of several books, like *From Occupation to Independence: A* Short *History of Peoples of the English-Speaking Caribbean,* which probes decolonisation in Caribbean history, Jamaican-born Richard Hart (1917-2014) was also a founding member of the People's National Party (PNP) in Jamaica, in 1940, and a Marxist whose dedicated political activism, over half a century, entitles him to wear the mantle of the Anglophone Caribbean's Che Guevara. Unlike Guevara, though, who takes up arms, befitting a Latin American revolutionary, Hart adopts a more staid British model of agitation which did not absolve him from taint as a communist and, along with three other Jamaicans, Frank Hill, Ken Hill and Arthur Henry, being expelled from the PNP in 1954. He next worked as editor of Cheddi Jagan's party paper "The Mirror," in Guyana, from 1963 to 1965, and served as Attorney General in the short-lived People's Revolutionary Government of Maurice Bishop in Grenada, in 1983, before settling in England where he died.

Occupation sketches events in the political development of the English-speaking Caribbean from the sixteenth to the nineteenth century, including the arrival of slaves from Africa, followed by indentured workers chiefly from India, Madeira, and China, to continue the plantation work of slaves emancipated in the 1830s. As proof of the cruelty of the Atlantic slave trade, Hart cites a debate in the British House of Commons, in 1792, when Prime Minister William Pitt admitted: "the dreadful enormities of that unhappy continent [Africa.]" (p. 21)

Hart links efforts of well known British abolitionists like Thomas Fowell Buxton and William Wilberforce to the prosperity gained by British business directly from slavery, and notes that Buxton owned a brewery while Wilberforce was a banker. He also points out that although the organisation of these abolitionists was popularly known as the "Anti-slavery Society," its formal name was "The society for the Mitigation and Gradual Abolition of slavery" (p. 33) conveying an impression of caution or gradualism that does not quite convey the nobility of altruism and self-sacrifice for which these abolitionists are today revered.

Hart further claims that: "Buxton's gradual plan [for abolition] would have taken at least fifty years for completion," (p. 34) with the yet further implication that, rather than the altruism of white abolitionists, what speeded up the enactment of the Emancipation bill on first August 1834 were slave rebellions on Caribbean plantations, notably in Barbados, British Guiana and Jamaica: "Slavery was abolished by parliamentary legislation, but it was the rebellious slaves who expedited the process and dictated the necessity for emancipation in accordance with a precise timetable." (p. 39)

After emancipation and the introduction of indentured workers, which helped to control/suppress the demands of freed Africans for better wages and conditions, British officials devised a new type of constitution, Crown colony government, when: "control was exercised by the appointed [British]

Governor without the assistance of an elected Assembly, subject to directions from the Colonial Office in London." (p. 58) Even after emancipation, Caribbean colonies were still regarded as ripe for continuing economic exploitation: "Goods from the metropolis were allowed to enter the colonies and exports from the colonies to enter Britain on payment of duties lower than goods imported from non-empire sources." (p. 89) This piece of artifice, shamelessly termed "imperial preference," meant that colonial goods could be sold cheaply in Britain while the colonies provided a ready market for thriving British manufactures. "Imperial preference," in other words, made it: "desirable to hold other countries in colonial subjection." (p. 89)

In time, however, injustices of colonial rule stirred up unrest in British Caribbean colonies, and gave birth to a movement toward decolonisation, perhaps inchoate at first, but through shared revulsion against a growing sense of inferiority, gradually acquiring the resolve that would eventually propel former colonies to independence. Hart quotes from an English magistrate in Jamaica: "Our rule exists in the last resort in a carefully nurtured sense of inferiority in the governed. As soon as we lessen that we lessen the security of our laws." (p. 94)

To resist colonial subjugation expressed a desire for justice and self-respect. Titles of Hart's chapters recognise stages of decolonisation, for example, "Pioneering Nationalists Organise" and "Labour Unrest and Organisation." Hart is convinced it was working-class unrest and organisation through protests, strikes and rebellions rather than British benevolence that pushed the British government to appoint a West India Royal commission, led by Lord Moyne, in 1938/39: "to investigate social and economic conditions in [British Caribbean colonies] and matters therewith and to make recommendations." (p. 135)

The Commission's Report was submitted in December, 1939: "It revealed such extreme poverty, poor housing, malnutrition, unemployment and illiteracy, that the war cabinet decided not to publish it" (p. 133) so soon after the beginning of World War Two. Two factors influenced Britain's response to the Report: the loss of British prestige "in the eyes of subject peoples" (p. 137) following their military defeats by Japanese troops in Malaya, Burma and Singapore, and their increasing financial and military dependence on the US which: "wished to obtain access to Britain's colonies in terms of equality to American exporters and investors." (p. 137)

Although British Prime Minister, Winston Churchill, made a defiant radio broadcast in November 1942 proclaiming: "I have not become the King's First Minister in order to preside over the liquidation of the British Empire," the die of Caribbean decolonisation had already been cast. British concessions to Caribbean demands became clear in 1943 when Jamaica was offered a new constitution that included full adult suffrage: a clear sign of independence to follow more widely in English speaking Caribbean territories by the 1960s.

REGENERATING CARIBBEAN INNOCENCE?

Keith Jardim
Near Open Water, Leeds, Peepal Tree Press Ltd., 2001, pp.168

The twelve stories in Keith Jardim's *Near Open Water* depict life in the Caribbean through events based, usually in Trinidad, or another unnamed fictional island like it. A graduate of the creative Writing program of the University of Houston in the US, Jardim has taught in Kuwait, but his earliest experience is in Guyana and Trinidad & Tobago, and his stories which generally deal with the Caribbean or South America, have appeared in journals such as *Kyk-Over-Al, Wasafiri,* and the *Journal of Caribbean Literatures.*

"In the Atlantic Field," the opening story in *Near Open Water,* exhibits Jardim's expertise in creative writing through crisp, precise, closely observed and professionally drawn portraits that marvellously evoke the seascape/landscape of the Caribbean in all its tropical grandeur and glory. No names are given and not much happens in this first story, a spare and taut narrative about a boy and his mother at a beach where he goes off to play by himself, and observes a young woman, probably a tourist. Upon re-joining his mother, the boy notices that her dress is torn and her skin bruised which causes her to beat him, and send him running off again. Everyday or casual happenings may appear aimless or innocent, but take on the powerful suggestiveness of dark deeds in an idyllic environment of sun, sea and sand, partly because of a strong erotic current that runs through the whole story, and indeed most of the volume.

If dark deeds are hidden or not clearly visible in the condensed, taut text of the first story they can scarcely be missed in the second, "The Marches of Blue," which is more expansive about the feudalistic social structure of an island where a boy narrator, Nicholas, lives with his grandmother and people of a different class and race, for instance, George the gardener, and an old village woman Albertine. To young Nicholas, his surroundings appear mysterious or confusing; but his grandmother instinctively fobs off any questions from him, probably because she is embittered by decline of her (white) class, and the gradual withering of social structures around her: "Since independence ... the island had lost any real sense of discipline and responsibility." (p. 18)

Nicholas's grandmother seems more resigned than angry: "age dries up things in you, even poetry, like this damned island. Damned because everything that has ever happened here over the last 500 years was never meant to happen, was a mistake, wrong." (p. 41) This sense of disillusionment seems widespread since Albertine is just as explicit about it: "So much of them wrap up in that drug business with the government and selling land for the hotels and tourism to all them world-class crook." (p. 24)

In Jardim's third story, "The Visitors," more details of dark deeds and disillusionment emerge when two armed officers from the island's Defence Force, on mere suspicion that he is a revolutionary, cruelly interrogate Trevor, a young man whose family is in the shipping business. Jardim's contemporary Caribbean is a typically post-colonial or Third World society where suspicion and violence reign because some politically weak leader is nervous about insurrection in his own state. News from the wider world is little better, reflecting similar insecurity and impending disaster: "weather disasters, failing economies, war, famine, revolution, environmental destruction, and the resurgence of diseases thought to be extinct." (p. 50)

Upheaval seems universal, afflicting both the developed and undeveloped world, rich and poor, Whites as well as Blacks. A black maid who refers to her white employer as "Old Bitch" in the next story "The White People Maid" is as bitter as Nicholas's grandmother in her morbid, caustic appraisal of Trinidad: "I cry for this whole blasted island... I cry for my mother's early death; I cry for "Old Bitch" how she so lonely and how she can't get a man again; I cry for the poor children it have in this island – the richest country in the Caribbean – and I cry for the future and the past. And I cry for myself, for the education I never get." (p. 71)

Although other stories in *Near Open Water* dwell on this Naipaulian theme of chaos and corruption in post-colonial societies, the title story celebrates the solitude and bounty of the pre-Columbian Caribbean: "What we had were gods of our choosing. God of the blue, the sea, the air, the green mountains, the sand." (p. 148) Not only does Jardim fail to produce clear evidence that indigenous Caribbean people enjoyed a landscape free of violence, corruption or disillusionment, but at the end of Naipaul's *In a Free State,* the author confesses that it is hard to believe in such primal innocence, and one of the narrators in "Near Open Water" seems to agree: "Your Caribbean ecological lament is dishonest, yet truth escapes somehow." (p. 150)

Since indigenous Amerindians did not possess as destructive weapons as European conquistadors, perhaps what the European colonial conquest destroyed in the Americas and Caribbean was primeval enough to be considered similar to the innocence of the Garden of Eden. This possibility appears in two stories: "In the Cage" where a couple make love in front of a jaguar in a cage, and in "The Jaguar" where a jaguar becomes symbolic of a reconnection of the Caribbean with Edenic innocence.

The erotic charge of the first story carries a Lawrentian message of pure sex as a means of regenerating human sterility and decadence, while the animal in the second story apparently originates in South America which shared an identical history and ecology with Trinidad before the island became separated by volcanic action from its "parent" continent. In "The Jaguar" Dr. Edric Traboulay, Zoolologist and Conservationist, explores the possibility that the jaguar, which is rooted in Aztec folklore and culture, may serve as a symbol of reconnecting Trinidad to South American innocence.

"A SWIFTLY DISAPPEARING WAY OF LIFE"

Lawrence Scott, Ed.
Golconda: Our Voices Our Lives, Arima, Trinidad, The University of Trinidad and Tobago Press, 2009, pp.146. ISBN 978-976-651-000-8.

Golconda: Our Voices Our Lives collects verbatim comments, stories or memories from villagers in Golconda, Trinidad. Their village began as a sugar estate for Indian, indentured labourers in the first half of the nineteenth century when, it seems, the English proprietor George Monkhouse named his property after "Golconda" a former fortress near Hyderabad, in India, which he remembered from his days in the East India Regiment. The aim of the volume is to catch the experience of villagers in their own direct speech rather than through academic or second hand commentary. The whole enterprise of recording and transcription from more than a dozen Golconda villagers required, apart from the editor Lawrence Scott, the collaboration of three assistant editors – Naila Arjoon, David D.A. Maharaj and Marilyn Temull, and two local Consultant Historians - Angelo BIssessarsingh and John Ramsaran, all of whom doubled as contributors.

With so many contributors chiefly of short (usually one page) prose narratives and even shorter poems, the editor exhibits the patience of Job combined with the judgment of Solomon to contrive order out of disorder, and produce a text arranged in six main sections labelled: Sugar; Estate Life;

Religion, Traditions & Festivals; Childhood & Schooldays; Marriage; Life Stories. If some repetition creeps in, it enhances the oral medium, since it is natural, especially for a speaker providing two or more contributions, to slip into repetition.

For all its concern with naturalness, credibility or truth, *Golconda* advertises itself as a volume with thick pages of sumptuously glossy, white paper and lavishly coloured photographs, a format suggesting that even if the volume begins as a simple, community project in cultural retrieval, it transforms itself into a genuine labour of love, destined for display on coffee tables, rather than arcane research that fills otherwise empty space on a library shelf.

Historically, after all, sugar became the lifeblood of Caribbean plantations, never mind lesser crops like coffee, cotton, cocoa or citrus in the beginning. More importantly, according to Angelo Bissessarsingh in his "Prologue," indentured Indian labourers who first arrived in Golconda, Trinidad, around 1850, became: "the dominant fibre in the fabric of life in Golconda for more than a century thereafter." (p. XIII) Service by Africans to the Caribbean sugar industry, during slavery, and by Indians during indenture, for example, with Caroni Limited in Trinidad or Bookers Brothers in Guyana, identifies both ethnic groups as common victims, although, as Moonan Amichan correctly asserts, more than once: "They [indentured Indians] worked as slaves but they were never slaves." (p. 74)

Life for indentured Indians in the "poverty stricken barracks" (p. 59) of Golconda was as bare, basic and brutish as for Africans in former slave logies. Accommodation consisted of one room divided into a kitchen and a "gallery" which served as living room, bedroom and everything else. (Bath or toilet facilities are not mentioned.) What this could mean for Jhaimany Seeta Seebaran's family of fourteen or Radha

Benjamin's of sixteen we can only imagine! In Jhaimany's case: "Sometimes I use to go to school without anything to eat and I drink water until I come home." (p. 75) Meanwhile, from Jaitoon Mahabir we hear: "Sometimes we going to school, we eh even have a underwear to wear. Had to wash [same] clothes to wear next day." (p. 19) It would take more research than a thousand academic treatises to match the eloquence of "a underwear to wear."

Working conditions in Golconda were just as grim. Sookier Amichan explains that she was forced to work despite being ill. She speaks for her group: "We putting sugar shit on we head in basket (that was cane manure, we used to say sugar shit) ... And all that thing used to come down in we face. Rain could come, sun could come, you have to go and do that work, and that's it." (p. 34) This supports the notion of Golconda as a gigantic prison where workers lived in constant fear of resisting authority, violating inhumane rules and regulations, or objecting to enforced browbeating, further compounded by abuse from drivers, foremen and overseers while, according to Moonan Amichan: "drivers used to take advantage of the ladies working with them, [and] the ladies who gave in to the drivers got the easier jobs to do." (p. 14)

Despite trial and tribulation in prison-like conditions, with the rum shop and cinema as their only outlet of dubious social relief, the resilience of Golconda residents is nothing short of miraculous, for example, their survival techniques of maintaining kitchen gardens and farm animals, and resourceful improvisation of commonplace objects for household purposes. Most miraculous of all was the effort in building fresh community out of ethnic and cultural fragments from the colonial era, not only social differences of caste, but of religion too - Hindus, Muslims, Catholics, Anglicans and Presbyterians – and contrasting cultural preferences between Africans and Indians.

The result was a mixed, creolising effect: "I [Bernadine Sandiford] get on good with the Indian. *Bhagwat* I there. They never look at me bad. As a negro they always have me as their own. "(p. 114) If there is lingering doubt about the value of these comments and recollections, consider that the Golconda barracks were demolished in the 1960s, the cane railway discontinued in 1998, and Caroni Limited itself closed for good in 2006. As the editor of *Golconda* rightly claims: "one of the main values [of the Golconda Project is] to record a swiftly disappearing way of life." (p. 135)

"LIFE, DEATH AND LIFE AGAIN"

Lelawattee Manoo-Rahming
curry flavour, Leeds, Peepal Tree Press Ltd., 2000, pp. 120,
ISBN 1 900715 35 X.

When *curry flavour* first appeared there was no other volume
of poems like it, flaunting female Indian-Caribbean identity
with such panache. Lelawattee Manoo-Rahming's title
proclaims curry as an emblem both of Indian cookery and
Indian-Caribbean culture, and in sixty-five short poems,
spread over one hundred and sixteen pages, she invokes both
male and female, Hindu deities, through prayers placed at
strategic positions in her volume, pleading for peace, happiness
and guidance in the midst of turmoil and travail in everyday
matters. Unlike Guyanese Sasenarine Persaud, for example,
who writes about Hinduism as almost unchangeable, Manoo-
Rahming's Hindu faith appears supremely flexible, capable of
mixing freely not only with other faiths such as Christianity
or Islam, but also with other non-Christian beliefs, and non-
puritanical codes of conduct.

In the first dozen or so poems in *curry flavour* we encounter
the persona of an Indian-Caribbean woman plagued by
deep longing for lost [Indian] roots and a nagging need: "to
belong somewhere." (p. 13) (Manoo-Rahming who was born
in Trinidad of Indian indenture stock, is married to a white
Bahamian with whom she now lives in the Bahamas.) In
another poem "Footsteps in this Land," the persona's tone

becomes almost plangent: "I am alone/ without a story .../ in this land/ where I have/ no umbilical cord." (p. 23) Again, in "Footsteps," the persona prays to: "Atabeyra/ Great Mother of the Caribbean Sea/ Goddess of Childbirth") (p. 23) for children to bring her: "a voice/ from my ancestral spirits/ in that faraway land [India]/ in the east." (p. 24)

Despite ethnic, Indian (Hindu) origins, Manoo-Rahming's persona invokes an indigenous Caribbean deity that might discover a new sense of belonging in her Caribbean experience, as we see in poems in *curry flavour* that celebrate the pristine, natural beauty of the poet's native landscape, and the rampant exuberance of its flora, fauna and culture. Although she has observed similar beauties of nature in other lands, such beauties, she pleads: "are not mine." (p. 108) Instead, in "Waterfalls and Winter Streams," she extols her Caribbean: "Where the only falls are waterfalls/ and summer is perpetual," (p. 108) while in "Dreaming of Places I Have Seen," she boasts: "till my death I shall marvel at the beauty of the symmetry / of the curly tailed lizard and watch it close its eyelid." (p. 109)

But nature is not all. We have only to look at "Down Home for Christmas" to relish: "Fruitcake steeping/ Benny cake drying/ Ham still baking/...Poinsettia scarlet and green/ Brazilian pepper berries/ Red like English holly," and all the boisterous clanging and clamour that announce our right to: "Have a rake n'scrape/Slammin', jammin'/ Down Home Christmas." (pp. 86-87) As we learn from "Carifesta Five – Rebirth," such uninhibited boisterousness is part and parcel of a history in which the: "lifeblood of Caribs and Arawaks/ Africans and Indians [is] /buried forever in the/Caribbean Sea," (p. 112) and to clinch the matter, in the same poem, while acknowledging that: "genocide/indentureship and slavery/ [are] hidden behind carnival masks," (p. 112) the poet recognises the Indian goddess of wealth, Maha Lakshmi, side by side with iconic figures from Caribbean history, for example, Dessalines

(Haiti), José Marti (Cuba), Garifuna and Kuna (black Caribs from St. Vincent), together with the calypsonians Invader and Destroyer, and dreams that: "Hanuman [the Hindu monkey god] has been reborn/ in this Carifesta Five/ of my Caribbean Sea." (p. 113) What could be more cosmopolitan or creole!

One of the most innovative aspects of *curry flavour* is its witty, iconoclastic approach to gender on the back cover which announces Manoo-Rahming's attack on: "stereotypes of gender, the sexual and spiritual, and the personal and political." Flexible gender borders are exposed, for instance, in "Trini Tabanca – Carnival '92" where, amidst the frenzy of carnival, the persona defiantly, and scandalously, advises: "If yuh cyar get ah woman/ Take ah man." (p. 106) Many other poems including "The Earring," "Woman Love" and "Come into my Garden" just as defiantly celebrate Sapphism, the love of women by women, while the title poem, which compares various parts of a woman's body with spices that go into the making of a curry, is both a masterpiece of erotic writing, and a rare celebration of the sensuousness of Indian-Caribbean cooking, also exhibited in Lakshmi Persaud's novel *Sastra*.

Yet poems in *curry flavour* can hardly be said to blaze with celebration, optimism or promise. For all their spirited quality, as mentioned earlier, theirs is a universe overshadowed by travail and turmoil. In "Eve of Creation," for example, although the persona adopts a womanist portrayal of Eve as creative and liberating, she speaks of death as: "no longer the end/ but the bridge with which we cross/the blackness/ of our unfolding universe." (p. 73) Pleasure and pain are intermixed as basic elements of experience: "Is nothing like good and bad/ is only life, death and life again." (p. 15)

If this mixed vision calls for special technical skills, Ms. Manoo-Rahming is not wanting, for her poems abound with vigorous wordplay, comic inventiveness, and daring wit, not to mention arresting images, original expressions and fresh ways of looking at commonplace events, for instance in "Passing Places" with: "hens prancing around you/ like puppies on two legs," (p. 67) or "Between two Worlds" where a trailer is: "parked like a shipwreck," and in "Waterfalls and Winter Streams," where we can almost taste the alliteration of "s" sounds in: "sweet spring water satisfies the thirst." (p. 108)

A UNIQUE, FEMALE, CREOLE VOICE

Lelawattee-Manoo-Rahming
Immortelle and Bhandaaraa Poems, Hong Kong, Proverse
Hong Kong, 2011, pp.176. ISBN – 13:9789881932136

Immortelle and Bhandaaraa Poems, Lelawattee Manoo-Rahming's second collection of poems, appears eleven years after her trail-blazing first volume *Curry Flavour,* and it confirms the author's versatility through works of sculpture, drawing and painting, and nine paintings each of which is associated with a particular poem in *Immortelle.*

Titles of five sections into which *Immortelle* is divided announce the pan-Caribbean, and global scope of its themes, for example, Hindu goddesses Bhavani,Durga,and Shakti in titles of Sections One, Two and Five respectively, Coatrische an indigenous Caribbean goddess in section Three, and the classical Greek goddess Hecate, Queen of Night, in Section Four. These goddesses point to the poet's devotional approach, and reliance on the influence of divine intervention in human affairs. Manoo-Rahming's devotion, particularly to female divine beings, betrays distinctly feminist concerns, although, as hinted in the title to the volume's fifth section describing the goddess Shakti, who "Surrrounds and Animates the Energy of the Male God," these concerns generally appear within a larger, more all-embracing framework of human equality, irrespective of gender.

Manoo-Rahming's collective title speaks volumes, in defining two focal points of her inspiration: the immortelle, planted as a shade tree on cocoa plantations in Trinidad & Tobago, in colonial times, proclaiming the Caribbean as the physical location of her subjects, and "bhandaaraa" which identifies the Hindu metaphysical structure of many poems in the volume. As "Immortelle" grounds the volume's poems in a Caribbean history of cultural deracination and political and economic victimisation, "Bhandaaraa," a Hindu ritual that assists the soul to achieve release from the body of a dead person, provides a theology for discussing limitations of human finiteness.

Awareness of finiteness, an inherent gap between human aspiration and achievement, inspires some of Manoo-Rahming's best poems when, upon the death of close relatives or friends, they lament the mortal curse of our deepest strivings and aspirations, for example, of family loyalty, solidarity and love, being controlled by universal processes of change, decay and dissolution. A natural instinct to probe the mystery of death, appears in devotional writing by many English poets from George Herbert to John Donne, William Blake, Christina Rosetti and Gerard Manley Hopkins, although there is nothing borrowed or derivative in the authentic, Caribbean context of creole, Hindu, pantheist, or Christian reflections of Manoo-Rahming's poems.

In "Deya for Ajee," the first poem in *Immortelle*, the persona pleads with her dead, paternal grandmother, her Ajee, for wisdom: "To see in you my goddess Durga [one who can redeem situations of utmost distress] / Helping me to battle the demons of this life." (p. 23) While death causes pain through loss and grief, life is no picnic either. True safety or security must be sought through metaphysics, in a sphere beyond life. In her second poem "Mirror Glimpses" in memory of her dead mother and sister Sally, the inevitability of grief is again acknowledged when the persona detects, in the simple incident of a scorpion being found in a bag of cookies, evidence of predestination: "I took it as a sign/ Sally will die." (p. 24)

By repeating the name "Sally" in the last line of each of the poem's four stanzas, the crashing finality of the last line of the fourth stanza: "Sally is gone." (p. 24) packs a punch of eerie, supernatural power that leaves no doubt at all about the brittle impermanence and discontinuity of our lives. Then, with a glorious burst of alliteration and onomatopoeia, "Washerwoman" celebrates Sally's resolve to overcome the harshness of her life as an impoverished single parent, by comparing her sorry life/death to mere sounds of someone handwashing clothes: "Just your spirit escaping squooshhhhh/ Like air in the squish, squish, squish." (p. 27) That the supreme sacrifice of Sally's lowly life is worth no more than passing sounds of washing dirt away is no different from feelings of the brutally blinded Gloucester when he realises in *King Lear* that human life is just as temporary as the lives of: "flies to wanton boys." Act Four, Sc..i, l. 37)

Other poems illustrate Manoo-Rahming's inventiveness in choosing a variety of subjects and techniques. Some poems celebrate the lives of artists, musicians and murder victims, while others combine episodes from history with contemporary Caribbean scenes and incidents. In the process, literary and cultural references are boldly drawn from places as distant as Ireland, Malaysia, and Polynesia, while explicitly erotic poems like "My Coontie" and "Ghazal on Ageing" reflect equal fearlessness in confronting restrictive sexual attitudes, hidebound by prudish or sterile convention.

What stands out most in *Immortelle* is its deeply ingrained creole instinct, Trinidadian in flavour, for mixing and innovation. It is not just Manoo-Rahming's prodigal wordplay and coinages, for example, "MuchworsethanGodforlife," (p. 67) or "ovadotcom" (p. 93) and "planesforpeople," (p. 101) nor her comparison in "Immortelle" between Trinidad's Piparo forest, and the fabled forest of Rama's banishment in the*The

Ramayana: technically, it is her expertise with multiple devices, lines of different length in the same poem, varying numbers of lines in different stanzas of a single poem, the repetition of words or phrases as a structural device in many poems, and brilliantly original images, sometimes extended effortlessly over several lines, that clinches Manoo—Rahming';s uniquely creole voice, and her position as a leading poet in the Caribbbean today.

TRAGICOMEDY OF COLOUR-CASTE

Frank Hercules
Where the Hummingbird Flies, New York, Harcourt Brace &
Co., 1961, pp.212.

Where the Hummingbird Bird Flies is the first and *I Want
a Black Doll* (1968) the second of only two novels by Frank
Hercules, (1917-1996) a Trinidadian who studied law in
England from 1935 to 1939, and again in 1950. Hercules then
migrated to New York City and started a business which he
abandoned for a career in writing. As an African-Trinidadian,
he examines racism against Blacks both in his fiction, and
non-fiction works such as *American Society and Black
Revolution.* (1972) Although sadly neglected nowadays, *The
Hummingbird* delivers a devastating exposé of Trinidadian (or
West Indian) social foibles, as promised in a title named for
the hummingbird, national emblem of Trinidad & Tobago.

Hercules bluntly castigates Trinidadians for a social code
that regulates criteria of physical, racial features within a context
of White supremacy over Browns, Blacks, Indians, Chinese
and other ethnic groups in the British colony of Trinidad &
Tobago. When guests are invited to a dinner party, held by black
socialite, Mrs. Dr. James Napoleon Walker, the list exposes
her sycophancy: "the Honorable Goodboy Nicely, C.B.E., and
Mrs. Nicely, His Lordship the Chief Justice Sir Cato and Lady
Bombass, Sir Augustus Oilman, Bart., and Lady Oilman,
Sir Horace Sugar, K.C.M.G., and Lady Sugar, The Honorable

Bubulphat Dahlpoorie, O.B.E. and Mrs. Dahlpoorie. The satirical implication of names like "Goodboy, Bombass and Dahlpoorie" pours scorn on pretentious, Trinidadian dignitaries genuflecting so obediently, almost robotically to what they believe is due observance of British social rank and manners.

Other dignitaries such as light-skinned lawyer, Mervyn Herrick, are invited along with obligatory Whites from the Governor and Assistant Resident Surgeon down to less important British officials. Mrs. Walker's guest list flourishes an: "all-embracing cult of caste and engendering of hierarchy" (p. 148) within: "the tragicomedy of color-caste – the endemic vice of colonialism," (p. 210) as Hercules roundly excoriates West Indians for unctuous ingratiation in colonial relationships. Alliteration and assonance are deftly used, for example, to sneer at Mrs. Walker's gross physical appearance: "her umber bulk ensausaged in black bombazine."

Carlo Da Silva whose father is a Portuguese civil servant of middle rank, and his mother: "a mulatto woman of Anglo-African derivation," (p. 79) was a good athlete in high school, but was kicked out because of: "his imperviousness to learning." (p. 79) Carlo's: "dominant ambition ... was to be accepted without question as a white man." (p. 80) When his black girlfriend Mary Redeson becomes pregnant – "Too bad her skin wasn't lighter and her hair a little bit straighter" (p. 85) – Carlo is furious: "If you [Mary] think you'll get a damn cent out of me, or if you' brass-face enough to tell my father, I'll kick your stinking black bastard out of your dirty guts! You blasted nigger whore!" (p. 89) Mary's ill-treatment seems all the more vicious since her mother died tragically when she was young, and her father Henry wins sympathyy from the author: "for all his personal obscurity, [Henry] towered in moral isolation above the bobtail brigade whose primary loyalty was to their private appetites and who licked the hand that fed them." (p. 151)

The Hummingbird is less a tightly structured narrative than a flexible assembly of scenes or events characters, relationships, commentaries and conversations within a mix of mayhem and moral corruption that form standard, building blocks of social infrastructure in British Caribbean colonies. Among the few characters who either resist or rise above the mix are home-grown exceptions like Henry Redeson and Mervyn Herrick, or Dr. Ivor Griffiths, a Welshman who serves as Assistant Resident Surgeon. Herrick's own estimate reveals Griffiths as someone: "who did more to civilize the concept and practice of Empire than a whole pride of proconsuls.[he is] no molasses-minded sentimentalist, but a clear-eyed, firm-footed realist who was predisposed by neither race nor creed nor color to regard anyone as... anything but a person manifesting...the illegibility of the human palimpsest." (p. 151)

The last quotation illustrates the author's prodigal gift for florid phrase-making in a work of exaggerated, linguistic exhibitionism. Hercules's Trinidadian speech appears as the antithesis of V.S. Naipaul's demotic high jinks in *Miguel Street* when, in *The Hummingbird*, for example, sundown is described as: "the slow suspiration of the afternoon," (p. 80) while the educated class in Trinidad is: "a smug coterie of synthetic Englishmen – definitive blacks and dissembling mulattoes," (p. 122), bad luck is: "perverse accretions of persistent mischance," (p. 151) and Trinidad society is: "clamant, prismatic, pungent, volatile." (p. 211).

Such deliberately erudite diction is a satirical dagger that neatly punctures bubbles of colonial mimicry and exhibitionism, even if its very bluntness risks being taken as unconscious self-parody by the author. The redoubtable Mrs. Dr. James Napoleon Walker herself betrays a whiff of social change when, only a few years later, she composes her guest list for another party, and feels compelled to invite a: "nigger man" because he is: "in a big position in the civil service" because: "things getting upside down in this place, yes." (p. 211)

"WHEN DE CANE ... DONE WE FINISH"

Clem Maharaj
The Dispossessed, London, Heinemann Educational Books
Incorporated, 1992, pp. 137. ISBN 0435989246

The Dispossessed, only novel of Trinidad-born Clem Maharaj,
mounts a scathing indictment of the indentured labour system
of workers brought chiefly from India to Trinidad between
1845 and 1917. The focus is mainly on Highlands sugar estate
which Donald Scott inherited as a prosperous business from
his parents before they returned to Scotland. Despite lapses,
prosperity continued through World War Two when there was
a demand for sugar, and Donald was able to invest in racehorses
and provide lavish entertainment for soldiers and sailors; but a
sharp decline soon afterwards caused bankruptcy, and placed
Highlands in the hands of a receiver. During this period of
decline Maharaj examines working conditions at Highlands
when Donald simply wallows in despair, resorting to drink
and aimless carousal, surviving mainly due to the love and
loyalty of his African-Trinidadian maid Bella.

Living in "ramshackle barracks," (p. 4) huts and shacks,
Highlands' Indian workers survive on bare necessities, with
men, women and children confined in large, family clusters
like prisoners in overcrowded cells, their only "amenities"
being smoking, drinking and gambling! Parents would rather
their children work than go to school, for which they can
be penalised by "school police" (p. 11) such as Mr. Mitchell.

Sankar, for instance, sends his two children, Dano and Sakina, to a grocer and his wife who abuse them with so much work that the children escape back home, which is scarcely any better since Sankar who lives with his common law wife Suraji, can be found at home only on Saturday nights when he is drunk. Suraji's thoughts sum up her downtrodden feeling: "Dis me lot in de world, a one-night-a-week husband." (p. 11)

Resistance to these conditions is surprisingly muted. Eddie's suggestion that his fellow workers take up market gardening in a big way is discounted because they need: "a big estate [to] feed and clothe all ah we." (p. 53) Workers who are dispossessed and forced by poverty or other reasons to abandon India for impoverishment in Trinidad are frustrated by their sense of dependency: "de problem is we doh know to do anyting except how to grow cane an wok in de factory. Dat is what dey brought our [indentured] parents foh. We need to know more dan cane." (p. 53) Indian Indenture began as a means of solving the labour shortage when African slaves became emancipated, and abandoned work on sugar estates but, according to Tex: "all me have from de time me born is to know how to work in one place, no odder skill, notting to depend on. We is cane people and notting else and when de cane is done, we finish." (p. 53) Colonialism, in the form of a tunnel-visioned reliance on a monoculture of sugar cultivation that satisfies British trade needs or requirements instils a seemingly permanent sense of dependency in indentured, Indian sugar workers.

While dependency corrupts the lives of both male and female workers, women come off worse partly as victims of indenture, but mostly of their male partners. The plight of Suraji is typical. To some extent, she may be regarded as slightly better off than other women since her service as an untrained midwife wins a semblance of respect. She also deserves credit for unselfish service as surrogate mother to Dano and Sakina, but she becomes addicted to smoking and alcohol after Sankar whose children she has cared for, marries a part-time prostitute, and turns her into an object of pity, public ridicule, and a common street woman who is easy pickings for any man who buys her a drink. The author's laconic comment on her fate is pointed: "The rum flowed, the men came and went. Some even stayed for two days. At times when the hunger and thirst for rum was acute, she [Suraji] would hang around the shop to beg for money." (p. 103)

Suraji's degradation is a sexist cross carried by many of Highlands' women. Her friend Sadwine, for example, is coerced into sleeping with the receiver's agent Goddard, a white man, as part of his agreement to continue giving work to women workers. Such "official" sexual exploitation at least assigns a degree of perverse agency to Sandwine, whereas most Indian women are largely passive victims of sadistic physical violence from their own men. Sadwine who is married to Sadhu, has an affair with the night watchman Harry, and in a revolting scene where she and Harry meet for a lover's tryst in an outdoor toilet: "with white maggots circling the pit underneath their feet," (p. 74) Harry flies into a temper and slaps her until she spits blood, then punches her uncontrollably. Similarly, toward the end of the novel, feelings of sexual inadequacy drive Sankar to attack Suraji and Sadwine with a cutlass. Suraji is nearly killed, and Sadwine expelled to a nearby shanty town where she is later found: "bruised, battered, blood trickling from her mouth" (p. 134) shortly before she dies.

Maharaj's portrait of grinding poverty, brutal victimisation and dehumanising degradation among Indian indentured immigrants in post-war Trinidad may appear too extreme or exaggerated, lacking, if not in concerted protest, at least in credible thoughts of protest or gestures of resistance. But, as we see, Tex and fellow workers briefly entertain such thoughts before giving up to limply accept the futility of resistance. Not that it is either unknown or implausible for victims of abuse to inflict further abuse on themselves: it is just that, although historically accurate, artistically, the unrelenting record of uncontested oppression in *The Dispossessed* appears a little too pervasive and perverse.

"BRITISH BUT...FROM ANOTHER VINE"

Lakshmi Persaud
Daughters of Empire, Leeds, Peepal Tree Press Ltd., 2012,
pp.332. ISBN 13:97818445231873.

In *Daughters of Empire,* her fifth novel, Indian-Trinidadian
author Lakshmi Persaud continues her probe into Indian-
Caribbean, family dynamics that she started in earlier novels
like *Butterfly in the Wind* (1990) and *Sastra* (1993); but her
fifth novel introduces political implications by probing post-
colonial aspects of ethnic, cultural and social problems faced
by the Indian-Trinidadian immigrant family of Santosh and
Amira Vidhur, and their daughters Anjali, Satisha and Vidya
who have lived in London since the 1970s. The novel's title
"Daughters of Empire" applies directly to Anjali, Satisha
and Vidya - Vidhur daughters who were born in Trinidad &
Tobago, a former British Caribbean colony.

While Indian-Caribbean characters in early West Indian
fiction, for example, Edgar Mittelholzer's *Corentyne Thunder*
(1941), Samuel Selvon's *A Brighter Sun* (1952), and V.S. Naipaul's
The Mystic Masseur (1957) tend to be unsophisticated country
folk, engaged mainly in agricultural pursuits, now, fifty years
after Independence in Trinidad, the Vidhurs are seen, in the
words of Amira's sister Ishani as: "a family of substance"
(p. 237), and according to Amira herself, as: "a serious,
thinking, professional family." (p. 242) Vidya describes her
parents as taking: "very seriously the skills of living a good

life, a considered life [trying] their best to understand the drift of current thinking ... [and getting] high on knowledge, reason, on discovery, on enlightenment." (p. 301)

This seems too good to be true, since it carries some of the revolutionary flavour of Salman Rushdie's celebrated phrase, "The Empire writes back," in so far as Amira's family change to become more Western than Westerners themselves in claiming highly developed, individual skills and a pronounced sense of citizenship. Similarly, in Trinidad & Tobago, Lily and Palli's school transforms the poor health, daily hardships and frustrations of impoverished sugar cane workers in the village of Penal by: "sowing the seeds of a quiet revolution." (p. 55)

At the beginning of their life in London, post-colonial adaptation seems arduous to Amira who is frankly perplexed in contemplating inter-generational difficulties within her family: "I expected my children would behave towards me as I did to my mother. Whether my mother was right or wrong we listened respectfully... Sometimes I feel I'm losing authority. I don't know anymore what I'm meant to do." (p. 91) But anticipating the action of the novel, Amira wisely concludes: "I fear that if their [her children's] lifestyle becomes so different from ours that I shall have to learn to accept it." (p. 91)

Fortunately for Amira, the process of adaptation is smooth for her family: her daughters all complete university level education. Anjali the eldest, sets the pace and, despite one severe setback which leads her to take up karate, is able to repulse an attack from thugs and, in due course, marry an Indian-Trinidadian medical doctor, Praveen Mahesh. After an M.A. from the London School of Economics, Satisha begins a promising career at a prestigious London bank, then shifts to the research department of the Commonwealth Secretariat, before she too marries an Indian-Trinidadian medical doctor, Amru Sen. Vidya not only becomes a teacher in London, but marries a fellow teacher Mark Baverstock, an Englishman, in a humanist wedding ceremony when Amira and one of her neighbours read poems, and guests listen to the second movement of Mozart's Concerto for Flute and Harp.

Other post-colonial topics include the feminist issue of: "women fighting bravely for opportunities equal to men's," (p. 40) and the increasingly shifting notion of home or belonging: "Everyone needed to belong somewhere." (p. 58) But in a novel with a third person narrator, we sense the author's voice speaking, often through Amira, in numerous references to food as another example of resistance to postcolonial complications. The literary significance of food, after all, appears in one of the earliest English novels, Fielding's *Tom Jones,* where it combines with sex to reflect the eponymous hero's gargantuan appetite for life, or in the better known Dickens novel *Oliver Twist* where food proves to the undoing of Oliver when he asks for more.

The revolutionary aspect of food in *Daughters* appears in often lavish descriptions of delicious Indian-Caribbean or Western meals, or a mixture of both. The rich and sensuous quality of these descriptions gets to the heart of the matter by defining the delicately blended culture of the Vidhurs: "spinach with cherry tomatoes and fenugreek...grilled aubergine, cut open, flesh scooped out to which warm olive oil, sweet peppers, onion and roasted garlic, cumin and a single hot chilli had been added, bygan chokha, and fried ochroes, channa dhal, the flakiest paratha rotie possible." (p. 307)

Despite appearances, this meal is not purely Indian since it resists the snobbery of Indian (Gujarati) women who, at a wedding, dismiss Indian-Caribbeans as: "second class Indians." (p. 280) Neither are the Vidhur daughters purely British, as Satisha's English friend Edward Huntingdon concludes when he realises that Satisha: "was British but came from another vine." (p. 284) Far from being one thing or the other, the Vidhur daughters reflect a complexity found in novels by other female

Indian-Trinidadian authors, for example, Ramabai Espinet, Shani Mootoo and Niala Maharaj, which offer even more wide-ranging and challenging versions of mixed cultural legacies in the Caribbean.

A PAIR OF CHICKENS, A GOAT AND A BICYCLE

Badru Deen
Out of the Doubles Kitchen: A Memoir of the First Family of Doubles The Number One Street Food of Trinidad &Tobago." Miami, Caritrade Inc., 2013, pp.239 ISBN 06158555369 ISBN 13: 9780615855363.

Out of the Doubles Kitchen: A Memoir of the First Family of Doubles The Number One Street Food of Trinidad & Tobago is a biography of the author's father Emamool Deen (aka Mamoo Deen, 1917-1979) combined with a memoir of Badru's extended family. The focus is on Mamoo Deen's creation and marketing of Doubles, and Badru's own career in Banking, Human Resource Management, Marketing and Sales in Canada, Trinidad and the US. According to the author, Mamoo Deen's mission: "was not motivated by maximising profit but charitably driven to feed poor people like himself with a low-cost, high-protein, nutritious, vegan street food that was within their meager means." (p. 218) It was also: "to spread the spirit of entrepreneurship with his [Mamoo Deen's] Doubles business, which for him represented a celebration of struggle and triumph over an oppressive system." (p. 219)

The system was British colonialism, for Mamoo Deen and his wife Rasulan grew up, between World Wars One and Two, in Trinidad & Tobago, as descendants of Indians who first arrived in 1845 as indentured, agricultural workers on British-owned, Caribbean plantations. Badru sees his parents as "subsistence peasants" (p. 23) who: "radically and innovatively escaped their social circumstances in ... an act of resistance against the [British colonial] economic system of labor exploitation, subservience and poor living conditions." (p. 23)

"Chapter 3: The Origin of Doubles" describes the circumstances out of which Doubles emerged. One ingredient, chickpeas ("chana" in Hindi), was soaked overnight and fried the next day in onions, garlic, salt and hot peppers before being packed in small funnel-shaped, brown paper packets to be sold as a dry snack. In time, Mamoo Deen and Rasulan began to boil and curry the chick peas, and sell it as wet, spicy "chana" out of an enamel pot carried in a basket.

Mamoo Deen and Rasulan separately sold another Indian delicacy, "bara," or flat bread made of flour, turmeric, salt and ground mung beans. Thus, like many of the best-known inventions, Doubles was not planned or envisaged in advance but arrived, spontaneously, in a moment of inspired revelation: "In a Eureka moment, Mamoo Deen decided to incorporate his curried "chana" on a similar single "bara" with chutneys." (p. 9) The combination was so successful that customers requested an extra or "double bara," and this manoeuvre of placing wet, spicy, curried chick peas between two "baras," like a sandwich, heralded the "invention" of Doubles.

In Trinidad, in the 1930s, Badru's parents: "did not have the legal knowledge to protect their intellectual property." (p. 32) Since Doubles attracted other producers who claimed credit for its creation, Badru writes: "This memoir [*Doubles Kitchen*] of the first family of Doubles should finally put to rest the factual inaccuracies of the origin of Doubles in Trinidad & Tobago."(pp. 236/7) *Doubles Kitchen* diligently documents Mamoo Deen's energy and innovation in marketing his invention, while his Doubles Freight carrier and Doubles Box, an ingeniously adapted bicycle, with individual compartments for chana, baras, chutneys and wrapping paper, exhibit amateur engineering skills in targeting distant locations, especially schools which provided a "captive clientele"(p. 133) throughout the villages and towns in Indian-dominated Southern Trinidad.

It took courage and persistence to prevail against ethnic and class stigma ridiculing Doubles as coolie street food, for example, the refrain: "Coolie, coolie come for roti; all de roti done.' (p. 132) In colonial Trinidad, just after World War Two, for instance, class and ethnic divsions were noticed when when Mamoo Deen moved to a North-Trinidadian district like San Juan: "Here [San Juan] an illiterate Indian family was surrounded by middle class Afro-Trinidadians who spoke proper English and wore neckties." (p. 105)

Mamoo Deen also prized his individuality: "He [Mamoo Deen] believed that being one's own boss was the greatest achievement for a man" (p. 87) He flaunted self-taught skills in music and Indian film songs, and played the harmonium and other Indian instruments such as the "dholak" (drum) and "dhantal" (percussion.) All this went hand in hand with alcoholism and domestic abuse prevalent in rural Indian-Trinidadian (and Indian-Guyanese) society at the time. Although he was a strong family man, Mamoo Deen had frequent outbursts of drunken temper, often beating his wife and children brutally, or engaging in frightening physical confrontations with neighbours.

These shenanigans, unflinchingly documented in *Doubles Kitchen*, are a by-product of the: "indenture system of subservience [that] denied the laborers – especially the males – their self pride, their self esteem and even their manhood." (p. 62) For all that, Badru still sees his father as a man who started marriage with: "a pair of chickens, a goat and a bicycle" (p. 164) and, through his adventurous, pioneering spirit, and irrepressible instinct for improvisation, created: "a delicious, substantial, and complete vegan meal for the man on the go." (p. 93)

At one level, *Doubles Kitchen* illustrates Trinidad's ethnic structure, and the solid agricultural grounding of Indian-Trinidadians, at least up to the first half of the twentieth century. On top of that, the book identifies an entrepreneurial penchant for business, allowing even illiterate Indian-Trinidadians (and Indian–Guyanese) as relative late-comers, to make a mark on the Caribbean scene. Most of all, by showing how a common street food, became a delicacy among all Trinbagonians, regardless of race, class or colour, *Doubles Kitchen* detects in Mamoo Deen's life and career, a transcendent example of the growth of Trinbagonian nationality, almost as genuine as carnival itself.

"THE SADNESS, THE GRIEF, THE TRUTH"

Earl Lovelace
Is Just a Movie, London, Faber and Faber, 2011, pp.353.

By winning the best book award at the 2012 Bocas Literary
Festival, Earl Lovelace's sixth novel *Is Just a Movie* seals the
author's reputation as the most distinguished contemporary
Trinbagonian novelist who still resides in his homeland; for
the novel's subjects and themes are wholly embedded in the
lives of ordinary Trinbagonians; but even if he won a prize for
his first novel, *While Gods are Falling,* as long ago as in 1963,
Lovelace's reputation should not now be admired only for its
prize-worthiness: *Is Just a Movie* wins attention purely as an
inspired vision of the author's countrymen in a style of utmost,
crystal clarity and grace.

Concerned with fictional events that occur in Trinidad
in the immediate aftermath of the Black Power revolution, in
1970, and full of richly realised, entertaining characters, *Is Just
a Movie* shuns a straight line, chronology. From the beginning,
when Errol and his friends become dissatisfied with their roles
in a film of Trinidad being made on their island, Lovelace's
characters reflect the somewhat improbable quality of being
drawn together, entirely by chance or impromptu motives, into
loosely connected sketches. If characters such as Kangkala the
calypso singer, or Dorlene Cruickshank the librarian/healer
hold our attention, it is partly due to their intrinsic interest
but, more importantly, to the improvised or chance nature of

their lives, not only in their village of Cascadu, but in Trinidad & Tobago, and the Caribbean as a whole.

In "Funeral," the first of several episodes recounting the funeral of Dorlene Cruickshank, we get a glimpse of Trinbagonian Prime Minister (Eric Williams) composing a letter of resignation when, after a long period in power, his party loses elections, and he is forced to accept failure of his dream of: "full and unqualified democracy and a West Indian nation from Cuba to Guyana." (p. 262) After Williams won Independence in 1962, his dream became: "the challenge of blending the discipline derived from the order imposed by the plantation, the creativity that came out of resistance and the anarchy of individual rebellion, and at the end still come up with one nation;" (p. 263) but this dream is stillborn.

The mores and values that prevail in Trinidad after this failure are what Lovelace excels in duplicating in the apparently structure-less plot of his sixth novel through the fluid or reverse moral values that prevail in Cascadu, and account for the novel's lack of structure, for these values are exactly what form the basic social structure of villages in Trinidad & Tobago and the Caribbean. As Sonnyboy's grandmother advises him with wise prescience: "Wickedness can flourish, it cannot reign." (p. 36) In other words, any gesture of resistance or non-cooperation with the structure of inherited, colonial values is preferable to full cooperation since colonialism too once flourished, but does not reign today; and when characters in *Is Just a Movie* engage in bizarre stratagems, ploys or contrivances that oppose their colonial inheritance they at least express a will to resist the effects of colonialism.

In "The Coming of Electricity and Clayton Blondell," an episode about Sonnyboy's recovery of his African roots, for instance, Blondell's name sounds as improbable as his entire episode which is associated with modernisation and progress, seen through the arrival of electricity in Cascadu. Lovelace's list of attendees at the event takes up almost a whole page, (p. 175) and speaks for itself since, as pure exhibitionism, it consists of a weird, mixed, not to say freakish assembly of Pentecostal preachers, Adventists, Hindu pundits, Muslim imams, Hare Krishna, Shouter Baptist mothers, Shango leaders, and Clayton himself: "at the head of a group of women variously dressed in army jackets, in dashikis, some with caps, others with dreadlocks, others in turbans." (p. 175)

Since he has already recovered his African roots, Blondell is asked how, as a descendant of African slaves, he can return to being African in a place like Trinidad with so much racial mixing. His reply brooks no dissent: "Return? You have never not been African." (p. 180) So it is no surprise when Sonnyboy follows Blondell and also finds: "a secure place as an African," (p. 183) except for the telling irony with which Kangkala, narrator of this particular episode, describes Sonnyboy's African conversion: "We had gone forward to right back where we had begun." (p. 183) Incisive irony exposes self-contradiction both in the characters themselves, as well as in the novel's choppy, episodic structure.

The West Indian text closest to *Is Just a Movie* is Samuel Selvon's *The Lonely Londoners* which consists of loose, fictional episodes evoking the lives of West Indian immigrants, in London, in the 1950s. The wandering, vagrant and unstructured lives of Selvon's characters is a result both of their immigrant status, as of their Caribbean history of slavery/indenture; and just as Selvon's novel is written wholly in creole English, so is Lovelace's entire narrative enriched by pure, creole idioms blended into the living, musical rhythms of everyday Trinidadian speech.

Such is the clarity, grace and fluency of this narrative that they together transform apparently contradictory scenes, topics, thoughts and seemingly discordant emotions into a convincing vision of cultural rudderlessness that is as natural as tropical sunshine or fresh rainwater, all of which is celebratory rather than critical or farcical. The only difference may be that while Selvon's narrator, Moses Aloetta, admits grief over the misadventures of his fellow West Indians in London - "As if the boys laughing, but they only laughing because they fraid to cry -" Lovelace's characters are more confident and assertive in happily celebrating their misadventures. But when Errol confidently advises his fellow actors to leave the movie set with his sneering, dismissive gibe: "Is just a movie," the narrator, almost like Selvon's Moses, counsels: "you had to listen past the chuckle in his [Errol's] laughter to the subtle agony bubbling in his voice, the sadness, the grief, the truth." (p. 29)

"NERISSA...HAD LIVED...I HAD MERELY EXISTED"

Niala Maharaj
Like Heaven, London, Random House Group Ltd., pp.556,
2006. ISBN 9780099492276.

Like *A House for Mr. Biswas,* celebrated saga of the Tulsis, an
Indian-Trinidadian Hindu family during the 1940s and 50s,
Niala Maharaj's novel, *Like Heaven,* mounts a rousing recitation
of fortunes of another fictional Indian-Trinidadian, Hindu,
business family, the Sarans, during a period of about fifteen
years, immediately before the first ever Indian-Trinidadian-
led government was elected in 1995. *Like Heaven* is the third
book of Maharaj, an Indian-Trinidadian who studied creative
writing at the University of Boston, and worked as a journalist,
television producer and communications consultant before
settling in Amsterdam, Holland.

Following his father's heart attack, Ved Prakash Saran,
narrator of *Like Heaven,* gives up plans for university study
to tend his parents' small, furniture business and, through
enterprising innovations such as sponsorship of a steelband,
Saran's Symphonia, transform the business into a gigantic
commercial project spread over several districts in Northern
Trinidad – Croissée, Dorado and Balandra - all under the
banner of the "Saran empire." (p. 78) Such is Ved's boundless
energy, ambition, and success that the sudden rise of his empire
invokes suspicion that: "the Sarans practised some obscure
form of Hindu witchcraft." (p. 378)

The only witchcraft is Ved's entrepreneurial daring combined with unstinting labour and skilful marshalling of employees, imbuing them with similar enthusiasm. Ved's employees reflect the variety of ethnic groups brought to Trinidad under colonialism, slavery and indenture, for example, Suzanne his store manager who is of mixed (African and European) blood, Nerissa an Indian Muslim, and Charlo an African-Trinidadian, master carpenter and steelband leader who, in view of the sickness of Ved's father, may be considered as his surrogate father. Other workers include Bernard and Tony Antoine who are partly of Corsican ancestry, yet another example of Trinidad's polyglot ethnicity. Some of Ved's relatives too, his cousin Ashok and brother Robin, work for the Saran empire. But complications among female, family members, Ved's sisters and Anjani Gopaul (Anji) his wife, create ructions that puncture his get-rich-quick balloon of success.

Like Heaven is full of verve, vigour and a rollicking sense of fun mixed in between lavishly ladled layers of wit and irony. Ved's grand economic enterprise, for instance, involving huge sums of money, and extensive contacts with foreign business partners and local government officials, is simply denuded by the sleazy, ethnic slur of Hindu witchcraft mentioned above. The slur catches an essential, half-comic, half-serious paradox about Ved's society, conveyed by the author's direct commentary, and by opinions that characters express about each other, for example, Charlo's richly caustic comment on Ved's irresistible feelings for his white lover Janet Stevenson: "Tiger don't phase he. Hurricane don't worry him. Getting condemned by the archibishop does roll off he back like grease off a hot frying pan. But let one white woman leave him and he does dry up and shrivel." (p. 66)

Ved's mother, Ma, too, has a tongue hot like pepper, as he frankly admits: "My mother was one of the most difficult, obstreperous, demanding human beings ever created by the process of evolution, but in the midst of her unreasonable behaviour there was a kernel of irony." (p. 411) According to Ved, Ma never holds back with pronouncements such as: "What Trinidad know about civilised? Set of thief and robber running this country. All they know how to do is wine their waist at Carnival." (p. 378)

These quotations, neither arbitrary nor mischievous, tie snugly into one cardinal notion, Naipaulian in essence: that the Caribbean, Trinidad most of all, is perhaps more comic than tragic. Interestingly, Maharaj claims that she found it impossible to write about Trinidad until she read Naipaul's *Miguel Street*. One attraction must have been Naipaul's genius in illuminating tragic themes of loss, abandonment and corruption through exposure of their comic potential. The quotation from Derek Walcott's Nobel Prize lecture that serves as the main epigraph to *Like Heaven* achieves a similar, tragi-comic effect by describing Port of Spain as: "A downtown babel of shop signs and streets, mongrelized, polyglot, a ferment without history, like heaven."

A quotation from Walcott's poem "The Spoiler's Return" which serves as epigraph to Part Three of the novel claims that: "Hell is a city much like Port of Spain." Are heaven and hell the same? Although Naipaul and Walcott are nowadays at daggers drawn, so far as their art is concerned, they evidently could not agree more about the paradoxical, contradictory contrariness of their common Caribbean culture, especially in Trinidad.

For Walcott and Naipaul no less than for Maharaj, ethnicity is fundamental. *Like Heaven* is riddled with racial slurs by Indians against Africans, and anti-Indian slurs like the press report about Hindu witchcraft, and Anji's constant sneering: "That's what matters, eh! Property and inheritance. That's all Indian culture is about." (p. 212) All this makes Ved admit: "guilt and shame... with our [Saran or Indian] quarrelling and arrogance and greed;" (p. 539) it also makes him realise that reflection of the moon in the eyes of his loyal, long-suffering, Indian-Muslim employee Nerissa: "was like the gates to heaven." (p. 529)

No wonder that Ved comes to live with Nerissa and, after fathering her child, confess: "Nerissa had really lived, had lived in touch with the earth, while I had merely existed in a sort of fantasy." (p. 551) His confession not only brings the plot of *Like Heaven* to a fitting end: it extols Maharaj's feat in speaking with such warm and winning conviction, through voices of both her male and female characters, whether on business, ethnicity, culture, politics or food: "dalphouri and curried chicken ... home-baked bread and cassava pone, home-baked ham, home-baked piccalilli and black fruitcake." (p. 354)

"HIS [NAIPAUL'S] ACCOMPLISHMENT OUTSTRIPPED HIS CONTEMPORARIES"

Patrick French
The World is What it is, London, Picador, 2008, pp.555, ISBN 978-0-330-43350-1 HB, ISBN 978-0-330-45598-5 TPB

Not even his detractors deny Vidiadhar Surajprashad Naipaul's spectacular literary success: he won the Trinidad & Tobago scholarship that took him to Oxford University in 1950, and later gained a reputation as the greatest living writer in English. Lesser prizes and honours apart, in 1990, Naipaul received a knighthood in Britain where he lived since 1950, and the Trinity Cross, awarded by Trinidad & Tobago where he was born in 1932. His first response on hearing he won the Nobel prize for literature in 2001 was: "a great tribute to both England, my home, and India, the home of my ancestors," which, through neglect, lived up to a characteristic love-hate for the Caribbean homeland that inspires the author's best writing.

Although much critical commentary already exists on his *oeuvre* of twenty-five works of travel, fiction, history, politics, literary criticism and autobiography, no full length biography has related Naipaul's historical origins to his literary success until Patrick French's *The World is What it is* with its title quoted from the first sentence of Naipaul's eighth novel *A Bend in the River*: "The World is what it is; men who are nothing, who allow themselves to be nothing, have no place in it," which may be taken as Naipaul's own summing up of his writing as a whole.

With sumptuous photographs of family and friends, and helpful footnotes and index, *The World* offers a purple pageant of pictures and descriptions of people and circumstances displaying Naipaul's enwrapment in folds of an extended Hindu family: father Seepersad (Pa), mother Droapatie (Ma) with no one left out, neither brothers, sisters, aunts, uncles, cousins, in-laws, wives, nor literary agents, friends and acquaintances: a really full record, and one that makes for a greater sense of completeness.

The picture of Naipaul's English wife Patricia Hale is crucial, for the two met as students at Oxford university, and despite serious strains to their union, never totally lost connection with each other until her death from breast cancer in February, 1996. Hers was a rare and stoic combination of duty, self-sacrifice and love, since Naipaul often could not write unless she was present, and she was the first to read his manuscripts and give an opinion he trusted. Such astonishing love and loyalty, despite Naipaul's infidelity with prostitutes early on, and a mistress later, is perhaps best seen as the role of: "a great man's wife" who is: "absolutely convinced of their husband's genius and will do anything that the husband asks to promote that genius." (p. 364) More bizarre, since neither Pat nor Vidia held religious convictions, is French's account of Pat's funeral when Nadira Alvi, a Pakistani Muslim who became Naipaul's second wife, two months after Pat's death, scatters her ashes in woods in the English countryside, while intoning a Muslim prayer, as Naipaul silently weeps and waits.

French writes: "The best a biographer can hope for is to illuminate aspects of a life and seek to give glimpses of the subject, and that way tell a story." (p. xviii) If it does nothing else, *The World* tells a gripping story of the single-minded struggle and stunning success of a great writer, and the human expense they exacted, no less from Naipaul himself, than from Pat, family members, friends, and Margaret Gooding, the

Argentine of British descent who, as Vidia's mistress for over twenty years, was summoned and dismissed as compulsively as Pat, until being summarily paid off like no more than a common fish wife.

French does not merely tell a good story, or capture the personality of an eccentric genius: apart from interviewing countless people, reading Naipaul's entire oeuvre, including criticism, and studying correspondence or documents, in particular, Pat's unpublished but invaluable diary, French fully describes each book, and inserts critical comments of his own that help to estimate the ruthless ambition and sublime achievement that led Naipaul to: "sacrifice anything or anybody that stood in the way of his central purpose, to be 'the writer.'" (p. 366)

French correctly claims that: "his [Naipaul's] cumulative accomplishment outstripped his contemporaries." (p. 12) But Derek Walcott from St. Lucia also won the Nobel prize for literature without courting recognition as an eccentric, tormented genius, which may help to explain why Naipaul and Walcott are currently at daggers drawn, engaged in a literary war hurling insults at each other. The quarrel, like Naipaul's calculated slur on his homeland when he received the Nobel prize, has to do with peculiar traits of Caribbean history, its insidious mixture of race, class and ethnicity, and Naipaul's origin within a minority (Indian) ethnic group that forms merely twenty percent of the Anglophone Caribbean population. Perhaps Naipaul had something to prove that Walcott did not, which may be why Walcott would never be caught saying, what Naipaul does: "I am altering ways of looking and [altering] a set of values that have come down to us." (p. 296) The burden of genius may be harder to bear for some than for others!

BEYOND CONSOLATION OR REDEMPTION

V.S.Naipaul
Half a Life, New York, Alfred A. Knopf, 2001, pp.211. ISBN
0-375-40737-5 (First published by Picador, London)

Out of twenty-five books so far, *Half a Life* is V.S. Naipaul's
thirteenth work of fiction, with other titles devoted to history,
biography, criticism and, travel. Since his birth in Trinidad in
1932, and his first book, *The Mystic Masseur,* a novel, in 1957,
Naipaul has reaped universal literary acclaim, including the
Nobel Prize for literature in 2001. His writing traverses his native
West Indies as well as Africa, India, the US, Latin America and
England, where he has lived since 1950. Events in *Half a Life*
move from India to England, Africa and, briefly, Germany.

Chapter One of *Half a Life* supplies an outline by Willie
Somerset Chandran's father about their family's high caste,
brahmin background in India, and the childhood of both
Willie (named after Somerset Maugham) and his sister
Sarojini, along with a third person narrative by the author of
Willie's career as a student and writer in London in the 1950s,
his meeting in London with Ana, an African woman with a
white (Portuguese) grandfather, their move to an unnamed
Portuguese colony in East Africa, evidently Mozambique; and
the final narrative by Willie himself, describing his earlier life
with Ana in Mozambique, toward the end of that country's
colonial period of guerrilla warfare, and collapse of Portuguese,
colonial rule in 1975.

On page 131, after he arrives in Berlin at the end of his sojourn in Africa, Willie relates the story of his past life in Africa to Sarojini who has married a German and lives in Germany; but his narrative stops abruptly, at the end of the novel, in the midst of recounting events from the middle period of his past life. Nor is this structural disjunction either accidental or perfunctory: it deliberately confounds the linear sequence of ordinary events in order to capture the actual flux and change of real life. During the episode of his life in London, Willie is told by Roger, a young lawyer who has read his stories: "I know your great namesake [Somerset Maugham] ...says that a story should have a beginning, a middle and an end. But actually...Life doesn't have a neat beginning and a tidy end. Life is always going on. You should begin in the middle and end in the middle, and it should all be there." (p. 79) Roger also discusses narrative technique in Hemingway and Shakespeare, and confirms the emphasis Naipaul places on a disjointed, asymmetrical structure in *Half a Life*.

Asymmetry is an essential feature of the half life led by most characters in *Half a LIfe*. Willie lives half a life because he is always dissatisfied. Sexual dissatisfaction is fundamental. He has to rely on help from friends such as Percy Cato, a Jamaican with whose girlfriend, June, Willie has his first (dissatisfying) sexual experience. Then there is Serafina, friend of his publisher Richard, and, in Africa, his wife Ana as well as: "the paid black girls of the places of pleasure." (p. 190) He also has an affair with an estate manager's wife, Graca, whose mother was: "a mixed race person of no fortune; her father was a second-rank Portuguese, born in the colony." (p. 193) Considerations of race only make Willie's reactions appear more cynical. When Graca first meets him, Willie thinks she sees him: "as a man who had spent many hours in the warm cubicles of the places of pleasure," (p. 184) and he concludes: "Sex comes to us in different ways; it alters us; and I suppose we carry the nature of our experience on our faces. "(p. 185)

Elsewhere, Willie also speaks of: "my own sense of the brutality of the sexual life" (p. 196) And after admitting: "some half feeling of the inanity of my life," he feels: "the beginning of respect for the religious outlawing of sexual extremes." (p. 196) Perfervid agonising over sexual frustration or longing, at least in Willie's case, is a powerful sign of his own half-lived life that implies continuous need for penance or retribution.

No matter what specific form it takes, the half-lived life seems to be an affliction as universal as original sin. Willie's own half-life partly originates in sexual failure, and partly from his displacement in Britain and Africa. His background helps him to understand: "that the world I had entered was only a half-and-half world [in Africa,] that many of the people who were our friends considered themselves, deep down, people of second rank." (p. 150) For Willie, displacement is universal: not only is India displaced from the British empire, or Mozambique from Portuguese control, but displacement exists everywhere, within India, Britain, Mozambique and Portugal too. What is worse is that the half life caused by displacement requires penance, retribution or redemption that is unavailable, for example, although peace and normalcy are expected after the guerrilla war that ends in Portuguese withdrawal from Mozambique: "There were services of a sort again. The great hardship was over. But just at this time there were rumours of a new, tribal war." (p. 210)

Willie is dealt unrelenting affliction by his half life. On the last page of the novel he admits: "the best part of my life has gone [at age forty-one], and I've done nothing." (p. 211) He blames Ana for living her life, but she confesses: "Perhaps it wasn't really my life either." (p. 211) Themes of radical displacement and a primal sense of loss, exile and homelessness have plagued Naipaul throughout his career, and they always end in grief that is ultimately beyond consolation or redemption, bearable only through their appearance in prose of crystal clarity, pure simplicity and steadfastly uncompromising accuracy.

"THE NEW RELIGIONS ARE JUST ON TOP...
INSIDE US IS THE FOREST"

V.S. Naipaul
The Masque of Africa: Glimpses of African Belief, Toronto,
Vintage Canada Edition, 2011, pp.241
ISBN 978-0-307-39996-0

In *The Masque of Africa: Glimpses of African Belief,*
V.S.Naipaul, the Trinidad-born Nobel Laureate for Literature,
offers what may be his final work of non-fiction, capping a
literary career of interchanging works of fiction and non-
fiction, from early non-fiction titles like *The Middle Passage*
(1963) and *An Area of Darkness* (1964) through, for example,
India a Wounded Civilisation (1977) *Among the Believers:
An Islamic Journey* (1981) and *India: A Million Mutinies
Now* (1990) to *Beyond Belief: Islamic Excursions Among the
Converted Peoples* (1998).

The Masque of Africa relates visits made to six African
countries when, as Naipaul explains: "I had wanted, when I
began this book, to stay away from politics and race, to look
below these themes to the core of African belief." (pp. 213-214)
Even for a seasoned traveller and writer of Naipaul's calibre,
this is a tall order, not only because Africa is a huge continent
with ancient languages, cultures and beliefs, but because
Naipaul's reputation was sullied by negative or hostile
reactions to his previous writings on African subjects or
people of African descent.

In the first section of the book "The Tomb at Kasubi," about Uganda, Naipaul considers the general impact of two foreign religions, Islam and Christianity, on traditional, African belief: "The traditional African religion had no doctrine; it expressed itself best in its practices and in things like the hundred fearful charms the witch doctors present to Mutesa I before the naval battle against the Wavuma in 1875." (p. 34) The big question is: "Why had the foreign religions wrought such havoc with African belief?" (p. 7)

In the second section, on Nigeria, Naipaul speaks with several Nigerians including Adesina who: "had started with nothing, in a far removed world, [and] was now the managing director of a great corporation." (p. 53) The interview with Adesina shows Nigeria in throes of change and modernisation, and reveals Naipaul as past master of a literary form that mixes character sketches with astutely observed descriptions of landscape and commentaries into a captivating species of non-fiction writing, for example: "The road where we were was hardly a road. The drains were overfull; the flood had scoured the gutters into an unspeakable dark mess, added plastic bottles and other vegetable rubbish, and this all bounced and raged down." (p. 85) Unflinching observation entails an uncanny ability that can report the truth frankly, even harshly, yet not without a kind of hard-fought sympathy for his subject: the wretched condition of the road, for instance, implies natural sympathy for its users.

The third section of *The Masque of Africa*, "Men Possessed," on Ghana, touches on the all-encompassing problem of tradition v. modernity in Africa. According to one of the author's interlocutors, Pa-boh: "Traditional religion in Ghana is dying slowly...We have witches who fly in the air. But when we saw aircraft we came to abhor what was our culture. I think the modern African is in a very difficult situation." (p. 123) Yet "Men Possessed" turns into one of the happier episodes in the book after the author meets Flight Lieutenant Jerry Rawlings who, as son of a Ghanaian mother and Scottish father, became Nigerian head of state three times between 1979 and 2001.

Rawlings was first jailed for taking part in a coup in May, 1979, but shortly afterwards, other army officers staged another coup, and made him head of state. During his term in power, Rawlings cleared up corruption in the civil service, army and business, before voluntarily returning Ghana to civilian rule. Naipaul's withering comment on such selfless and high-minded patriotism is predictably reductive: "It was a romantic idea: if you cleaned up a country, it looked after itself. But people and countries were more complicated than he [Rawlings] thought; and a year later he led a coup against the people he had placed in power." (p. 141) Nothing proclaims Naipaul's sternly realistic and caustic reflection on corruptible human nature more than this; although admiration for Rawlings may not be completely lost, what remains is Naipaul's legendary conviction in the ingrained irreversibility of human frailty.

"The Forest King," Chapter Four, recalls an earlier visit to Ivory Coast in 1982 when the French-speaking territory seemed to flourish under Houphouet Boigny as President. Naipaul's views are seemingly dismissive perhaps because of an earlier essay "The Crocodiles of Yamoussoukro" that he published in 1984, in "The New Yorker," about Ivory Coast and Houphouet Boigny's grandiose construction of a cathedral with a dome intended to be higher than St. Peter's in Rome, and a moat with sacred crocodiles.

"Children of the Forest," about Gabon, another French-speaking country, is more substantial. Gabon was visited in 1893 and 1895 by Mary Kingsley, the English explorer and travel writer. It is also where, at Lambaréné, Dr. Albert Schweitzer, the renowned, Swiss philanthropist, established his hospital in 1915. Various local speakers discuss endemic issues about African belief already mentioned, for example, "The new religions, Islam and Christianity, are just on top. Inside us is the forest," (p. 161) or, expressed another way: "In the human beings you have divisions." (p. 16)

While, to some extent, by focusing on religious conflict, tensions between tradition and modernity, or other aspects of African belief, in the previous five chapters of *The Masque of Africa*, Naipaul is largely able to achieve his aim of avoiding problems of politics and race, his plan somewhat unravels in the final chapter on post-apartheid South Africa "Private Monuments, Private Wastelands" when he confesses: "I felt stymied in South Africa and saw that here race was all in all; that race ran as deep as religion elsewhere." (p. 214) Apartheid had turned race into religion, and Fatima, Naipaul's coloured guide: "understood... the deception for Africans, of political freedom and the end of apartheid." (p. 213)

"SO TRINIDADIAN CULTURE DON'T HAVE PLACE FOR INDIANS TOO?"

Ramabai Espinet
The Swinging Bridge, Toronto, Harper Collins Publishers
Ltd., 2003. 306pp. $32.95. ISBN 0-00-225520-0

Ramabai Espinet's writing, including poetry, children's fiction,
editorial and scholarly work, has been very promising; her
novel *The Swinging Bridge* fulfils the promise by reconstructing
Indian-Caribbean history, fleshing it out with characters and
events that take in the migration of one woman from India,
at the end of the nineteenth century, through her settlement
in Trinidad as an indentured immigrant, and her family's
fortunes, four generations later, in the 1960s, when family
members are driven to migrate once more, this time to Canada.

The Swinging Bridge is narrated by Mona Singh, a forty-two-
year old Indian-Trinidadian woman who, with her parents,
brother Kello and sister Babsie, emigrated from Trinidad to
Canada in 1970. Despite different directions taken by family
members, tragic news of Kello's illness and impending death
suddenly brings the family together, although because of
puritanical inhibitions at the time, Kello's parents are told he
suffers from cancer, not Aids. This tragic turn inspires Mona's
reflections not only on the family, but on her own identity
as an Indian-Trinidadian woman, and on the fate of Indians
in the Caribbean as a whole. Her reflections and subsequent
visit to Trinidad, in search of family history, form the text of

The Swinging Bridge. Mona's reflections centre on one main question as expressed by her cousin Bess: "So Trinidadian culture don't have place for Indians too?" (p. 285)

The theme of a place for Indians in Trinidadian society contradicts an Afro-centric view of the Caribbean that has prevailed from the beginning, and intensified since the Independence era of the 1960s. Originality of theme is matched by an innovative structure dividing the novel into three parts, each preceded by a brief passage "Kala Pani" that sketches the haunting story of Mona's great grandmother Gainder, who came as an indentured immigrant from India to Trinidad, on the ship "The Artist", in 1879. At the time, Gainder was only thirteen years old, but her parents had died prematurely and she was forced into marriage to an older man. She escaped only to be caught in a trap set for her by agents recruiting immigrants for the Caribbean.

If that were the end of Gainder's troubles it would be harrowing enough, but on board ship, she is attacked by a white sailor and is rescued by a fellow, indentured immigrant, Jeevan, a stick fighter who kills the sailor, and receives summary (in)justice of abandonment, in prison on the tiny island of St. Helena, off the West coast of Africa. The final, suspenseful climax of Gainder's story is only tracked down by her great granddaughter at the very end of the novel, when it completes a structure that is seamlessly circular, beginning and ending with Gainder.

In *The Swinging Bridge* we follow Gainder's hapless victimization as a woman, through her entire progeny, down to the narrator's generation, and observe its searing indictment of the violence to which Indian-Caribbean wives, mothers and daughters have been consistently subjected. By the author's account, it seems that virtually no Indian female is safe from sexual harassment or violence either within or outside her family. Mona herself, her mother and other female characters in the novel are all victims; and she adds the horrifying story of her school friend, Rosanna, whose boyfriend was found in her bedroom chopped up "fine, fine" by Rosanna's father and uncles. Even if this account of sexist violence seems excessive in *The Swinging Bridge*, the historical record of wife murder, choppings, beatings and general abuse among Indian indentured immigrants is indisputable.

Its innovative structure, and relentless indictment of sexism are what most account for the triumph of *The Swinging Bridge* as an educated meditation on the fate of Indian-Caribbean culture in the post-colonial Caribbean. Since the novel's Indian-Trinidadian protagonists emigrate from Trinidad to escape discrimination, only to find the same thing in Canada, they may be said to run from pillar to post. Mona's mother tells her: "I didn't grow up like you all, you know, pitching here, there and everywhere. I came from somewhere." (p. 253) Still, although Mona's generation is more footloose than her mother's, they are all forced eventually to migrate to Canada. The swinging bridge on which Gainder boards "The Artist" in 1879, and which Mona later encounters in a game that pitches her here, there and everywhere, is a perfect symbol of her fragmented identity.

On one hand, while *The Swinging Bridge* faithfully chronicles each painful moment of Gainder's tortuous journey from India to Trinidad, the trauma of her family's second migration, and the disturbing dilemma of Mona's crisis of identity and placelessness, the novel also records Mona's umbilical identification with every aspect of the Trinidad landscape, from its trees, flowers, crops, fruits, and animals to its food, calypso and carnival which conclusively confirms her both as ethnically Indian and, culturally, one hundred percent Trinidadian. Thus the answer to Bess's question about a place for Indians in Trinidad is a resounding capital "YES," which is just as resoundingly vindicated when, partly to satisfy the dying wish of her brother, Kello, Mona returns to Trinidad to re-purchase the land where she grew up before her father sold their house.

The epigraph to the novel: "I enter as one who raises/ a cloth from a covered face,/ not knowing what the narrow/ almond husk of my house holds for me - /my salvation or my ruin" a quotation from the Chilean poet Gabriela Mistral - encapsulates the unrelieved tone of Mona's narrative which fearlessly lifts a veil to reveal hidden, unsavoury truth that could spell either "salvation" or "ruin;" for not only does *The Swinging Bridge* herald salvation: it also blazes a fictional trail that takes in the troubled totality of Caribbean experience from India via the Caribbean to Canada, just as the fiction of other writers, notably Caryl Phillips, meditates on similarly troubled Caribbean experience from Africa to the Caribbean and destinations beyond.

SECRETS OF SIN IN TROPICAL EDEN

Kelvin Christopher James
Secrets, New York, Villard Books, 1993, pp.197
ISBN 0-679-42409-1

Secrets is the second book and the first of four novels by Trinidad-born Kelvin Christopher James who has lived in the US since 1970, and produced two volumes of stories. While the action of stories in James's first book *Jumping Ship and Other Stories* (1992) are divided between Trinidad and the US, events in *Secrets* are located entirely in Trinidad, in rural surroundings, without definite indication of a specific time period. Uxann, the chief character, is a teenager who has her first period early in the novel, while she lives with her father, a plantation overseer known as Seyeh or Paps.

Relationships between Uxann and Paps, or between Uxann and her best friend Keah, are unusual. Paps who banished Uxann's mother because he suspected her of infidelity, addresses Uxann as "Girl Chile" throughout the novel, and betrays typical British Caribbean, colonial, class consciousness when he advises her: "You better than dese common people 'round here." (p. 28) Paps believes his position as an overseer counts for something among fellow villagers, and when he hires Keah as part-time housekeeper to settle a debt that her family owes him, he warns Uxann against socialising too much with Keah because of their changed relationship: "Remember she [Keah] working for you." (p. 30)

Upon hearing of Keah's new working arrangement, even the school friends of both girls share Paps's social prejudice when they eagerly ask Uxann: "Is it true Keah working servant for all you?" (p. 30) From generation to generation, a master/servant relationship has been handed down through the community's consciousness, carrying continuing resonance of an hierarchical, plantation system, based on African slavery, as the region's most formative institution. Paps's explanation of a rainbow period in human history when: "mankind discover work and profit, and all a sudden, when a man was weak he had to work for a man who was stronger or die one way or de other... Strongman call dat system profit. Weak man call it slavery," (p. 87) establishes crucial grounding of the mythic or folkloric terms and structure at the heart of *Secrets*.

Because their community is small, isolated and ethnically uniform, consisting only of African or mixed, African/European people, issues of class do not mix as freely with problems of ethnicity in more urbanised communities on the island; but lives confined in a social cocoon so close to nature inevitably develop ingrown habits and practices of their own, for example, when Uxann's school friend Eralee tells her, Keah is expelled by the nuns at their Catholic school after: "Sister Moran ketch she [Keah] and Preddy [Keah's boyfriend] behind de tool shed in de vegetable garden doing nasty... Yeah, like a cow in heat in de bull pen. " (p. 22) In a remote agricultural community, observation of farm animals is perhaps children's only resource of sex education.

Still, when Paps says to Uxann: "Leh me tell yuh, Girl Chile... yuh body not a keepsake...yuh have it for use. Harder de better, I say," (p. 86) it is scarcely a father's caring, nurturing homily to his adolescent daughter! But the whole narrative of *Secrets*, both in its choice of sensuous words and inventive coinages, fulsomely celebrates the satisfaction of natural, bodily functions with both enthusiasm and something close to reverence. Uxann's alimentary habits and need to relieve herself are frequently mentioned at the same time as her desire for food. Along with her preparation or consumption of ravishing meals, she relishes nothing better than repeated raids on Dosaro's property for fruits of all shapes, colour, variety or size: "Although normally she [Uxann] drooled over the fat plums and sweet, crumbly meat of the crusty sugar apples, these days it was less-sweet fruit that she craved, like the sour sweet pomme-rac." (p. 93) Uxann indulges herself until she is: "sated and well stocked." (p. 94)

It is no coincidence that satisfaction of her appetite for fruit should lead Uxann to observe a couple's secret love-making in the same vicinity: "As if he [the man] were a macawoeul [boa constrictor] and she [the woman] a chicken hypnotized and ready to be consumed, but uncaring of the peril, even courting it."(p. 96) Description of the unknown man's love-making as a "serpent's bite" (p. 96) is also no coincidence, since *Secrets* clearly re-enacts a tropical version of the Edenic story in which original garden guardians are seduced by a serpent, to set in motion a fatal catalogue of interaction between corruption, transgression, indulgence and calamity.

After she starts working for Uxann and Paps, it does not take long for the extroverted and promiscuous Keah to become pregnant by Paps himself. Worse still, although it is somewhat unconvincingly draped in mystery, Uxann too becomes pregnant, most likely by Paps since her baby looks like him; and in a macabre ending that clinches the mythic significance of *Secrets*, Uxann kills her baby without any concern or mention of legal sanctions against her. More than anything else, myth justifies the potent title of a novel which regularly refers to multiple secrets between characters themselves, and between them and the mystery of their world which, not unlike ours, has much to learn from myth, folklore or revelation.

When Paps mysteriously disappears, and signs of Keah's pregnancy become more visible, it is no wonder that Keah fears her mother will turn her out, and implores Uxann to take her in because Paps has revealed "all kinda secret" (p. 191) to her, notably that he has officially bequeathed all his assets to Uxann but, more importantly, that he is not Uxann's biological father. (p. 191)

LIMITS OF AMERICAN POWER

Joseph O'Neill
Netherland, New York, Vintage Books, 2009, pp.256
ISBN: 978-0-307-38877-3

As a novel about cricket played mainly by West Indian and South Asian immigrants in New York City, *Netherland* is the handiwork of an intriguingly, half-Irish, half-Turkish novelist, Joseph O'Neill, a lawyer who grew up in Holland, studied at Cambridge University, practised law for ten years in England, and now lives with his wife, also a lawyer, and children in New York city. If fiction about cricket is rare, a novel of *Netherland*'s curiously mixed provenance is a hundred times more so.

Shortly after the 9/11 catastrophe, the narrator Hans van den Broek, a Dutch equities analyst who lives with Rachel, his English wife, and son Jake, in uptown Manhattan, New York, recalls dealings with Chuck, an Indian-Trinidadian immigrant, whose corpse is found floating in a New York canal at the opening of the novel. In flashback, Hans first meets Chuck at a New York cricket match in which Chuck is the umpire and Hans the only white player among immigrant team-mates from Trinidad, Guyana, Jamaica, India, Pakistan and Sri Lanka. From his unique, ethnic vantage point, Hans relates all he learns about English-speaking West Indian and South Asian immigrants in New York City and environs, from the 1990s until about 2005, much of it directly from the ever loquacious Chuck, alias Khamraj Ramkissoon.

So consuming is Hans's larger-than-life, mythic portrait of Chuck that he leaves little space for details about his own job, or his son or the impact of Rachel's separation after she leaves for London with Jake, and has an extra-marital affair there. Chuck's fellow ethnic immigrants or business contacts, except perhaps the Jewish businessman Abelsky, fare little better than the narrator's family so far as fully fleshed portraits are concerned. But this neglect means that Chuck is etched all the more imposingly in the full panoply of his ethnic regalia as natural, self-appointed leader, maestro, impresario and almost divinely consecrated President of the New York Cricket Club.

Chuck's interests range far beyond cricket, for example: "American history, birding, sales of Brooklyn real estate, meteorological phenomena, interesting economic data, resonant business stories." (p. 101) His insatiable curiosity combined with boundless enterprise, energy and eloquence transform Chuck into an archetype of the American dream that embodies hallowed virtues of intense energy, individualism and optimism reminiscent of iconic heroes like the real life, rags-to-riches Horatio Alger, and the fictional, self-inventive Jay Gatsby.

When Chuck first meets Hans in 2002, he was fifty-two years old, having arrived in America in 1975 as: "A fat coolie from the bush. No job, no money, no rights." (p. 133) Employing a common immigrant strategy, Chuck's wife works as baby sitter to a well-to-do family, while he plunges into: "Painting, plastering, demolition, cement work, roofing, you name it." (p. 133) Observing his single-minded climb to prosperity, Hans assesses Chuck as: "a wilful and clandestine man who followed his own instincts and analyses." (p. 71) Hans also sees in Chuck both "deviousness" (p. 71) and an "immigrant's credulousness" (p. 71) that produces: "machinating and trusting selves." (p. 71) For: "Chuck was a know-it-all on everything from South African grass varieties to industrial paints," (p. 71) and his histrionic speeches, egregious ebullience and self-aggrandising business ventures, for example, his project of a: "sports arena for the greatest cricket teams in the world" (p. 79) seem to play fast and loose with the law, which explains why Hans sadly concludes: "there was nothing, or very little, I could have done to produce a different ending for Chuck Ramkissoon." (p. 71)

Chuck's eager participation in the American dream is ironic because it is not certain if this dream was even intended for his ethnic group. If West Indian authors evidently find this dream problematic for their own immigrant brethren in America, imagine how hard it would be for a foreign author to interpret West Indian pursuit of the same dream through cricket in America! In his classic work *Beyond a Boundary,* C.L.R. James celebrates the liberating role of cricket for West Indians, just as in *Netherland,* Chuck impulsively argues: "people, all people, Americans, whoever, are at their most civilised when playing cricket," (p. 211) and, launches into a preposterous claim: "With the New York Cricket Club we could start a whole new chapter in US history." (p. 211) No wonder Chuck's attempt to advance American history ends with his corpse being ingloriously dumped in a New York canal!

But we should not forget either O'Neill's title or his Dutch upbringing, for in *Netherland* he addresses an ethnic, immigrant community on the outer or lower limits of New York (American) society just as, historically, Holland or the Netherlands represent outer or lower regions of formerly central, Germanic lands. The final line of *Netherland*'s epigraph to Whitman's *Leaves of Grass*: "I dream'd that was the new City of friends" expresses the poet's dream of universal peace and brotherhood, including, presumably, for those who are from "outer or lower [peripheral] regions" of the world.

In a crucial conversation, Rachel suggests that US President George W. Bush's plan to invade Iraq is: "about a life and death struggle for the future of the world" (p. 98) in which the US: "is the strongest military power in the world. It can and will do anything it wants. It has to be stopped." (p 98) As we know to our cost, the US was not stopped, and Whitman's dream now floats as lifelessly as Chuck's corpse because President Bush, like Chuck, confuses Whitman's true vision with the more common, illusory American dream of quick riches or unlimited wealth and power. Whatever else it may be, *Netherland* remains a powerful parable of limits of American power that will likely become more clearly visible in the twenty-first century.

QUIXOTIC FANTASY RELIEVES COLONIAL GUILT

Robert Antoni
Carnival, New York, Black Cat, Grove/Atlantic Inc., pp.295.
ISBN 0-8021-7005-6

Carnival is the third novel, after *Divina Trace* (1992) and *Blessed is the Fruit,* (1997) of Robert Antoni, a white Trinidadian who was born in Trinidad, grew up in the Bahamas, and now lives in New York city. Antoni's characters in *Carnival* are diasporic Trinidadians who pay a return visit to their homeland partly to savour the glory of carnival, but also to meet villagers, the Earth People, who live close to Nature in a rainforest district, provocatively named Hell Valley. Their visit occurs during the 1980s when costume designer Peter Minshall, friend of the author, plays the role of a character in *Carnival* as he prepares to stage the story "River" for his band in the 1982 carnival.

In an interview with fellow Trinidadian novelist Lawrence Scott, Antoni explains that he was inspired by Ernest Hemingway's novel, *The Sun Also Rises,* which relates adventures of a group of English and American expatriates who live in France and go down to Spain to attend a fiesta, very similar to the Trinidad carnival, in which revellers immerse themselves in an elemental spectacle of saturnalian music and dance that, they claim, will refresh their jaded spirits and revive burnt-out emotions.

Carnival contains three main characters, the narrator William Fletcher who is a white Trinidadian living in New

York City, Laurence de Boissière a black Trinidadian scholar and poet who lives in England, and Rachel, William's cousin and childhood sweetheart who lives in France. Entirely by coincidence, the three expatriates meet in a New York bar where their plan is hatched for spiritual renewal in Port of Spain, Trinidad's capital city.

In the Trinidadian hierarchy of skin colour and class, William belongs to the high social level of local Whites, just below the top rank of foreign (pure) Whites, and there is no better proof of this than a private cemetery for his family, in the middle of the Savannah, the largest, promenade in central Port of Spain. But times have changed, and since the cemetery is constantly desecrated by trespassers, William's mother orders it razed. As William's cousin, Rachel is of similar ethnic stock and is described as "café au lait" in colour, while Laurence's father: "Like most intelligent, black, middle-class West Indian men of enterprise in those days, [had] gone to foreign;" (p. 129) but with support from his mother, a school teacher, Laurence wins scholarships and becomes educated.

The chief characters in Hemingway's novel mentioned above are literary types nursing a mood of despair and disillusionment that was widespread in Europe in the 1920s and 30s following World War One. One Hemingway character is made impotent by a war injury; another, of English, aristocratic stock, is driven to serial promiscuity; and together with others they form the "lost generation" or well-to-do drifters indulging themselves aimlessly in drinking, fishing and going to bullfights.

It seems far fetched to compare these (European) characters afflicted by fresh and direct damage from the universally documented destruction caused by World War One with Antoni's protagonists who appear some sixty years later claiming to be scarred by a history of Caribbean colonialism. It is not that Caribbean colonialism has not left deep scars of confused identity, homelessness and diasporic wandering on West Indians: in fiction by Trinidad writers such as Ralph Deboissiere, Alfred Mendes, Samuel Selvon, V. S. Naipaul and Earl Lovelace, these scars are comprehensively depicted in all their psycho-sociological, economic and spiritual aspects in characters of all ethnic groups.

In West Indian terms, problems of identity stem from post-slavery issues of race, class and colour. So although William, Rachel and Laurence are not directly touched by the futility that prevailed in Europe between two World Wars, their sense of being lost and helpless is not only similar, but more deeply ingrained. One central incident that hovers like a brooding presence over the whole novel, is an attack that William and Rachel suffered when they were teenagers and were both raped by a group of Rastafarians, in almost ritual enactment of revenge for past wrongs inflicted by Whites on Blacks in the Caribbean.

This deeply rooted sense of what Derek Walcott calls historic "passion and wrong" is evident throughout the novel's action, for instance, during the carnival when William kisses and dances with a local reveller Monique who, as they pass by the savannah cemetery, pees on the spot where generations of William's ancestors are buried: "Yellow urine catching the sun and bouncing up off the shining plaque like golden beads... Monique staring into my eyes, smiling at me maliciously, deliciously" (p. 194)

The frenzy and violation of carnival match turbulent inner feelings of the main characters, and Antoni's language captures both public and private turmoil whether in commentary or dialogue. Here is a glimpse of his public view of carnival: "A solid mass of humanity, indistinguishable, embracing each other. Covered, head to toe, in every imaginable nastiness: axle grease, baby oil, flour, Quaker Oats, tar, mustard, peanut butter, Hershey's chocolate syrup. In addition to the paint, mud." (p. 159) Antoni quotes Freud on the efficacy of carnival:

"Licensed excess Freud called it, the tribal cure." (p. 109) As Freud implies, accompanying this frenzy of excess is a natural awareness of need for restraint which represents a tension between letting go/retrieval, abandonment/ rescue, disease/ cure that runs right through the novel.

If, as expatriate or diasporic Trinidadians, the main characters in Antoni's novel are looking for healing or home, their quest seems in vain. Twice policemen warn them to stay away from the villagers, Earth People, whom they [the police] consider simply as "bush niggers," (p. 282) and when Edward Baptiste aka Eddoes, who is crowned as King of the carnival bands, tries to force himself on Rachel, he is beaten by fellow villagers. Earth Mother, the villagers' leader, claims that Eddoes was dragged by the police jeep, but it seems he will survive. After all the sound and fury, perhaps because their quest is nothing more than quixotic fantasy, William, Rachel and Laurence quietly return "home."

"HER COUNTRYMEN'S THIRST FOR ANYTHING INDIAN"

Ariti Jankie
Hush Don't Cry, Trinidad and Tobago, Shiksa Publishing
House in conjunction with Magic Words Publications, 2010,
pp.183. ISBN 978-976-8226-57-0

Ariti Jankie's novel *Hush Don't Cry* dramatises the experience
of Indian-Trinidadian Meera Roopnarine and an Indian
national, Kapil Verma, chiefly in Trinidad. Meera's story
exposes her Indian-Trinidadian community's natural but
sentimental, perhaps superstitious interest in India as the
motherland of indentured Indians. Once, during Meera's visit
to India, she: "understood her mother's devotion to the land
of her ancestors, and her countrymen's thirst for anything
Indian." (p. 96) The subject seems well suited to an author who,
herself Indian-Trinidadian, worked as a journalist in Trinidad,
England and India where she studied at the Indian Institute
for Mass Communications in New Delhi. Jankie migrated to
India in 1992 and, in 2005, returned to Trinidad where she
worked at the *Trinidad Express.*

By the 1990s when the action of Meera's novel begins in
Trinidad, Indians were no longer fresh arrivals of impoverished
coolies from India. After one hundred and fifty years: "They
[Indian-Caribbeans] had conquered the degradation of
poverty, to climb the economic ladder during two oil booms
that played midwife to an Indian middle class with some
Indians knocking on the doors of high society." (p. 7) Despite

being the last child in a family of ten who live in the rural Trinidadian village of Merauli, Meera advertises in an Indian newspaper and finds an Indian husband who, by sheer virtue of his Indianness, assumes exalted prestige as: "the doctor from India in a land [Trinidad] where India was worshipped from afar." (p. 45) Such is their affluence that, Meera's family think nothing of the expense of air travel and having two wedding ceremonies, one in New Delhi, India, followed by honeymoon in England, and another wedding ceremony in Trinidad.

Ceremonial excess and ostentation indicate that all is sweetness and light for Kapil and Meera who live in her family home while he works as a doctor. Soon afterwards, her pregnancy announces great expectations. Meera was: "one of the lucky girls of Indian origin on the island who had the chance to marry an Indian." (p. 124) But Meera also notices Kapil's aloofness, his refusal to share his earnings with her, and his apparent plan to: "live off her [Meera's] family." (p. 38) Worst of all, when Meera introduces her idea of opening a hair dressing salon, Kapil reacts by kicking her severely. Suddenly, great expectations decline into fear, terror and premonitions of horror: "She [Meera] looked at him [Kapil] and saw herself buried alive." (p. 39) By this time too, who can blame Meera for thinking, so far as married life is concerned: "Hers was melting into a continuing nightmare!" (p. 40)

Adding insult to injury Kapil has affairs first with a woman named Jennifer, then with Kathy Ann, and the author now sees Kapil as "a bomb waiting to explode." (p. 45) The explosion comes when he performs an abortion on Kathy-Ann and she dies. Kapil and his family hurriedly leave for India to avoid prosecution. On their way, they stay with another of Meera's relatives in New York where, in assessing his chances of working in the US, Kapil divulges that his prestige and professionalism as a doctor were entirely bogus: he had spent only one year in medical school in India, and admits: "how easy it was to have certificates copied at Indian street corners."(p. 76) Despite all that, Kapil's violent behaviour continues after the birth of his son, Kabir, in New York, his drunken abuse leading eventually to intervention by police and deportation with his family to India.

Life with Kapil's family in his home village of Lakhanpur turns out even worse for Meera who becomes a virtual slave not only to Kapil, but to his mother and sister. In one incident, because he considers her improperly dressed, Kapil grabs Meera by the hair and smashes her against a wall and, in another, because Meera serves an insufficiently cooked chapatti, her mother-in-law clamps her hand down on the "tawa" or hotplate until she screams. Exposure of such gross, intra-family victimisation in India, another theme in *Hush Don't Cry*, is second only to the superstitious glorification of India by Indian-Caribbeans, and, along with: "stories of bride burning" (p. 114) is: "common behaviour meted out to daughters-in-law throughout the country [India]." (p. 114)

Meera escapes back to Trinidad where she quickly builds up a prosperous business as a caterer. Then, partly influenced by traditional injunctions of her duty as a Hindu wife, she and her children return to Lakhanpur where she helps Kapil financially to build a house. When Kapil's abuse resumes, however, Meera appeals for help to the embassy of Trinidad & Tobago in India, and the title of the novel is the consoling greeting of an African-Trinidadian embassy official when he first observes Meera's battered condition, and decides to help her return home. An "Epilogue" recounts events ten years after Meera has become: "an independent, wealthy businesswoman," (p. 177) and her family are reunited with her in Trinidad. But Kapil's violence flares up yet again except, this time, Meera's daughter Kavita defends her mother, staying with her, while Kapil and his son Kabir return to India.

Although some readers may not be entirely convinced by the author's often swift, melodramatic, and somewhat mechanical changes of mood and action, for example, Kapil's seemingly genetic predisposition to violence, Meera's resilient and miraculous powers of physical and financial self-regeneration, and Kapil's escape, scot free, from legal implications of causing Kathy-Ann's death, Jankie's exposé of female victimization in *Hush Don't Cry* catches an aura of wife abuse and female victimization partly authenticated through hints of personal experience, but also through historical records of Indian indenture, and novels like *The Swinging Bridge* by another female, Indian-Trinidadian author, Ramabai Espinet.

"MEN...ROUNDED UP TO ATTEND ANY FUNERAL FOR RUM"

Ingrid Persaud
If I Never Went Home, London, Blue China Press, 2013, pp.292, ISBN: 978-09926977-0-9

If I Never Went Home, the first novel of Ingrid Persaud, trips smartly between episodes in the US (Boston) and the author's homeland of Trinidad & Tobago. The novel opens with Dr. Beatrice Clark, (Bea) a twenty-nine-year old Trinidadian professor, now living in Boston, being admitted to a psychiatric hospital suffering from clinical depression. Through morbid confessions and flashbacks to scenes from her Trinidadian childhood, Bea reconstructs her lapse into depression as an immigrant, overcome by diasporic alienation in Boston. We can gauge the depth of her alienation from the black humour of her confessions claiming, for instance, that it would be easy to arrange a funeral for her in Trinidad where: "there are men who could be rounded up to attend any funeral for rum or a few dollars. Knowing the dead person is optional," (p. 83) or from more bitter sarcasm when she suggests to her psychiatrist, Dr. Payne, that: "For my funeral they're going to have to pass by a rum shop and bribe a few guys to come and mourn for me just to have a decent show." (p. 83)

Such self-laceration has deep roots in Bea's memories of home when, at the age of thirteen: "friends would taunt her about her long rod-straight hair." (p. 99) Ethnically, Bea is of mixed parentage, her mother Mira being Indian and her father,

Alan Clark, of mixed African-European blood. It is no secret that ethnicity, identity, race and colour complicate the lives of Caribbean people, whether at home or in the diaspora. In one flashback, Bea is hectored by her maternal grandmother for: "being lucky to have good hair from we side of the family" (p. 100) and not the "picky-picky" hair from her father's side; and in the same incident she is further humiliated by her mother's open discussion of her with a salon of female hair dressers who: "picked her [Bea] over with their gazes like vultures pecking on a rotting carcass." (p. 101)

Technical originality, evident in these brief quotations, hint at Persaud's expertise in managing action that includes two locations, Boston and Trinidad, and two narrators, Bea and a younger relative, Tina Ramlogan, who lives in Trinidad. At first, this combination may test our patience in relating events between the two narratives but, scarcely one third of the way through, the novel gathers surprising speed when both narratives suddenly merge and intensify, step by suspenseful step, into an explosive climax. This structure is, if not the mature handiwork of a seasoned artist, surely the masterstroke of an inspired beginner.

The title "If I Never Went Home" is another masterstroke that highlights a duality inherent in the word "diaspora." According to Salman Rushdie, Indians in the diaspora are so overcome by feelings of homesickness, while living away from India, that they invent imaginary homes for themselves in lands where they settle. More than for most other communities, this concept of "home" as shifting or fluid is, perhaps, best suited to West Indians who, as displaced persons from Africa, India, Europe, Madeira, China and elsewhere, often experience feelings of homelessness both at home and abroad.

After Bea returns "home" to Trinidad to escape psychological breakdown in Boston, the author discerns desperation and distress in her thoughts: "All that resolve about going back, straightening out her life, and she [Bea] had returned to Boston as lost as ever." (p. 288) Bea's disturbing discovery of loss illustrates a sense of homelessness generic to West Indians. If she had not gone back home she might never have discovered the truth about her family, her relationship with Tina, or her identity as a Trinidadian and Caribbean person; for by shining more light on herself, the heightened awareness of her origins and consequences of her depression, mixed ethnicity and chaotic family relations now appear as positive, illuminating.

Bea's experience also illustrates fundamental features of her Trinidadian/West Indian manners, identity and culture that include not merely her diasporic depression, sense of homelessness or tangled relationship with Tina; nor the ramshackle disunity of the Clark family whose historic, coloured middle class status now seems in disarray; nor even the vulgar lustfulness of Uncle Fred's attempted rape of his thirteen year old niece: it also advertises the unique adroitness of Trinidadian speech with which a potential employer rejects Tina's application: "Darling, don't take this the wrong way, but you will need training up and I too busy for that;" (p. 204) the equal directness with which another employer accepts her: "All right. I know I going regret this, but I'm giving you a chance. You could start now;" (p. 205) and the wilful desecration of Great-Aunty Sonia's funeral by a stepson: "emboldened by the weed of wisdom." (p. 213)

Also revealing is similarity between the desecration of Great-Aunty Sonia's funeral and the gallows humour in Earl Lovelace's 2012 Bocas Festival, prize-winning novel *Is Just A Movie* when, during a funeral, the coffin is reopened and grieving mourners stunned by the supposed corpse getting up by herself: this type of humour in *Home* is spot on about a culture that instinctively frowns on universally accepted norms of careful conduct in preference of what is unconventional, irreverent or gratuitously rebellious.

"ALL THAT TO SAY I WAS BEREFT."

André Alexis
Childhood, Toronto, McClelland & Stewart Inc., 1998,
pp.265, ISBN 0-7710-0665-9

Childhood, André Alexis's first novel (and second book)
comes with glittering credentials, having won the Books
in Canada First Novel Award, as well as being co-winner
of the Trillium Book Award in 1997, after which Alexis
completed eight other books, including a children's novel,
a play and novel *Fifteen Dogs* that won both the Scotia Bank
Giller Prize and the Rogers Writers' Prize in 2015. Born
in Trinidad, in 1957, Alexis migrated to Canada when he
was four years old, and *Childhood* is the fictional biography
of Thomas Macmillan who, like the author, is both of
Trinidadian parentage and similar age. At the age of forty,
and living in Ottawa, Tom begins narrating the story of
his life from early childhood in the small, South Western,
Ontario town of Petrolia, to the age of ten when he arrives
in Ottawa, Canada's capital city.

After his grandfather dies and his mother Katarina leaves
home, Tom grows up with his Trinidadian grandmother,
Edna Macmillan. At the time, the 1950s and 60s, Petrolia was
a typical Ontario town whose small-minded, racial attitudes
were not exactly welcoming to a black family from Trinidad.
One neighbour is: "wary of a certain tendency in Negroes,"
(p. 39) and notices that Katarina: "was even darker than Edna ...

[who] had hoodwinked people into treating her white." (p. 39) As an illegitimate child living alone with his grandmother, it is only after Edna dies in 1967, that Tom faces the bleak truth of his fate as an outsider, without strong roots either of family or community in Petrolia: "Aside from this house [his grandmother's] my own room, my clothes, and the books my grandmother had given me... I had nothing at all. All that to say I was bereft." (p. 70)

As for Katarina, she is a virtual stranger to her son when, after Edna's death, she arrives to take Tom away from Petrolia. On their way to Ottawa, as they are driven by Katarina's boyfriend, Mr. Mataf, Tom becomes more aware of the down-and-out, street-smart lifestyle of his mother when she and Mr. Mataf set him up to steal food from a shop. He is caught by the shopkeeper, reprimanded by his mother, and taken back to their car, only to find out that the shopkeeper was forewarned to observe him [Tom] closely because he was a kleptomaniac, merely as a ruse by Katarina and Mr. Mataf to enable them to steal as much food as they can carry without being noticed. Cunning duplicity, at the expense of both Tom and the shopkeeper, is followed up by Mr. Mataf, the next morning, when he silently abandons Tom and his mother, asleep in their tent, while he unloads their suitcases from the car and drives away, never to be seen again.

Katarina hurls vain imprecations at their predicament before she and Tom trek wearily to Ottawa, as she struggles with their suitcases, and they eventually reach the home of Katarina's old friend Henry Wing: "a black man with Chinese blood, handsome, tall, forty years old, in love with a woman [Katarina] eleven years younger, at work on an encyclopedia of limited appeal." (p. 137) It adds to Henry's eccentricity that, while Tom and Katarina live with him, we never find out whether he is Tom's father or not: he denies it, and Katarina is non-committal on the matter.

Eccentricity stretches further when Katarina develops a dislike of Henry's Trinidadian housekeeper, Mrs. Williams, and forces Tom to say that he witnessed Mrs. Williams steal Katarina's shoes, leaving Henry no option but to fire his guilt-less housekeeper. Worse still, Tom himself regularly pilfers small items of clothing and personal effects, from both Henry and his mother, and when caught and questioned, not only does he falsely claim that Henry had asked him to steal, but Henry admits he had asked Tom to steal. It is difficult to understand the bizarre motives and actions of all three characters. Katarina suspects that Henry dislikes her clothes and asks Tom to pilfer some items which might encourage her to change her way of dressing, while Tom, who is still only twelve, admits: "It hurt me to keep quiet, but I wanted them [Katarina and Henry] to suffer now that it had come to suffering." (p. 195)

The tangled psychology and intriguing complexity of the main characters in *Childhood* are enriched by the simple, precise language of an adult narrator, and a beguiling tone of innocent bewilderment voiced by Tom's child persona to produce a combined effect of haunting, aching sadness that pervades almost the entire narrative, as Katarina and Tom move from Henry's house to an apartment of their own, and later as Tom starts to live on his own. Later still, Katarina returns to live in Petrolia, and eventually dies there. After managing her funeral and settling her business affairs, the narrator returns to Ottawa and, by unhappy coincidence, finds that Henry too has died, leaving proceeds of his will, nearly seventy-nine thousand dollars, to him Tom and his mother.

By wrestling with strange motives and desires of characters amidst picaresque adventures and bizarre events, *Childhood* plumbs mysterious depths of sadness in the human psyche, as when Tom acknowledges his mother's numerous relationships and vagrant lifestyle, and tries his best to understand her: "though she [Katarina] loved Henry, she thought herself happier away from him, "(p. 215) or when Tom himself admits: "With my mother, I always felt, no matter where we were or what we were doing, an underlying restlessness...the only moments when this wasn't so were when she first sat with Henry, in silence, and on her deathbed when she was with me, again in silence." (p. 216) Strange how the puzzling, contradictory or bizarre quality of these reactions is exactly what makes them so captivating!

"DEATH IS NOTHING AND LIFE IS EVERYTHING"

Dionne Brand
Love Enough, Toronto, Alfred A. Knopf Canada, Toronto, 2014, pp.180, ISBN 978-0-345-8088-2

Dionne Brand who was born in Guayaguayare, Trinidad & Tobago, in 1953, and has lived in Toronto since 1970, is author of ten volumes of poems, five works of fiction, and producer of seven documentaries, four of which are films for the National Film Board of Canada. *Love Enough,* her fourth novel, explores the texture and quality of life in contemporary Toronto, recording change from the 1970s and 80s, a period dramatised in Brand's first collection *Sans Souci and Other Stories,* (1988) when the city reeled from the fresh impact of newly-arrived West Indian and other immigrants to twenty-first century Toronto, a city bristling with new, multicultural artefacts and trophies, and surveyed with the self-satisfied air of someone not merely aware but proud that she herself contributed to the change.

The best guide to Brand's twenty-first century Toronto is June, a middle-aged social worker who served in El Salvador, Mozambique, South Africa, Zimbabwe, Nicaragua, Ghana and Mexico City, and now lives in Toronto with her female partner, Sydney. June's career not only boasts of exciting travel or anticipation of revolution and love, but invites connection with the author's own Marxist adventures in Grenada in October, 1983 when she cowered in ruins of Maurice Bishop's revolution, in mortal fear and terror of invading American troops launched by US President Reagan.

We also connect June's feelings with those of the author when she writes: "The sky was violet; a violet soft with polymers and hydrocarbons, and June saw two small blue butterflies mating near the lake. It was just beside the dogwood bushes. Summer Azures. She stopped. Her heart felt feathery at the sight. She was on the verge of crying." (pp. 2-3) June's reactions cause her partner Sydney to classify her among: "people who watch everything all the time," (p. 7) betraying exactly the observant, acute and practical sensitivity that tempts June to remember when she was young and in love, and tried to analyse love or love enough, until she wondered about the futility of: "simply teetering on the thin filament in the brain between the insula and the striatum." (pp. 7-8) In some respects, June's portrait recalls the flower power generation of the late 1960s, those for whom love, in any quantity, could be relied on to put the world instantly to rights.

As a middle-aged social worker who is gay and lives with a female partner, June joins other characters in *Love Enough* who are somehow regarded as misfits, either sexually ambiguous, dubiously artistic, or outright car thieves, drifting in one fashion or other, and needing help from social services. Family names are not given, not even those of June and Sydney, the two main characters, who can scarcely be regarded as a conventional family. As for other characters, Lia and her brother Germain, alias Ghost, grew up in foster homes while their mother Mercede and grandmother Renata are as lost as their children. Germain and his friend Bedri are car thieves. Bedri's sister Hela works in a hair store and their father Da'uud is a Somali who speaks Italian, English, Arabic, French and Somali, and was trained as an economist in Switzerland, although he now works on the night shift as a taxi driver.

With such a diverse cast, talk of revolution and love seems inappropriate or futile, as June realises during one of her affairs with Isador, a Chilean man. For June: "Revolutions were so wonderful for sex...[but] sex is a limited idiom, not a whole language – it gets exhausted." (p. 57) June has many affairs, male and female, as with the Tamil Tiger who gave her a thousand sarungs: "he had not been a complete waste of time, they [the sarungs] were a presence, an extravagant after-image of a fact. Love is Love. It wears off," (p. 155) which virtually puts paid to any nympholeptic dreams of flower power, or love and revolution. In one of her arguments with Sydney, June claims that she [Sydney] mistakes consumerism for optimism while she [June] sees the world more clearly: "We are just hanging on a ball of hard mud spinning in space at a ridiculous speed. That's us, that's the earth. A ball of mud, hanging and hurtling nowhere." (p. 136)

In one incident, June and Sydney witness a scene where a man, woman and their daughter stand on the street staring into a shop window. June catches a look on the girl's face, one of: "a desire that would not be satisfied," (p. 111) and gets the impression that the parents had promised their daughter something: "a promise they would never fulfill. So the girl has a future happiness on her face, but even she understands the futility of it." (p. 111) While June believes that so-called misfits, immigrants or whoever, emphasise their difference as a defence mechanism against anticipated mainstream disapproval, and are left: "inconsolable, irreconcilable and sharp," (p. 112) Sydney regards this emphasis as a sign of happiness and hope.

Perhaps these conservative v. liberal attitudes are unlikely ever to be reconciled, leaving us with the author's assumed triumph in her past battles over racism and sexism in *Love Enough,* and fresh delight in a new Toronto where Beatriz, for instance, one of June's lovers, can tell her: "I have held someone dying. Death is nothing and living is everything," (p. 116) or when June can describe their city as an artifice in which: "it is as if you will miss something if you die:" (p. 160) all this in rich, epigrammatic language that proves the girl/poet from Guayaguayare has finally arrived in Toronto.

A MIRACLE OF MODERN MULTICULTURALISM

Dionne Brand
What We All Long For, Toronto, Alfred A. Knopf, 2005, pp. 319,
ISBN 0-676-97169-9

As Dostoevsky and Dickens respectively immortalised St. Petersburg and London in their fiction, so nowadays, do West Indian writers imaginatively re-create modern metropolises in which they settled. But Dickens's dour and grey portrait of nineteenth century London contrasts sharply with the 1950s British capital city in Samuel Selvon's novel *The Lonely Londoners,* (1956) with the seemingly resplendent gaiety and raillery of its black, West Indian, immigrant characters. Similarly, while 1930s Toronto (unnamed) appears as somewhat dull and staid in the novels of Morley Callaghan, it emerges in the fiction of Barbadian-born Austin Clarke, by the 1970s and 80s, as a scene of endemic racial discrimination and police brutality toward black West Indian immigrants. Against this background, Dionne Brand's *What We All Long For* proclaims Toronto of the 1990s as a city of the ages, a miracle of modern of multiculturalism, and a veritable haven for immigrants from the four corners of the earth.

Brand is perhaps better known as a poet, her volume of poems *No Language is Neutral* having won [Canada's] Governor General's award for poetry in 1990. She first turned to fiction in a volume of stories, *Sans Souci* (1988) which provides nostalgic evocations of her Trinidadian childhood, and starkly realistic portraits of West Indians in Toronto. Her first novel *In Another Place Not Here* (1996) probes inner lives of characters displaced from their Caribbean homeland, and in search of a new home in Toronto. *What We All Long For*, Brand's third novel, is a paean of exultant praise for Toronto.

What we all Long For contains four main characters, young Canadians all, although they come from differing racial and cultural backgrounds. Tuyen, a visual artist, is the child of refugees who fled from Vietnam during the Boat People crisis in the 1970s, while her lesbian lover Carla is a bicycle courier whose father is black and mother white. Oku, the only male member of the quartet, is a black poet in love with Jackie, the fourth member, a black woman whose parents come from Nova Scotia. As these protagonists eat, drink, make love, and pursue dreams of self-fulfillment in downtown Toronto, their family relationships reflect a common misunderstanding that bedevils relations between many first-generation Canadian immigrants and their children. Brand's portrait of this misunderstanding and observation of niceties of cultural emphasis between different ethnic groups reveal unusually deep understanding of her characters and their contrasting cultures.

But strangely for what looks like a drama of high excitement, the action in *What We All Long For* is surprisingly static. Although family backgrounds of the main characters are systematically organised, chapter by chapter, they do not really advance the action. Forward plot movement emerges chiefly from the story of Tuyen's brother Quy who is lost, at the beginning of the novel, during the refugee exodus of Boat People from Vietnam, and is sought by his parents throughout the rest of the novel. There is also some suspense when Jackie's brother Jamal is detained by police and becomes impatient with efforts to release him. Yet slow-moving action is no handicap to an author with Brand's superb skills. Oral resourcefulness and original imagery combine with the masterly touch of a born poet in *What we all Long For* to transmute even common subjects into pure literary gold. For example: "The barber shops were universities of a kind and repositories for all the stifled ambition of men who were sidelined by prejudices of one sort of another" (p. 189). Nothing could be more concrete, concise or incisive.

The thematic focus of the novel lies in its title. Brand's past activism on behalf of Marxist, feminist and anti-racist causes is unlikely to allow her to propose multicultural Toronto as the crowning achievement of her characters' deepest longings. Her quartet of protagonists do not simply cavort and carouse: they also struggle with grief, pain and trauma caused by dysfunctional family relationships and restrictive social attitudes. Toronto is no bed of roses. Yet relish of the author and her characters for the city is inescapable.

Relish culminates in the central image of the novel: a free standing artwork or "lubaio" on which Tuyen assembles bits of wood, photographs and other Toronto-based items that might be used, like the trend-setting "oeuvre' of the American painter, Jackson Pollock, to create: "alternate, unexpected realities" (p. 224). The real significance of Tuyen's 'lubaio' may be elusive: it seems to represent the spontaneous expression of instinctive human aspirations which appear to thrive in such a congenial place as Toronto.

Despite congenialness though, Brand's Toronto appears somewhat synthetic, embodying multicultural theory rather than multiculturalism itself. There is a difference, for example, between Brand's enthusiastic vision of a lively, emergent Toronto and the settled yet changing nature of the Pakistani immigrant community in Zadie Smith's novel *White Teeth* (2000) set in London, England, at the end of the twentieth century. There has always been something new or undefined about Canada, a quality of continuous self-discovery that once led Northrop Frye to describe Canada as "next year country."

It is not entirely surprising that something of this new, untried quality should rub off on Toronto, Canada's flagship city. What is surprising is Brand's success in capturing this quality in an imaginative work. It is the sort of success most Canadian writers or artists would die for. That it is achieved by a Canadian writer who was born in Trinidad, and did not come to Canada until she was seventeen years old, is breathtaking!

SEWING NEEDLES THROUGH EACH FINGER NAIL"

Neil Bissoondath
The Unyielding Clamour of the Night, **Toronto, Cormorant
Books, 2005, 350pp, ISBN 1-896951-87-2.**

Neil Bissoondath's stories and novels establish him as a leading
Caribbean-Canadian writer, although his fiction seems to
focus, less and less, on the Caribbean. Action in his fourth
novel, for instance, *Doing the Heart Good* (2002) takes place
entirely in Canada, with only white Canadian characters, and
action in *The Unyielding Clamour of the Night* unfolds on an
unnamed island, formerly a British colony, somewhere in the
Indian Ocean. The island's population have Indian names and
eat Indian food, while their politics seem vaguely similar to
events in post-colonial Sri Lanka, when the government and
a Tamil, separatist movement were locked in deadly combat.

The central character in *Clamour of the Night*, Arun Banerjee,
comes from a well-connected family in the north of the island
where a majority of the population live, and where the capital city
and government are located. As the story opens, Arun travels to
the town of Omeara in the south of the island where local people,
pejoratively called "two- percenters", are represented by "The
Boys" - freedom fighters, guerrillas, revolutionaries, subversives,
outlaws or terrorists: "a band of fighters who had been sent from
the rebel stronghold farther south to take the war to the army"
(p. 99). In short, it is all out civil war; which takes deadly toll on
soldiers and civilians alike, with little hope of resolution.

The strange thing is that, for all the horror and trauma, causes of the conflict are not disclosed. Since post-colonial conflicts in the second half of the twentieth century generally have to do with religious, linguistic, economic, cultural or ethnic problems, one suspects that one or more of these factors is relevant here; but the focus is solely on the military conflict and its potential for indiscriminate terror and destruction. One gets a sense, in other words, that neither the actual details of the conflict nor its geographical location matters as much as the stark and comfortless fact of internecine conflict as an apparently inevitable, perhaps ineradicable aspect of human existence, especially in contemporary post-colonial states.

After his arrival in Omeara, Arun's closest contact is with the family of Jaisaram, an illiterate butcher who happens to be vegetarian. It is not only the handling of meat by a vegetarian that is improbable: much about Jaisaram's family seems mysterious, contradictory. His wife seems too docile and domesticated to be true, while their daughter, Anjani is the exact opposite: an absolute live-wire, culturally sophisticated, sexually liberated, daring and decisive. Living in a remote town on an island consumed by civil war, Anjani also seems almost too good to be true, especially her skill in mixing cocktail drinks, combined with her expulsion from school for: "behaviour inconsistent with the moral standards of Holy Faith Convent." (p. 202)

Anjani's affair with Arun follows almost inevitably, as does her subsequent kidnapping and murder, and a situation where the army and terrorists appear to compete in inflicting the most ingenious and murderous atrocities on each other. No doubt "The Boys" are responsible for the carcasses of dogs left hanging on a row of telephone poles, with one pole carrying the dead body of Arun's student Mangal Pande, a soldier. When the army captures a terrorist sympathiser, they lock him up for one week before they release him unharmed, and advertise the false rumour that he has turned informer. It is only a matter of time before the sympathiser is found tortured and killed, presumably by his former comrades, "The Boys", who have also driven sewing needles through each fingernail and pounded a railway stake through his heart.

This phantasmagoria of horror somehow strikes a chord of recognition because of contemporary news that we get daily from areas of conflict all around the world. Perhaps this is why, although he writes about a country that we do not confidently identify, we feel surprising sympathy for people so helplessly caught in an atmosphere of constant fear, suspicion and alarm, aptly described as: "the unyielding clamour of the night"; for the author deftly weaves different threads of rumour and deception into an intricate web of suspense and terror that gradually enmeshes everyone in the novel.

Arun, for example, believes that his parents were accidentally killed by terrorists who bombed their plane because a deputy minister's wife was on board; but he has a rude awakening when he learns that the real target was his parents who secretly acted as government collaborators, importing instruments of torture for the army. Similarly, the story Arun hears from Anjani about her brother Nagarat who absconded to Canada to escape persecution from the army, turns out to be completely false: Nagarat died when a bomb he was carrying went off prematurely. Such twists and turns keep the reader guessing, and entertained, while they transform the action into a torrid and suspenseful narrative that mixes adventure, romance, and violence with deviant, political skulduggery.

Yet, however suspenseful or gory events in the novel may be, frequent discussion about the nature of violence and amorality of politics suggest that *Clamour of the Night* is no simple thriller. While authorial neutrality allows Bissoondath to abstain from taking sides in the conflict between "The Boys" and the government, it also appears to nourish a cynical notion of both sides pursuing violence for the sake of itself. There is no doubt that a spate of decolonization, worldwide, during the mid-twentieth century, produced numerous post-colonial nations subject to ethnic, linguistic, religious, poltical or regional conflict and seemingly endless strife. Bissoondath does well to dramatise such conflict and strife in stirring, or even shocking action; but the implication that scenes of gruesome cruelty are inevitable, or relished by contestants, in a post-colonial context, is more the stuff of political thrillers than serious fiction.

"SECRECY HAS BEEN WELL TERMED THE SOUL OF ALL GREAT DESIGNS."

Neil Bissoondath
The Soul of all Great Designs, Toronto, Cormorant Books, Inc., 2008, pp.223 ISBN 978-1-897151-32-7

The unsettled, roving nature of Bissoondath's settings is striking in his most recent fiction: his early stories and novels are set either in his native Trinidad, in Canada where he lived since his university days, or in foreign places, while his fifth novel The *Undying clamour of the Night* takes us to a remote island that looks like Sri Lanka, but the action in his sixth novel *The Soul of all Great Designs* swings back to Toronto, Canada's largest city which, although not remote like the island in the previous novel, is just as nameless. A settled sense, either of place or belonging, is clearly problematic in Bissoondath's fiction, implying not only shifting, physical restlessness, but uncertainty, doubt, turmoil, in the inner lives of his characters.

Soul is divided into three parts the first of which is narrated by a young man living with f his conventional, working class parents in the fully earned comfort of their suburban home. The young man dislikes his parents' practical-minded conventionality and, entirely to please them, takes a job in a painting company without abandoning his secret yearning to become an interior decorator. As he asserts at the beginning of his story: "Everybody has secrets. I have a secret. Don't you? Deep down, in your heart of hearts as they say?" (p. 3)

One secret is that while employed at the painting company, unknown to his parents, he also works as an interior decorator. Another secret is that he uses his good looks to pass himself off as the stereotype of a gay interior decorator.

This double life creates inner strain. Our hero who prefers not to give his name, yet another secret, frets about leaving home and breaking free from parental control when, abruptly, his parents die in a traffic accident, and by the end of Part One of his story, he is left enjoying complete independence and success with his own interior decorating company - New World Designs. In Part One at least, carefully observed detail combines with sharply analytical character studies to produce a taut, diverting and wholly compelling narrative, the work of a true master.

In a complete change that seems wholly disconnected from the serious or sober manner of Part One, Part Two revels in delightfully comic episodes about an Indian, immigrant family and their frantic, if clumsy match-making efforts on behalf of daughter Sumintra (Sue). When her parents contrive a meeting with an Indian bachelor, eligible because of his professional qualifications, money and family status, Sue's cutting sarcasm is hilarious in confessing to her suitor: "Sometimes my folks can be as subtle as an earthquake." (p. 92) Yet the ironic portrait of Indian immigrants struggling to survive in North America, fighting for acceptance of their foreign qualifications, settling for second or third best, then greedily acquiring conspicuous wealth, is both amusing and soberly realistic. The comment:" The idea of 'going to the cottage' was alien to people whose spare money was sent back home to relatives or hoarded for plane tickets to the land they had only left physically" (p. 101) confirms Bissoondath's authoritative grasp of immigration and ethnic issues.

As if to redeem the disconnection between the first two parts of the novel, the nameless hero of Part One meets Sue when he buys a bottle of water from her father's food truck at the end of Part Two. Part Three opens with our hero's confession that "Alec" the false name for himself that he gives Sue, is a total fabrication, yet another secret. Then follows a frenzied sexual relationship between Alec and Sue in which they often use an apartment of Kelly, Sue's trusted friend. There is another episode of ludicrous, failed match-making between Sue and an ageing Indian widower Professor Mukherjee; but by this time, Sue's secret erotic encounters with Alec are too binding.

The secrets in *Soul* aid and abet the artificial and flexible quality of identity which is an essential part, or soul of the novel's design. Alec quotes Shakespeare's "All the world's a stage and all the men and women merely players" (p. 201) in justification of the roles he plays, and adds: "These selves of ours we're supposed to be true to our constructions – the roles we play, roles that are either given to us or that we invent ourselves." (p. 201) This is a frankly frightening confession. For Sue is ineluctably drawn to Alec: "She [Sue] wanted to know who I am. But who I am is what I have constructed – ungraspable and enigmatic, fluid even to myself." (p. 202) This enigmatic, artificial identity is what leads to the bizarre climax of the novel.

From his earliest fiction Bissoondath has been attracted by the quicksilver nature of identity whether conditioned by race or ethnicity, as in the Caribbean, or by immigration, language and class as in Canada. But secrecy is crucially linked to the formation of identity in *Soul*. Bissoondath takes his cue from the novel's epigraph: "Secrecy has been well termed the soul of all great designs. Perhaps more has been effected by concealing our own intentions, than by discovering those of our enemy." The quotation is from an English clergyman Caleb. C. Coulton remembered chiefly for his aphorisms and sayings.

The author's skill in *Soul* is beyond dispute: his taut, intricately designed and potently succinct narrative, relieved by witty, comic sketches, is the work of a master technician. But the link between secrecy and identity produces too horrific a climax in the novel. Nor is such horror justified by Colton's epigraph which both eulogises secrecy and connects it to "great designs." Alas, not even irony can pass off the final horror in *Soul* as part of a great design.

THE ORIGIN OF BLACK BRITISH FICTION

Andrea Levy
Small Island, London, Headline Review, 2004, pp. 441
ISBN 07553 0749 6

If Andrea Levy's earlier stories in *Light in the House Burnin'* (1994), and novels such as *Never Far From Nowhere* (1996), and *Fruit of the Lemon* (1999) created scarcely a ripple on the literary scene, her fourth novel *Small Island* was greeted by a splash of acclaim, with four distinguished literary awards, the Orange Prize for fiction, the Whitbread novel award and Whitbread Book of the Year, and the 2005 Commonwealth Writers' Prize for best book.

Levy was born in England of Jamaican parents and her story in *Small Island* is narrated by four main characters, Gilbert and Hortense, Jamaican immigrants, no doubt based on the author's parents, and Bernard and Queenie, an English couple. The action takes place during two periods of time, "1948," the year when Gilbert and Hortense arrive as immigrants in London, and "Before," the period before 1948 which fills in the early family history of both sets of narrators. Despite shifts between interchanging periods of time or transitions from one narrator to the other, there are no gaps: everything makes for a coherent whole.

The title of the novel tends to suggest that *Small Island* is concerned mainly with the fate of Jamaicans, or West Indians generally, many of whom flocked to England from small,

Caribbean islands shortly after World War Two. Gilbert, for instance, had already lived briefly in England while serving in the Royal Air Force (RAF) during the war; but after going back home to Jamaica, he returns to England on the ship Empire Windrush whose arrival, on 20th May, 1948, marks the beginning of the post-war inrush of West Indian immigrants to Britain.

Levy's portrait of West Indians in England, in 1948, is backed up by solid detail. Deluded by misguided, colonial expectations, these West Indian immigrants come up against deep-seated racial prejudices of a homegrown English population; and Gilbert, Hortense, and other West Indians suffer bitterly in their attempts to find housing or employment in London. Hortense's colonial innocence, in particular, is touching as a West Indian who harbours her own brown, middle class prejudices against her fellow black Jamaicans, while betraying an obsequious and unrealistic over-evaluation of English culture and manners. One can imagine the calamity of her shock and pain upon discovering that her highly prized qualifications, proud badge of Jamaican, middle class respectability as a teacher, are blankly rejected in England, and contemptuously ignored by seemingly racist or prejudiced education authorities in London!

Small Island seems entirely reliable so far as its social portrait goes, for instance, of restrictive English provincialism and quaint practices and rituals such as the courtship of Bernard and Queenie. But the author captures an international flavour of attitudes toward race by also including episodes of racial discrimination by white American soldiers against fellow black Americans serving in the US army, in England, during World War Two. In addition, we get a rather lengthy account of Bernard's military service in India, which helps to enlarge the focus of *Small Island* from a social portrait merely of England to one of wider impact of the war on Britain and its far-flung empire.

According to Bernard: "The war was fought so people might live amongst their own kind. Quite simple. Everyone had a place, England for the English and the West Indies for the coloured people" (p. 388). The trouble is that such pious, hypocritical and unrealistic fantasies are shattered by the end of the novel, when Bernard's marriage to Queenie is shaken to its foundations, and Gilbert and Hortense are asked to bring up Queenie's baby, conceived while Bernard is away in India.

This intermingling of fortunes of the main characters with events of the war is foreshadowed by a strategically placed Prologue that reflects on the wider impact of the war on ordinary people in England, and the empire as a whole. Although the link between characters and the wider impact of the war is eventually vindicated, its effect in clinching both a dramatic climax and a coherent plot, may come later than some readers may wish.

In spite of this, *Small Island* offers a brilliantly evocative portrait of post-war England, in early days of the large-scale arrival of West Indian immigrants. Levy's research cannot be praised enough for its varied details, accurate report on the military and social history of her parents' generation, and its deep understanding of ethnic issues, then only beginning to be discussed or even recognised. She should also be praised for her intuitive, subtle and flawless grasp of traits of English culture, speech and personality. Bernard's racism, for example, is totally plausible, perhaps because it appears, side by side, with his wife's more tolerant attitude toward black West Indians.

Levy's command of Jamaican speech and manners is inspired, even if Hortense's mistaken, school teacher's sense of colonial propriety, Jamaican style, is slightly exaggerated when she uses words like "perchance" or "agape" as part of her everyday speech; for in vocabulary, attitudes, gestures and manners, *Small Island* establishes roots of the cultural mixing out of which black British society would later spring, and, more than anything else, explains the extraordinary success of *Small Island*, in which West Indian protagonists appear as precursors to characters who would later be seen, in full splendour, in the work of Samuel Selvon, the first true master of black British fiction.

"EVERYONE SHOULD KNOW WHERE THEY COME FROM"

Andrea Levy
Fruit of the Lemon, New York, Picador, 2007, pp. 340.
ISBN – 13:978-0312-42664-4.

Like her earlier novels *Every Light in the House Burnin'* (1994) and *Never Far From Nowhere,* (1996) Andrea Levy's third novel, *Fruit of the Lemon,* considers the fate of black, Jamaican immigrants in England. After growing up in London, Faith Columbine Jackson, narrator of *Fruit,* describes a visit to Jamaica where she is caught in an unexpected orgy of cultural exploration and self-discovery. Like Faith, the author herself was born in England of Jamaican parents who, in 1948, had made an historic voyage on the "MV Empire Windrush" the first of many ships that would bring tens of thousands of West Indians to settle in England, their "mother country," during the 1950s.

Part One of *Fruit* describes Faith's growing up in London, Part Two her mind-blowing sojourn to her ancestral homeland, while Part Three, consisting only of half a page, supplies a rather perfunctory conclusion to the novel by noting the narrator's return from Jamaica to London on 5th November, Guy Fawkes Day, the very date on which her parents had arrived in England, in 1948.

Levy's first two novels boldly expose racial prejudice against black immigrants, in England, in the late 1970s. Race and colour seem prescriptive: they appear, either when Faith applies for a job or, for example, she observes a blatantly racial incident in which a black woman, owner of a book shop, is randomly attacked by a young white thug. Not that she gives an impression of black immigrants living in constant fear from attack: it is just that Levy acknowledges racism and seems to relish her use of wit, innuendo and insinuation in exposing it.

In Chapter Twelve, for instance, race lurks in conversations between Faith and the parents of her white boyfriend Simon, particularly with a friend of Simon's parents – Winston Bunyan. But preoccupation with race is not all on one side: Faith's parents foster a relationship between her and Noel, a black work mate of her father's, presumably because they think she should marry black; and her brother Carl's white girl friend, Ruth, who also sees race in every nook and cranny, impulsively counsels firm, militant action against "European oppression" (p. 141) when she hears about a job interview in which Faith thinks she may have got the wrong end of the stick. Ironically, Faith does get the job, and Ruth's militancy turns out to be misguided.

Fruit's real appeal is in Part Two of the novel with Faith's account of staying with her mother's sister Coral in Jamaica, and meeting members of her extended family like her cousin Vincent, aunt Coral's son, and his wife and children. Although impressed by Jamaica's tropical sunshine, luxuriant growth and outdoor life, Faith is jolted by cultural differences between herself and "fellow" Jamaicans. From the beginning, minutes after her arrival, at the airport itself, she is reduced to tears when someone steals five dollars from her, and her luggage is misplaced. Then there is growing awareness that these incidents are accepted as normal, airily dismissed with a familiar shrug; and it makes her realise she is now part of a culture that prides itself on improvisation and random impulse rather than preparation, order or consistent planning.

Faith also realises how fundamentally Jamaican society is regulated by values of race, colour and class. This is not the racial discrimination of Whites against Blacks that she knows in England. Race in Jamaica is physical, spiritual, endemic, as in the description of Gloria, her cousin Vincent's wife: "Gloria's nose was flat and broad and her hair which was straightened, was round and curly on her head. She had very dark skin. A rich dark blue-black that had no highlights of a paler colour." (p. 206) Faith also condescendingly associates Gloria with the Black and White Minstrels show, although she later confesses: "I was ashamed of the thought." (p. 206)

Tortured exploration and bitter recognition of ancestral roots in the six chapters of Part Two narrated by Faith's relatives, mostly her aunt Coral, display fully fleshed sketches of older family members. Even if they look like individual lectures on family biography, theycollectively provide a record both of Faith's family history, and conditions of poverty and unemployment that drive Jamaicans either to emigrate or, for instance, register for service in the First World War.

Hinting at Jamaica's deceptive appeal as a tropical paradise, the novel's epigraph consisting of one four-line stanza from the folk song by Will Holt, compares love to a lemon tree which may look pretty and have sweet flowers, but produces bitter fruit. More to the point, the epigraph confirms that Faith's well intentioned search for roots, following her mother s advice "Everyone should know where they come from," only leads to bitter-sweet discovery of ingrained racial ethics inherited by Jamaicans from their colonial history of African slavery and racial mixing, That such tragic historical circumstances should inspire a narrative of richly individualistic characters, superbly described scenes, pungent speech idioms, and bubbling wit is nothing short of a feat.

Perhaps Levy's *pièce de résistance* is the twisted mind-set and frenzied attitudinizing of Faith's light-skinned cousin Matilda who not only brings up her "pass-for-white" daughter Constance to eat lemons in the English way, and become an Anglophile, educated in England, but also marries a Rastafarian, gives her son an African name "Kofi," and travels to Africa where she changes her name to "Afria" and wears African clothes: "Fruit of the Lemon" indeed!

"MINOR INLETS, NOT PORTS SUBLIME"

Cecil Gray
Careenage, Toronto, Lilibel Publications, 2003, 84pp,
ISBN: 0-9681745-3-1.

When, in 1994, he published his first book of poems *The Woolgatherer*, in Toronto, Cecil Gray was already seventy-one years old, and an immigrant since 1988. Gray was born in Trinidad & Tobago, and had a distinguished career as Director of the In-Service Diploma in Education Programme at the University of the West Indies in Jamaica, where he produced twenty-five text books for use in West Indian schools; but *The Woolgatherer* was no flash in the pan, trial run, or stopgap to while away idle hours in an unfamiliar landscape, for it was followed by *Lilian's Songs* (1996), *Leaving in the Dark* (1998), *Plumed Palms* (2000), and now *Careenage* - Gray's fifth volume of poems.

In celebration of typical childhood joys in Gray's native city of Port of Spain, many poems in *Careenage* evoke familiar, everyday, Caribbean activities, incidents, transactions or scenes, for example, lorries: "with flour/ Or Irish potatoes or rice in jute bags tied/ Down with ropes" (p. 64) and a Chinese shop that: "always smelled of saltfish and olive oil" (p. 64) both of which strike an immediate chord of recognition in older West Indians.

Some poems reflect on historical, West Indian topics such as slavery, exploitation, poverty, immigration, or their psychological and cultural off shoots like mimicry and problems of identity. "Hijackers" (p. 58) laments the suffering of "revered ancestors," African slaves, whose bones have been swallowed up by the Atlantic ocean "without a murmur". Not only did many slaves perish in "The Middle Passage," the journey from Africa to the Caribbean, what is worse is that accounts of slavery by colonial authors hijack "the truth of history" by erasing its details.

"As a former publisher of school texts, Gray is acutely sensitive to the role of authors who, during colonial times, routinely popularised views of colonial history. In "Forts," for instance, ruins of British-built forts are presented as exotic reminders of post-imperial glory, instead of what Gray regards as: "our [West Indian] story/ The real one written with slaves' scarlet/ Blood in ledgers abroad." (p.58). Betraying what seems like an instinctive spirit of resistance to oppression the world over, Gray's poems convey heightened awareness of the continuing victimisation of West Indians, and a strong sense of solidarity with these and other examples of colonial injustice.

Other poems in *Careenage* consider reactions to family and friends, impressions of travels in foreign lands, or mixed feelings of exile in Canada. Like poems in the author's previous volumes, those in *Careenage* conjure up loving tribute to West Indian landscape and seascape, manners and culture, sights and sounds, the historic colonial past as well as the post-colonial present. If poems in Gray's five volumes are all of a piece, what distinguishes those in *Careenage* is an apparently fresh preoccupation with themes of loss, decline, disappearance, transience, ageing, and the inevitable finality of death itself.

As the persona confesses in "Gestures" (p. 34), he now hears news only: "of endings, of final farewells, and ghosts", which makes him see himself as: "a simple sojourner afraid that he is losing: "cherished companions who once walked with him/ as they slide down a slope and go into nothing." (p. 34) A sense of deprivation, dwindling and drain is inescapable in these poems; but there is no sense of fear or complaint. Rather the tone is one of calm assessment in settling accounts, or satisfied contentment over the mystery of universal change and decay.

In the title poem of "Careenage" (p. 81), the persona prays that every: "weary seafarer who has finished the course" will find: "a tranquil harbour ... a careenage" where he and his friends will swap stories. Although this may be final, it is not regarded with dread. The tone is one of finality and fulfilment as in Keats's great ode "To Autumn" which speaks less of drain or dwindling than of ripening and maturity. This even-tempered acceptance of life's transience, and the unstoppable passage of time, is perhaps the most notable feature of Gray's poetry, and may be found, for instance, in "Jacob and Otty" where the persona's long separation from two cherished, childhood friends arouses no: "wistful longing for their return." (p. 30) There is a touch of nobility in facing death and dissolution with such studied equipoise!

Gray's poems consist mainly of short lyrics, no more than one page each in length, like the sixty-eight examples in *Careenage* which vary stanzaic form and metre strategically to suit each subject. For instance, although written mostly in free verse, a poem like "Her Name" pays homage to the persona's grandmother, and uses rhyme effectively to lend an air of rhythmic, bouncing light-heartedness and warm affection. In general, Gray's imagery revels in naturalness. When thoughts of airline passengers waiting in a departure lounge are compared to tightly packed suitcases: "each with his freight/ of thoughts, weight of baggage" (p. 10) the experience appears natural, unforced, yet arresting. Skill with alliteration and assonance is also striking in "Silhouettes" where vowel sounds: "the owl's/ monotonous, boring and foreboding hoots" (p. 65) make the hooting of the birds almost audible.

With such technical skill and commitment to West Indian themes, history and culture, it is surprising that Gray does not enjoy higher standing among West Indian poets. In "Minor Inlets" (p. 23) he admits that he: "never promised a rare, special vision" or "epiphanic revelation". His aim was more modest: "my prow is set/ for minor inlets, not ports sublime." (p. 23) Even if he does not yet rank with leading names in West Indian poetry like Derek Walcott, Edward Brathwaite, Lorna Goodison or Dionne Brand mainly because of his late start, Gray's even-tempered reflection and technical sophistication suggest that his ranking will rise as his work becomes better known.

"I AM GLAD THAT I HAD DAYS TO DO WHAT I DID"

Cecil Gray
Possession: Poems, Toronto, Lilibel Publications, 2009, 71pp.
ISBN 978-0-9681745-5-5.

Possession, Trinidadian Cecil Gray's sixth volume of poems, continues his compulsive meditation on the fate of Caribbean nations despite colonial victimisation by slavery, indenture and much else. One poem "At the Sea's Edge" recognises the fate of victims of empire worldwide: "Today Iraq, yesterday all of Africa, and before that / the land and people of what's called America." (p. 65) The persona finds it hard to stomach the fact that European imperialists who conquered and dispossessed an entire continent, had the gall to name "America," after themselves instead of their dispossessed Amerindian victims, the true "Americans" who are: "stepped on like roaches by imperial boots." (p. 65)

In "Coast Road," the persona recalls abuses of empire in Trinidad: "blindfolded years of slums and subjection / when smooth roads were closed to those with complexions / a bit too swarthy, and their sweat could not earn / enough to relieve them from hunger, nor from / compounds they lived in like horses in stables." (p. 68) Such dehumanising conditions, based on race and colour, are bad enough. What is worse is fear that the sordid truth may be lost in mists of history. So far as ethnic mixing goes, "Bugles and Drums" acknowledges rhythms of Africa and Shango worship in Trinidad where: "beliefs had to come from Europe's scripture ... and to be African / was an offence." (p. 8)

Not all poems in *Possession* are weighed down by the heavy hand of history however: some poems focus on everyday events and personal relationships, for instance, "Sceptre" which celebrates the piety and patience of the poet's grandmother, or "Jimmy King" which recalls fond memories of a friend, and "Goodbye" which gives thanks for forty years of friendship with Freya Watkinson, an English woman who dies before the poet can pay one last visit to her. In "Epitaph," Gray pays homage to P.E. Ferdinand who was his teacher seventy years earlier, but now: "has sunk like a stone into oblivion." (p. 11) Unsolicited expression of gratitude, so long afterwards, when no one might even have noticed if the poet had remained silent, hints at our capacity, too rarely perhaps, for selfless actions of pure goodness.

In an unusually satirical poem "Cutting Edge" Gray sneers at poets who indulge in avant garde literary gimmicks, implying preference for his own more conventional style, mixing iambic pentameter and free verse, with varied stanzaic forms and lines of varying length. When it suits him, though, as in "Well," he is versatile enough to display his own dalliance with avant- gardism through an idiosyncratic arrangement of lines on the page.

Although many poems in *Possession* consider commonplace scenes or events in Canada, England and India, there is no denying the relentless, haunting effect of the poet's post-colonial, Caribbean origin on his imagination. The opening poem in the volume "Always the Sea" quotes two lines from the Barbadian poet Frank Collymore as an epigraph: "Like all who live in small islands/ I must always be remembering the sea." (p. 1) The crucial role of small islands in shaping Caribbean consciousness is again driven home by the final lines of "Bounty," which declare that mere sight itself of the

Caribbean landscape evokes: "the love for an island that was not yours but / which claimed your faith and reshaped your ends." (p. 70)

What also haunts *Possession* is a sense of loss and transience when: "All things sink out of sight," (p. 5) or: "Expectations have withered to straw;" (p. 9) for youth, ambition, energy and enthusiasm all fade away in due course. In "Fragrance," for instance, the poet recalls the bubbling zest and energy of his schooldays which brought: "the scent of burgeoning hope;" (p. 9) but: "None of that happens today." (p. 9) "Take Five" also recollects the poet's youthful excitement over particular musicians, Brubeck, Desmond, Billy Eckstine, and particular tunes – "Tenderly," "Moonglow," "Over the rainbow" - which gave irrepressible delight and led the persona and his young friends, during one of their music listening sessions, to burst out in gushing song for neighbours to hear. Inevitably, the poem ends with two unanswerable questions: "What heavy roller through the years crushes such zest? / How is celebration so ruthlessly suppressed?" (p. 15)

Still, plaintiveness signifies neither bitterness nor complaint: the persona probably feels no more than natural concern over his own process of ageing, as in an earlier poem, "Cool Now, Calm," where he confesses: "I wish for nothing more, merely to endure / a pebble on memory's soft powdery strand." (p. 5) If this sounds pretentious, consider other lines in the same poem: "despite comforting myths / like warm blankets" that is to say, systems of belief that promise spiritual transcendence in some form of eternal life: "dissolution comes to end / every trivial parade." (p. 5)

This sounds more like tough-minded acceptance of finiteness or transience in all living things, especially when it is followed by: "Twilight has its own comforts like any age." (p. 5) Sunny acceptance of inevitable loss or human mortality, within a universe of ultimate secrecy and unfathomable mystery, gains even stronger conviction from the simple majesty of the final two lines of "Cool Now, Calm": "I am glad that I had days to do what I did / but I'm cool now, calm, as it fades away." (p. 5) Here, surely, is both contentment and gratitude!

"YOUR VILE RACE IS OF SUCH A NATURE THAT NURTURE CANNOT STICK"

Elizabeth Nunez
Prospero's Daughter, Ballantyne Books, New York, 2006, pp.316 ISBN 0-345-45535-5

Prospero's Daughter is the sixth novel of Elizabeth Nunez, a Trinidadian who, after secondary school in her home island, moved to New York where she gained Masters and Doctorate degrees. In 1972 Nunez began teaching at Medgar Evers College and today she is Distinguished Professor at Hunter College. Through remarkable creativity and energy as editor, author, and promoter of black writers, Professor Nunez has won numerous awards and, in *Prospero's Daughter,* focuses on relationships between Caliban and both Prospero and his daughter Miranda, three main characters in Shakespeare's last play *The Tempest.*

In Shakespeare's play, Prospero, rightful Duke of Milan, uses magical powers to entice his usurper brother Alonzo into shipwreck on a remote island over which Prospero assumed ownership. Events are manipulated by Prospero until he regains his rightful position through an arrangement of marriage between his daughter Miranda and Alonzo's son Ferdinand. But although she was one of few native people on the island before Prospero's arrival, Caliban's mother, Sycorax, gets little sympathy from Shakespeare: being a witch banished from Algiers to the island does not bolster the genuineness of

Caliban's claim of dispossession on grounds of her being the original owner of the island.

During a period of decolonisation in the mid-twentieth century, however, when many European-owned, Caribbean colonies gained independence, the dispossession of Sycorax, a black native, by a white usurper/coloniser, Prospero, became a hotly debated topic of colonial liberation, with Caliban regarded as an emblematic colonial victim linked to themes of dispossession, exploitation, racism and hypocrisy, vigorously championed by Third World artists, authors and scholars. This led to a more partisan re-interpretation both of the poisoned relationship between a benevolent, paternalistic Prospero and his servant/slave Caliban, and of Prospero's allegation that Caliban had sexually violated his daughter Miranda.

In the post-colonial reinterpretation followed by Professor Nunez's novel, Shakespeare's story is removed from a North Atlantic location to Chacachacare, an island off the coast of Trinidad, near to Venezuela and the South American mainland. At the time of the action in *Prospero's Daughter*, probably shortly before independence in 1962, the island was used as a leper colony, and provided refuge for Dr. Peter Gardner, an English medical doctor and researcher who is portrayed in a rather less benevolent light than Shakespeare's Prospero since he changes his name and flees in haste from England after causing the death of a female patient on whom he had tested an experimental drug. In remote Chacachacare, however, Gardner sets himself up as a botanical consultant.

Gardner's arrival in Chacachacare with his three-year-old daughter Virginia brings him in touch with Carlos Codrington, a Caliban figure whose parents are an Englishwoman Sylvia Codrington and a local fisherman who was a poet and dreamer, later killed by drug dealers. Like Sycorax, Sylvia came from Algiers, and after she dies, leaves her possessions in care of her housekeeper Lucinda Bates. Following a storm, Gardner insinuates himself by helping to rebuild Sylvia's house, but after Lucinda's death, he seizes ownership of the property which Carlos assumes is his inheritance from his mother. A bitter conflict over dispossession, racism and exploitation erupts, chiefly between Gardner and Carlos, creating a complicated intertwining of Carlos's growing love for Virginia over their twelve years together on the island, with Gardner's own incestuous relations with his daughter, and sexual exploitation of Ariana, Lucinda's doogla daughter who is Gardner's cook.

At first, Gardner acts as a mentor and instructor teaching Carlos about plants, literature and music; but this cooperation disappears when Carlos and Virginia fall in love, and Gardner accuses Carlos of raping her. Gardner calls Carlos "filth" (p. 143) and "lazy bastard" (p. 144) and treats him like a servant/slave, eventually locking him up like an animal in a wooden cage. Animosity increases when, from his cage, Carlos accuses Gardner of obeah and devil worship, and shouts: "You cursed my mother. I curse you in the name of my mother" (p. 220) But Gardner gives as good as he gets: "Your vile race is of such a nature that nurture can never stick," (p. 220) and in a final scene where Gardner and Carlos continue screaming barbed insults at each other, Gardner pleads with Virginia for forgiveness, without success, before suddenly hurling himself over a precipice, in his outstretched cape, as he falls to his death on rocks below. His daughter sums him up as a boil which was lanced and: "spewed out the years of obscenities he had hoarded, defiling Ariana, defiling me." (p. 254)

If Gardner's pitiful appearance succeeds in ripping away the rotten web of falsehood, racism, concealed repression and hypocrisy that surround colonialism in general, the novel's female characters, from Sylvia Codrington and Lucinda Bates to Ariana and Virginia, also succeed in advancing a feminist note of toughness and endurance in surviving abuse. From the confident, adventurous spirit of Sylvia, in her worldwide travels, to Virginia's innocent belief in the inherent humanity of African slaves, Nunez celebrates an astonishing capacity for resilience in her female characters.

In a scene where Carlos wonders whether English-born Virginia could acquire West Indian identity by living with him, he is assured by Gardner himself that a rose that is grown in West Indian soil becomes West Indian, no matter its origin. This not only assures Virginia of West Indian nationality: it also suggests that processes of persistence, survival and change are best left in female hands.

"WORDS SHOULD NOT HAVE BEEN NECESSARY"

Elizabeth Nunez
Not for Everyday Use: A Memoir, New York, Akashic Books, 2014, pp.256, ISBN-13;978-1- 617775- 233-9

Born in Trinidad and working in the US since the 1960s, Elizabeth Nunez, author of eight novels, written between 1986 and 2011, and currently Distinguished Professor at Hunter College in New York, is also author of *Not for Everyday Use: A Memoir* both a portrait of her family and a confessional of her deepest feelings: "I am a writer. My business is to tell everything...here I am telling all, writing the all I think is all." This sounds like a deeply considered resolve to face up to truth, despite its perils.

Growing up in a British Caribbean colony, Elizabeth imbibes colonial values of intellectual confusion and cultural and emotional self-hatred; and not until the civil rights movement in the US, in the 1960s, does she understand: "the extent to which slavery had existed on my island...African Americans were digging into their past [of Atlantic slavery] and they retrieved mine. I was horrified to learn about the cruelty of the British." (p. 120) Her colonial, Trinidadian upbringing had taught her that: "they [the British] had come to our island and blessed us with their culture and largesse... [for which] we were expected to be grateful." (p. 120) We can see why Caliban, from Shakespeare's *The Tempest* becomes a compelling symbol of colonial dispossession and resistance in Nunez's *oeuvre.*

Elizabeth's first person narrative in *Everyday Use* meditates on the death of her ninety-year old mother in Trinidad, and convergence of family, her father Waldo and ten siblings, who arrive from various parts of the US and Trinidad for the funeral. Elizabeth's own concerns are mixed with sketches of other relatives/friends, particularly her parents and chiefly her father. Her meditations mix sketches from the past, with present reminders of ongoing funeral preparations, a neat, technical exploit that heightens both the volume's coherence and suspense. Chapter Fifteen, for instance, mostly discusses the turbulent inner struggle of the narrator, a divorcée, against the inflexibility of Catholic proscription, before ending with a brief review of practical arrangements for the High Mass at the funeral.

In typical Caribbean fashion, Elizabeth's family is a mixture of African and European with Madeiran (Portuguese/Jewish) elements. Race, colour and class are paramount both in Elizabeth's own family and students in Trinidad and the US: "Like the amazing diversity of skin colour and hair texture in Trinidad, my students are dark-skinned, cocoa-pod brown, chocolate brown, cafe au lait, pale cantaloupe, sun-kissed pink." (p. 231) Her mother whose lighter colour assigns her to middle class Trinidad: "does not understand why here [in the US] her class does not trump her colour." (p. 202) Meanwhile: "My grandfather, like my father, was dark-skinned, the colour of a ripened cocoa pod." (p. 169) Still, the Nunezes were: "one of the island's most distinguished families," (p. 156) and: "Deep down, I think she [Una Nunez] always felt as if she did not, could not belong to the Nunez family." (p. 156)

Despite aberrations or hardships, for example, her mother's orthodox Catholic belief that saddles her with fourteen pregnancies and eleven children, Elizabeth's family portrait is one of stunning achievement from family members who include doctors, business executives, actuaries, a lawyer, an entrepreneur, midwife and a university professor and writer. There are also rich details about Trinidad's history, geography, food, culture and politics; but the main focus is on family relations especially between her parents whose love for each other inspires one of the narrator's most striking revelations: "I wanted to die in the presence of someone I loved, someone who loved me, someone who... had cared about me, who had supported me through good times and bad. Someone with whom I had history." (p. 192)

Another striking revelation is the author's acceptance of the numinous as central in everyday actions and relationships. When Elizabeth informs her mother that the novel she is then writing, *Anna In-Between,* includes a character based on someone like her, Una replies: "Write what you want to. I won't mind, no matter what you say," (p. 251) leading Elizabeth to wonder: "Was she giving me permission? Did she already know what I had written? " (p. 251) This awareness of the possibility of intuitive, spiritual or non-rational communication between mother and daughter reinforces similarities between *Anna In-Between* and the author's novel immediately following – *Boundaries* - and corroborates Elizabeth's sense of mysterious interdependence between fact and fiction, reality and truth: "I think to some extent all novels are camouflaged autobiography. The facts may be inaccurate, even false, but the emotions and ideas resonate from the writer's experience." (p. 253)

This may explain why Elizabeth and her mother find it so hard to divulge their deepest feelings to each other. Once, when Elizabeth buys her a cookware set that she badly wants, Una puts it away and never uses it. The same thing happens with a dishwasher. The cookware set and dishwasher are not for everyday use: they are symbols of deepest feelings between mother and daughter which each woman finds too sacred (numinous) to express in words; Elizabeth and Una realise they can depend on each other when needed: "Words should not have been necessary. For either of us;" (p. 245) which is why Elizabeth's eulogy for her mother claims that she was the best wife and mother, that her heart was her china cabinet, and that: "she [Una] had unlocked that heart whenever we [her family] needed her." (p. 245)

"FEELING THAT YOU WERE AWAY FROM EVERYTHING, EVERYWHERE"

E.A. Markham
Against the Grain: a 1950s memoir, Leeds, Peepal Tree Press
Ltd., 2008, pp.192, ISBN13:9781845230258.

For an author of ten volumes of poetry, six of fiction and five
edited collections of poems and prose, plus an account of his
travels in New Guinea, Edward Archibald (Archie) Markham
has not had the impact he deserves, mostly in Britain where he
lived until his death in 2005. He was born on the Caribbean
island of Montserrat in 1939, finished high school in Kilburn,
London, and took post-secondary studies at what is today
the University of Wales, Lampeter. Markham then taught at
different colleges in Britain, wrote under different pseudonyms,
and participated in numerous cultural projects, readings and
conferences that make him an inexhaustible source of restless,
immigrant energy, ambition and creativity, all of which he
seems to have poured into *Against the Grain: a 1950s memoir.*

If immigration is a lifeline to West Indians, the Markhams
immigrated with a vengeance: Archie's father first left Montserrat
to work on the Dutch island of Aruba before absconding to
Montreal where he became a priest; Archie's two brothers, Joe
and Norman, chose Canada, but had moved to London by the
time Archie arrived, along with his mother and sister Julie,
in 1956. Nor was this toing and froing inspired by traditional
Caribbean motives of seeking higher education, skills or

employment, at least not entirely; for Mrs. Markham could afford to send money to her sons to buy a family home in London before she even arrived.

There is no denying some ambivalence: "We were comfortable in Montserrat and yet, we looked forward to leaving." (p. 36) Archie blames the family's leaving on a sense of remoteness, dependence and alienation inherited from a colonial legacy of: "feeling that you were away from everything, from everywhere; from where things happened; you were at the furthest point from where things in the world came." (p. 36) Politics also drove Markham immigration. By the 1950s, old, feudalistic/colonialist ethics were on the run in the Caribbean: "in the changed political atmosphere pioneered by the early trades-unionists, we were part of the employer not worker class;" (p. 37) but in London, when plans to buy a house did not work out, the narrator's mother: "felt the loss of status keenly. She never complained. Except about the cold, but she never hid the fact that she had had five houses 'at home' and had had five maids (though not at the same time) to do her bidding." (p. 163)

While Part One of *Against the Grain* "Over There" celebrates the glamour and grandeur of the family's inherited wealth and social status in Montserrat, Part Two "Over Here" contrives a bittersweet saga of immigrant life in London, and Part Three "Against the Grain" sums up the profit and loss of it all. Mrs. Markham did not only feel socially adrift: "she feared for us [her children] in England, "(p. 163) and an "Afterword," which includes a eulogy by the narrator for his brother Joe who dies of cancer, catches a genuine sense of grief felt by the family.

The encounter between an immigrant family like the Markhams and the host culture in London leaves a lasting impression; for the Markhams react with a self-contradictory but all too plausible mixture of awe, wonder, trepidation and fear, when Mrs. Markham feels it strange for them to be lumped together with Jamaicans, simply because the large majority of West Indian immigrants in London are Jamaican. It is also strange for them to see an African or an Indian (with a turban) for the first time. As for sliced bread, the narrator regards it as: "unbelievably grand, each white slice was the same thickness throughout and the bread was wonderfully moist. It all seemed so much of an advance on the little rolls we used to get at Mr. Lee's ... when my grandmother's stock from Saturday baking had run out." (pp. 87-88)

And don't talk about such a new fangled contraption as a gas meter! Readers of Samuel Selvon's *The Lonely Londoners* will remember the frantic struggle with gas meters faced by West Indians, newly-arrived in London, in the 1950s, or the jaunty antics of the old, Jamaican lady Tanty, who was so dismayed by her first venture on board a red, double decker, London bus, that she felt it would topple over or "capsize." Such reactions register the shock of moving from one society where personal relations are all loose, flexible or informal, to a technologically developed one, that is more organised, ordered or controlled. As the narrator observes, when British passengers on an underground train appear to unfold their newspapers at one stroke of the clock: "it seemed like being part of people in a book." (p. 91)

Not that uglier aspects of immigration such as racism are ignored! Rather than give vent to outrage, Markham prefers the simple, matter-of-fact blend of candid observation with tolerant, free-wheeling informality and humour which reports, for instance, that: "queuing was a fairly painless lesson in democracy," (p. 168) or notes, when his father blames his mother for their separation: "how unconvincingly he managed to put his case of wronged innocence." (p. 64) His gift for witty phrase-making alone affirms Markham's enviable literary reputation, and along with his industry, versatility and artistry, may yet catapult *Against the Grain* to a position not far behind some of the best West Indian memoirs so far, for example, Austin Clarke's hilarious *Growing up Stupid Under the Union Jack*, (1980) Roy Heath's more sombre but exquisitely moving *Shadows Round the Moon* , (1990) or Lorna Goodison's wonderfully lyrical *From Harvey River: a Memoir of my Mother and her People*. (2007)

"WHAT IS THAT? BLACK POWER? BLACK DIRTINESS!"

Merle Collins
Angel, London, Women's Press Ltd., 1987, pp.294.
ISBN 0 7043 4082 8

Born of Grenadian parents in Aruba, in 1950, Merle Collins has so far written two novels, *Angel* (1987)and *The Colour of Forgetting* (1995,) three volumes of poetry, and two collections of stories, plus works of criticism while working as Professor of Comparative Literature and English at the University of Maryland in the US. Collins studied at the University of the West Indies in Jamaica, and at the London School of Economics. She supported the People's Revolutionary Government (PRG) led by Maurice Bishop in Grenada, before it collapsed from internal divisions, and Grenada was invaded by American forces, in 1983, during Ronald Reagan's Presidency.

Through a third person narrative *Angel* relates a story of three generations of the McAllister family, in Grenada, from the heyday of "Leader," fictional name for Eric Gairy, a school teacher and trade union leader, who ruled the island from the 1960s to 1979, in the dictatorial style of "Papa Doc" Duvalier of Haiti. As a black, working class family, the most senior member of the McAllister family, Ma Ettie, brings up five children in a one-roomed house during Gairy's régime until he was ousted by the PRG, in 1983. Ettie's daughter Doodsie and her common law husband Allan, are parents of Angel whose career, especially her education at the University of the West

Indies in Jamaica, and her political opinions, take up much of the second half of the novel.

The Grenadian social atmosphere in *Angel* is one of torrid, colonial upheaval, further heated up by unrest and violence, including burnt buildings, and poor living conditions of black workers on white-owned plantations. Discontent is fomented by low wages and injustice as hinted by Regal, Ma Ettie's son: "When cocoa price fall, everybody knowin, but you ever hear dem [white plantation owners] saying tings good, cocoa price really high, so we go give labourers a big raise? To hell was them! We fightin!" (p. 9) Inevitably, a strike erupts, but opinion is divided and Mano, a strike-breaker, is brutally beaten by his workmates. Workers' problems and possible solutions are hotly debated reflecting sharply conflicting attitudes toward the chief representative of the workers, known simply as "Leader," evidently based on the historical Eric Gairy (1922-1997.) The older generation, however, Ma Ettie, for instance, tend to be more complacent: "All you young people mus wait let ting work deyself out. Is God worl: he go fix it." (p. 28)

Angel is very successful in melding social and political concerns with inner, spiritual or philosophical reflections and family relationships of characters to create a plausible, social portrait of the black, Grenadian, working class. Doodsie, for example, disapproves of Angel's new-found awareness of Black Power during her studies in Jamaica, and asks derisively: "What is that? Black Power? Black Dirtiness! [coyly referring to Angel's informal mode of dress] With the education in your head...I not lyin chile, you spoil de way for any other girl children I have after you...Because no way dem would smell university and certainly not in Jamaica. Not when I see what it do to you." (p. 174) The implication again is that girls are somehow not suited to education.

No doubt differences in outlook are common between generations everywhere, but the degree and intensity of difference in a Caribbean, colonial context seems exceptionally divisive. Self-hatred, inculcated in Caribbean people during slavery, invokes assertion of Black Power as vehemently as did the slogan "Black is Beautiful" among African-Americans in the 1960s. Just as Ma Ettie is sceptical of the use of political agitation to correct social and economic inequality among Doodsie's contemporaries, Doodsie disapproves of the more strident opinions of her daughter on theories of race, colour, class and gender, for example: "this ting about who high brown an who black is nonsense. All of us black." (p. 201)

On political matters Angel is equally outspoken. She despises popular adulation of Leader, and smashes a picture of him on the wall in her parents' home, arousing blind anger in her father who cannot understand when she claims: "A man [Leader] who have a country in such a mess, we have him up on the wall like a hero. They [visitors] would think everybody in this house stupid." (p. 200) Angel's post-university views are so different from those of her family and their friends that they label her as a communist, in the idiom of ideological rivalry between the US and USSR during the Cold War. This only summons up bitter memories of her convent school days when she says: "endless prayers for merciful God to kill Castro and leave Cuba in the hands of beautiful America." (p. 200) This is when, at the very end, the Grenada revolution takes place led by the unnamed "Chief" based on Maurice Bishop.

The saga of revolution and the American invasion is narrated partly through reports on public media of a population randomly victimised by someone or other without knowing why. Angel suffers an eye injury during the invasion, but is well enough to conclude: "We [the Revolutionary Government] do wrong. We do real stupidness. But nobody don have a right to invade. We caan let nobody jus invade we country." (p. 274) This is further narrated in a variety of creole registers that include French creole subheadings and expressions, Grenadian creole and standard English, and poems, letters, songs underlining the essential orality of a text that is pure music in diction and rhythm.

"GRENADA MUST NOT BE ABANDONED TO THE COMMUNIST CAMP"

M. Paterson
Big Sky, Big Bullet: A Docu-Novel, Grenada, St. Georges Books Ltd., 1996, pp. 382.

Big Sky Big Bullet: A Docu-Novel is the revised edition of a book first published by Maurice Paterson in 1992 about the New JEWEL Movement and its charismatic leader Maurice Bishop, who was born in Grenada in 1944, studied law in England in the 1960s, and returned home in 1970 while Grenada was still a British colony. In 1972, Bishop brought various political groups together, for example, JEWEL or its inner core OREL Organisation for Revolutionary Endeavour and Education, and his own MAP or Movement for Assemblies of the People, into the New JEWEL Movement (NJM) or Joint Endeavour for Welfare, Education and Liberation. In 1974 Grenada achieved Independence, and in 1976 Bishop was elected to parliament where he became Leader of the Opposition.

In the early 1970s, Grenada languished under the despotism of Sir Eric Gairy, a local union leader who had begun as an anti-colonial fighter, but by 1974, had become, in Bishop's words, a "criminal dictator." (p. 31) Inspired by almost universal fear and hatred of Gairy, at a time when socialist or communist régimes had already taken root in Caribbean territories like Cuba, Jamaica and Guyana, the NJM sprang out of the crest of a socialist wave, in the midst of a Cold War of fierce ideological conflict between the US, champion of capitalism, and the Soviet Union (USSR), their socialist antagonist.

As the author implies, there was a sense of relief and expectation when, during a visit that Gairy made to the US in 1979, the NJM seized power from his army on 13th March, and formally installed itself as the People's Revolutionary Government (PRG). The coup aroused hostility in some Caribbean nations, while predictable support came from Jamaica's Michael Manley, Guyana's Forbes Burnham who had previously provided military training for NJM personnel in Guyana, and from Cuba's Fidel Castro who responded promptly with a substantial shipment of badly needed weapons. If, at first, regional prospects for the coup seemed favourable, they changed in 1980 when Michael Manley lost power to the conservative Edward Seaga and, more disastrously, the arch-conservative Ronald Reagan defeated Jimmy Carter to become President of the US; for as one of Paterson's anonymous commentators then saw it: "The most fundamental question the Grenada revolution faced was how to handle US antagonism." (p. 374)

Whether the NJM handled US antagonism badly or well, Bishop's quixotic attempt to reverse centuries of colonial damage through dreams of a socialist utopia that:"offered radical help for the Caribbean cause" (p. 224) was probably doomed from the start; not simply because Grenada was in the wrong place (the political orbit of the US) at the wrong time (the middle of the Cold War); but because the prevailing, geopolitical context of ideological warfare fostered divisions within the NJM, for instance, over strategy toward Cuba or the Soviet Union, and over loyalties of party moderates and radicals. Worst of all, the context generated bitter personal rivalries, including an alarming rift between the NJM leaders, Maurice Bishop and Bernard Coard. The potential danger of these divisions may be gauged from one of Paterson's informants who claims that Phyllis Coard (Bernard's wife): "was the single most destructive element to the party." (p. 60)

Big Sky Big Bullet accurately documents ideological divisions and personal antagonisms that fuelled a suicidal struggle between Bishop's faction of the party and its Coard-led Central committee, precipitating the detention of Bishop and seven of his supporters by fellow NJM comrades on 19th October, 1983, apparently for not cooperating with the more radical agenda of the NJM's Central Committee. Later the same day, Bishop and his group were freed by a spontaneous assembly of ordinary citizens; then they were re-captured by the PRA and shot.

According to General Hudson Austin of the PRA, the army's action was defensive because Bishop and his faction refused to negotiate and wanted to "wipe out" (p. 275) the Central Committee. Whatever the case, the Americans now had exactly the excuse they needed to invade Grenada, which they did on 25th October, 1979, ostensibly to restore peace and stability, although their real motive was given away by Eugenia Charles, Prime Minister of Dominica who, immediately after the murders on 19th October, journeyed to Washington to implore President Reagan: "Grenada must not be abandoned to the communist camp."(p. 265) This is similar to the early 1960s when the American CIA sponsored riots in British Guiana, and the British introduced a new voting system to remove the socialist régime of Dr. Cheddi Jagan.

Paterson's technique of quoting directly from private letters and reports, and reproducing views of commentators with different perspectives is intended to create an impression of objectivity, which may explain his sub-title of "Docu-novel" or partly documentary account; but despite broadly based sources, total objectivity seems elusive. What Paterson's multi-voiced narrative does achieve is a lively, dramatic and plausible re-enactment of much of the chaos, confusion, fear, terror, panic and hysteria that gripped Grenadians during October, 1983.

With Grenada as a mere pawn in a global game of super power *realpolitik*, and the Cubans claiming non-interference in Grenada's internal affairs, the US simply regarded the Cuban-built airport at Point Salines as a military base in their deadly game with Cuba (proxy of the USSR). "Ideology had been the key cause," (p. 374) said one commentator. In an era when ideological motives pitted American capitalism squarely against Soviet communism, internationally, for the PRG to support the Soviet Union's invasion of Afghanistan in 1979, without fully realising its international implications, was to give "carte blanche" to the US, to invade Grenada on virtually any pretext they wished.

"TO *NOT* BE BURIED IN ONE'S OWN LAND...THE ULTIMATE INSULT"

Caryl Phillips
A Distant Shore, London, Vintage, 2004, 312 pp., ISBN 0 099 42888 1. First published in 2003.

After his stage play, *Strange Fruit,* (1980) Caryl Phillips quickly clocked up nine novels, four works of non-fiction, a couple more plays, besides articles and reviews that placed his "*oeuvre*" on the cutting edge of writing by authors who, like himself, had moved from the periphery (distant shores) of former British colonies, to the English-speaking metropolis of Britain, Canada and the US.

In a strict sense, Phillips is no "immigrant", "new migrant" or "newcomer", all terms that frequent his seventh novel *A Distant Shore.* Although born in the Caribbean island of St. Kitts, in 1958, Phillips was taken as a baby to Britain where he is now rightly regarded as black British alongside the likes of Zadie Smith, Fred D'Aguiar and David Dabydeen, also of Caribbean origin, yet preoccupied with themes of diasporic communities in Britain including dilemmas of identity, nation and home.

These themes hark back to the generation of Naipaul, Selvon, Lamming and others who, half a century earlier, first plunged us into a universal drama of migration, and earnest quest for roots and home. But writers of diasporic communities, in contemporary Britain, now appear to plump for more tangled themes, not merely about immigrants, but a more nondescript assemblage of refugees, travellers or itinerants from a wider range of countries, euphemistically described as "developing." For, as they vie for survival among native Britons, the new arrivals, unlike black immigrant characters, in earlier West Indian fiction, are less deluded by the perceived stability, order or tranquillity in the Britain of Margaret Thatcher, Tony Blair or George Brown.

In *A Distant Shore,* the narrator Dorothy Jones, a retired, fifty-five-year old secondary school teacher in Weston, near a small town in the North of England, flashes back through a series of episodes that reconstruct her past career and relationships. We learn, for example, of her unhappy marriage with Brian: "the selfish pig [who] had walked out on nearly thirty years of marriage". (p. 207). Hardly more comforting is Dorothy's memory of her younger sister Sheila, a rebel who ran away from home and lived with Roger for twenty-five years, before discovering: "she wanted to be with a woman" (p. 242).

Later, Sheila's sudden death from cancer adds poignancy to Dorothy's story, making her seem faded, bereft, abandoned; and this impression gathers strength when we realise that she was forced to take early retirement for harassing a male supply teacher who was her lover, and that she was later humiliated, literally spat upon by Feroza, wife of yet another lover, Mahmood, a Muslim corner shop owner. If Dorothy's experience betrays any sign of the fate of middle-class Britons, in the 1980s and 90s, it is scarcely more reassuring or stable than the uncertainty of the immigrants or refugees who live among them.

Dorothy is one of two narrators in *A Distant Shore,* and her story accounts for roughly half of the action in the novel. During her retirement in Weston, she encounters Solomon Bartholomew, formerly known as Gabriel, a black handyman who is the second narrator. Gabriel's narrative recounts details of his past life in Africa, including wrenching departure from his family to fight in his country's civil war. Known as Major Hawk, Gabriel fights under Colonel Bloodshed, the names alone capturing the desperation and savagery that drive Gabriel to escape and, after many cloak and dagger adventures, make his way, via France, to Britain, where he is eventually processed as a refugee.

Such varied events, expertly blended together, make for an accomplished novel which won the Commonwealth Literature Prize for best fiction in 2004. One of Phillips's chief accomplishments, no doubt deriving from the duality of his Caribbean birth and English upbringing, is the confidence and authority with which he probes both African and English life. This is perhaps the chief difference between him and Caribbean writers of the Selvon era who saw their host society either as wholly foreign and/or uniformly stable and orderly.

Phillips, on the other hand, is particularly good on documenting provocations endured by non-white immigrants in Britain, or in exposing poisoned racial attitudes, for instance, when Dorothy's sister is mugged by a black man and resists cooperating with police, partly, one suspects, because she is more in sympathy with her mugger from a victimised community than with authoritarian white police.

The result is an illuminating meditation on the human cost, on both sides, when people move from unstable, poorer countries to those they expect to be more prosperous and stable. As Colonel Bloodshed affirms: "To *not* be buried in one's own land. Now *that* is the ultimate insult." (p. 100) This, alas, is exactly what happens to Gabriel/Solomon, when, without giving any provocation, he is killed and thrown into a canal by a gang of white youths; and even if his tragedy is probably a figment of Dorothy's deteriorating sanity, strangely enough, it only adds to our sense of conviction in the truth or relevance of disturbing events in Phillips's novel

STRANGERS FROM HERE AND EVERYWHERE

Caryl Phillips, Ed
Extravagant Strangers, London, Faber & Faber Ltd., 1997, pp.315. ISBN 0-571-19240-8

Caryl Phillips's anthology *Extravagant Strangers* looks at excerpts of prose and poetry by immigrants living in Britain, for expressions or feelings of nationality or home: three selections by Africans who were enslaved before they settled in Britain in the eighteenth century, and the final selection also by a contemporary African, Ben Okri, from Nigeria. Of the thirty-nine authors chosen over a period of nearly two hundred years, most are children either of British people who lived abroad, or of non-white parents in British colonies and former colonies. In other words, whatever else it might be taken for, *Extravagant Strangers* is a post-colonial text that includes some of the best known British writers from Thackeray, Conrad and Kipling to Doris Lessing, V.S. Naipaul and Salman Rushdie.

Phillips is nothing if not a conscientious editor: each excerpt is preceded by a perceptive biographical/critique, often no more than one and a half pages in length, placing the author's work in a general context that makes it easier to enter each excerpt's mood, medium and message. The critique in the first excerpt by the Nigerian Ukawsaw Gronniosaw, for instance, does not merely summarise his life, but observes his: "rather naive faith" (p. 2) in England upon his arrival. Gronniosaw's experience introduces a recurring pattern in the volume, of initial faith in England being shattered when an author later acquires: "a more realistic view of his new countrymen." (p. 2)

Although black or non-white authors complain about racial discrimination, it is only one aspect of a wider sense of alienation or failure to develop a genuine sense of belonging to Britain. Of white authors who lived in Britain but were born and/or brought up abroad, Jean Rhys describes her perplexity, as a white West Indian, shortly before World War One, when confronted by the calculation, regimentation and precise routine required simply to take a bath in a London boarding house: "My aunt explained the ritual of having a bath...you had to ask for it several days beforehand, you had to take it at that time and no other, and so on and so on." (p. 66) Similarly, William Boyd who was born of British parents in Ghana, is completely flustered by British manners of dressing and dealing with money which lead him to confess with relief: "I never felt like this in Africa where I roamed about the countryside, cycled through the streets [in Ghana]" (p. 265)

If it somehow seems out of proportion for a small and insignificant region like the Caribbean to claim eleven authors in *Extravagant Strangers*, the reason probably has to do with the editor's own background (Phillips was born in St. Kitts), and with a complex relationship between Britain and her West Indian colonies, since the sixteenth century, one deeply scarred by exploitation through African slavery and Indian indenture. African-Caribbeans and Indian-Caribbeans were historically conditioned to view Britain as much their home as Africa or India respectively, and characters of West Indian authors like V.S. Naipaul, George Lamming and Sam Selvon, who arrived in London as early as 1950, exhibit respect or warm feelings for Britain, at least initially.

For all his illustrious revolutionary credentials, C.L.R.James too, in "Bloomsbury: An Encounter with Edith Sitwell," where he discusses English literature with one of England's leading literary luminaries, in 1932, betrays strong Anglophile sentiments that are light years away from the searing indictment of exploitation of West Indian immigrants in England, denounced in Linton Kwesi Johnson's provocatively titled poem "INGLAN IS A BITCH" written, in 1980, in pungent Jamaican creole idiom: "Inglan is a bitch/ dere's no escapin' it/Inglan is a bitch/dere's no runnin' whey fram it."(p. 268) Similarly, the urbane elegance of V.S. Naipaul's writing in *The Enigma of Arrival* describing his arrival in London, contrasts sharply with the view in *Beyond the Dragon's Mouth* by his younger brother Shiva, who arrived in London fifteen years later, in the mid-1960s and found, in the same Earls's Court district where Vidia had lived earlier: "dizzying vistas of anonymous urban housing," (p. 232) a drunk randomly throwing a brick into a shop window, and: "the transience of a purgatorial clearing house." (p. 232)

It is astonishing how a typical story "From Sour Sweet" by Timothy Mo (Hong Kong), about the adjustment of a Chinese family to life in Britain, strikes the same chord as excerpts from other authors. This is probably most evident in Doris Lessing's magnificently observant essay "In Defence of the Underground" which summons up a deeply thoughtful reflection of multicultural London as the living confluence of issues such as race/class/colour and a turbulent legacy of colonialism interacting daily with the very buildings, streets and people of the great city.

The title of the volume is taken from Act One of Shakespeare's *Othello* where Roderigo and Iago, more out of mischief than mercy, inform aged and respected senator Brabantio that his daughter Desdemona has committed the ultimate sin of indulging in an intimate sexual relationship with a black foreigner, Othello, "an extravagant and wheeling stranger / Of here and everywhere," (*Othello*, Act I, Sc. ii, ll. 137/138) quoted as part of an epigraph to Phillips's volume. As one of the more established West Indian writers in Britain, Phillips is among the most reliable interpreters of contemporary black British experience and, for him, *Othello* is a central text on race, colour and immigration suggesting that, in their common search for a sense of belonging and home in Britain, his characters are unlikely to succeed and may have to remain truly extravagant strangers, whether in Shakespeare's or any other sense.

"BLISS WAS IT IN THAT DAWN TO BE ALIVE"

Rachel Manley
Horses in her Hair: A Granddaughter's Story, Toronto, Key
Porter Books Ltd., 2008, pp.344. ISBN 978-1554702060

Horses in her Hair: A Granddaughter's Story is the third
volume in Rachel Manley's trilogy of family memoirs that
began with *Drumblair,* (1996) largely about her grandfather,
Norman Manley (1893-1969), which won [Canada's]
Governor General's award for non-fiction in 1997, and was
followed by *Slipstream: A Daughter Remembers* (2000), about
Rachel's father Michael (1924-1997). Both Norman and his
son Michael were Jamaican politicians, Norman as Premier
from 1949 to 1962, and Michael as Prime Minister from 1972
to 1980, and again in 1989. As wife of Norman and mother
of Michael, Edna Manley (1900-1987) was steeped in politics;
but she also had an independent career as an artist, sculptor,
carver, diarist and editor; and, as announced on the jacket
of *Horses,* her impact is: "nothing less than the mother of
Jamaica's artistic soul."

Edna was the fifth child of Reverend Harvey Swithenbank,
a Methodist Minister from Cornwall, England, and Ellie a
mixed blood (Euro/African) Jamaican woman whom Harvey
met during a seven-year stint as a missionary in Jamaica.
Edna grew up in England, and for her granddaughter, born
nearly fifty years later, to re-create details of her life in *Horses*,
including those of her early years in England, is an inspired feat

of improvisation, imagination, research, and reconstruction from historical accounts, artifacts, family letters, diaries and personal memories.

It was at her home in Cornwall that Edna met Norman, her Jamaican first cousin, who had won a scholarship to study law at Oxford University. Together with their relationship we are told of Edna's studies at St Martin's School of Art in London, Norman's service in World War One, and the role of soldiers of the British West Indian Regiment in the war, reflecting beginnings of West Indian resistance against racism and colonialism that would spark strikes and riots in many British Caribbean colonies in the 1930s and lead, by the 1950s, to a credible movement for West Indian Independence.

Norman and Edna marry in London before travelling to Jamaica in 1922, and from her first glimpse of squalor and deprivation in downtown Kingston, Edna is dumbfounded as seen, for instance, in her reaction to domestic service pay: "She [Edna] was horrified by the few shillings all domestic staff were paid to work from dawn to late at night." (p. 99) Even if she was not overtly activist, Edna supported her husband's liberation politics of which the launch of his People's National Party (PNP), in 1940, was the crossing of the Rubicon for Jamaicans and other West Indians toward their goal of freedom from colonial rule.

As an Englishwoman, what particularly dismayed Edna, was the ingrained colonial-mindedness of middle class Jamaicans and their superstitious idolisation of English manners. "Nowhere [in Jamaica] was there a black hero depicted on a monument, only Nelson and Queen Victoria. Any book of history began with Columbus. How could history start at the moment of capture?" (p. 111) Rachel writes with conviction about her grandmother's earnest struggle to adapt her social, moral and artistic sensibility to Caribbean colonial conditions.

Paradoxically, Edna's struggle was artistically liberating from: "her armature of solid physical Englishness" (p. 151) the feeling of being "straitjacketed in England, even in art school." (p. 151) It was a crucial breakthrough when, in Jamaica: "she seemed to find the raw source of life and movement" (p. 151) and: "she knew in her heart that she had found her landscape... She had at last come home, spirit and flesh at one, combined in a medium." (pp.-151-152) Thus were Edna's carvings and sculptures nourished by the irresistible, political awakening initiated by Norman.

The triumph was that her work was recognised in England, for instance, by Apollo magazine, and by the association of her name with those of established British sculptors like Henry Moore and Barbara Hepworth. To consider all this today, and her equally ground-breaking editions of the literary journal "Focus" which first came out in 1943, it is no wonder that Edna's name: "is readily associated with the kindling world of Jamaican art and literature," (p. 202) and that she was awarded Jamaica's Order of Merit when she turned eighty.

Lavish pictures of Edna's work are reproduced in *Horses* accompanied by helpful commentaries on each item, in particular, "Horse of the Morning," carved out of Guatemalan redwood, which influences the title of Rachel's memoir by representing: "a young country's claim to name and place." (p. 185) But this optimism is counteracted by a sculpture "Ghetto Mother" partly inspired by bitterness over the 1980 Jamaican elections, when Michael Manley lost, and eight hundred people were killed in election riots. "Ghetto Mother" also laments the invasion of Grenada by the US in 1983, and the pitiful economic and military helplessness of the wider Caribbean: "an island, a lone atoll hunkered down, protecting itself from the onslaught of vaster powers, both economically and militarily." (p. 320)

Every page of *Horses* celebrates the contribution of the Manleys through Edna's artistic endeavours, Norman's visionary political initiative, Michael's revolutionary politics and, Edna's tireless efforts in the Manley house of Drumblair where, like Madame de Stael in an eighteenth century European salon, Edna played hostess to promising poets, artists, novelists and intellectuals debating issues of the birth of a new Caribbean nation: "Drumblair ... was the headquarters, the beating heart to which warriors came to report and complain and reconcile and decide " (pp.-178-179) about a revolutionary birth that inspired similar feelings to Wordsworth's delirius joy upon first hearing of the French Revolution:" Bliss was it in that dawn to be alive/ But to be young was very Heaven!"

"WHAT MAKE COW WALK OVER THE HILL?. CAUSE HIM CYAN'T WALK UNDER IT."

Barbara Lalla
Cascade, Kingston, Jamaica, University of the West Indies Press, 2010, pp.299. ISBN 978- 976-640-233-4

Cascade is the second novel of Barbara Lalla who, in 1976, left her native Jamaica for Trinidad where she later became Professor Emerita of Language and Literature in the Department of Liberal Arts, on the Trinidad campus of the University of the West Indies. Like the author's first novel *Arch of Fire,* (1998) *Cascade* studies Jamaican family and social relations, with special emphasis on perils of ageing in conditions of crime, violence and insecurity in post-colonial Jamaica. While the main action of *Cascade* takes place in Jamaica itself, characters communicate with each other in Trinidad and Canada and confirm ageing, nowadays, as an increasing, worldwide concern.

Three main characters, Rosemarie (Rummy) and a married couple, Ellie and Dan are Jamaican seniors who shun life in the crime-infested city of Kingston, for a guest house, Cascade, that is owned by their friend Ivy, and is being converted into a home for the elderly in the hills of rural Jamaica. Although Ellie and Dan move to Trinidad to be with their daughter Rachel and her Trinidadian family, contact between characters is maintained through accounts from multiple narrators, including Ellie, Rosemarie, Dan and Ivy, and a host of relatives, servants, care givers and other associates.

Different narrators create multi-faceted versions of events and characters, as many as twelve voices that may sometimes test the alertness of readers, especially in the case of minor characters with concerns of their own. Still, we do not lose track of the main topic of "elder rights," (p. 180) of protagonists threatened, partly by dementia in the normal process of ageing, and partly by machinations of family members or care givers who take advantage of protagonists' decreasing mental competence. Elder abuse may not be new, but the author's timely exposé reminds us of the recent spectacular increase in the life-span of populations in most countries, leading to a universal care-giving industry that is today more institutionalised and open to abuse of elders.

In *Cascade* the plan for Ivy's guest house depends on care-giving services from Rosemarie who has experience in a US hospital; but the plan is transformed into a more commercialised one of a sleek resort with luxury accommodation for tourists at ground level while, according to Sibyl, resident seniors are confined, in prison-like conditions, upstairs: "Don't talk bout iron bar, Missis... is crime they say. Stupidness. Whoever hear bout crime inna country? Besides, they not trying to protect us, is jail they jailing us." (p. 174) To complicate matters the person who engineers this transformation of Cascade is Scotty Cunningham, Rosemarie's stepson whose wife Pansy serves as his partner in crime as he gradually takes over control from Rosemarie.

Although Ivy, Rosemarie, Ellie and Dan grow up during the period of British colonialism in the Caribbean when human rights were more restricted, they paradoxically display more humane and caring attitudes than Scotty and his associate Ashmead who reflect ethics of a younger, more calculating generation of "free" post-independence Jamaicans. As Rosemarie says of her stepson: "Scotty is like a animal with the whip cracking over his head...Scotty mad fe money, and is that send him to Ashmead in the first place." (p.186) The author seems to make a clear, if ironic, distinction between the moral climate in colonial Jamaica, despite limits on political freedom, and the grasping greed that follows independence. For all its post-colonial coarseness and commercialism, however, Professor Lalla who is either author or co-author of several academic studies of Jamaican creole, contrives a fictional portrait of Jamaica that is, at least, partially, redeemed by her magnificent command of Jamaican creole speech as well as by other oral strategies that eloquently express the deepest thoughts and feelings of her characters, and elicit their resilient humanity in coping with what they consider adverse historical change.

Apart from the vocabulary, rhythms and cadences of Jamaican speech itself, the jokes of one narrator, Basil, have no more motive than comic relief. In one instance, water running down the hillside instinctively prompts Basil to ask: "Miss Petrona, what lie down inna bed an him bed always wet?" before he supplies the answer: "Ribba." (p. 30) Basil's pun on the word "bed" is not related to any activity or conversation he has with Petrona: it simply records his position as an underling within the hierarchy of Jamaica's class structure, and uncomplaining acceptance of his fate. Basil addresses another joke to Ellie: "What make cow walk over hill, ma'am?" and again answers: "cause him cyan't walk under it." (p. 190) Even if such jokes do not advance the action of the novel, they relieve tension.

One of the most effective oral strategies in *Cascade* is the author's use of aphorisms or apophthegms drawn from traditional Jamaican folk wisdom, for example, the delicious paradox of: "There are two tragedies in life, they say. One is not to get your heart's desire; the other is to get it," (p. 28) or the blatant sexism of: "Mankind nat to be hold in subjection to womanhood." (p. 31) The wonder is that such reflections accompany the spontaneous immediacy of outbursts from people who live daily under threat of violence from either police or gangs: "Bullet a rain – blam blam! Me' queeze under the divan. Yes, sah. Gunshat. 'Queeze me have fe 'queeze. Blam blam round me I smell de gunpowder inna de room." (p. 197)

"SHE IS NOT GOING TO MARRY NO MAN BLACK LIKE HER"

Pamela Mordecai
Pink Icing and Other Stories, Toronto, Insomniac Press,
2006, pp.241. ISBN 1-897178-32-8

Pink Icing and Other Stories, a volume of eleven stories, is the
handiwork of Jamaican author, literary pioneer and promoter
of women's writing, Pamela Mordecai who is credited with
more than thirty books, including poetry, fiction, anthologies,
text books, children's books and writing for and about women.
A charming photograph of Mordecai as a child appears on the
cover of *Pink Icing,* announcing the voice of a child narrator,
or at least a child's perspective in many stories as they unfold
in Jamaica.

The title story sets the tone of life in post-colonial Jamaica
with deceptively innocent observations from an eight-year-
old girl on her way home from school one afternoon. Nothing
could be more routine or everyday. Colleen comments on
what she sees: "I know that upstairs houses have a meaning
and upstairs people are important. That is because they are
classy and have clout and almost always have colour." (p. 44)
By "colour" Colleen means light coloured skin, and the lighter
the better. Her friend Miranda, for instance, tells her that: "She
[Miranda] is not going to marry no man black like her ... She is
going to marry a man with good [light] colour to improve her
children's own." (p. 44) Colleen's innocent report on the system
of race/class/ colour classification in Caribbean societies with

a history of plantation slavery carries twice its impact since, in her childlike simplicity, she is completely unaware of the vileness of self-hatred that this system breeds in descendants of African slaves.

Further on her way home, Colleen notices the unusualness of Tim Blythe, a white man, as a farmer: "White people own animals, ride animals, shoo away animals, but they do not herd animals." (p. 47) She also notices Blythe's high boots and whip even if she is too young to connect the boots and whip with standard accoutrements formerly used by (white) plantation proprietors to control their slaves. The appeal of "Pink Icing" rests squarely on the delicate poignancy of dramatic irony in Colleen's observation that she has never seen Blythe use his whip, when the coercive brutality of that whip (or one like it) on African slaves, has exercised perhaps the most formative influence on Jamaican history, society and culture.

At least Colleen realises that Blythe's white cut-stone house is not: "just a big upstairs house," (p. 48) for she is aware of an hierarchy of colour applying to Whites too, namely that the Sabgas, Middle Eastern Lebanese, are another [lower, non-European] category of Whites. As if she deserves a reward for exposing the perverse inhumanity of West Indian race/class/colour classification, Colleen ends her story by treating herself to a cake with delicious pink-icing, the final irony being that the cake shop is run by a woman, evidently a descendant of Chinese indentured immigrants, who replaced emancipated Africans on sugar plantations, and thus further complicates already tangled permutations of race/class/colour in Jamaica.

In "Hartstone High," halfway during the school year, Shirley Lyn, a Chinese girl, joins Hartstone High School, attracting suspicion because of her late entrance, and because her all-female class mates are unable to connect her with any of the well known Chinese families in their district. One day, when Alima, who sits next to Shirley in class, spills a bottle of ink all over her desk, Shirley springs into action leading cleaning operations that help to speed up her integration into the class. Later, another girl happens to glimpse their teacher, Miss Latty, in a compromising sexual situation with the headmaster on school premises, and the class decide to keep the matter secret; but when Miss Latty announces on the following Monday that Shirley has suddenly left the school, it awakens dormant suspicion among her class mates of Shirley's ethnicity betraying their class secret and causing her expulsion.

In "Alvin's Ilk," despite his reputation for mischief at Central Village All Age school, Alvin helps in the rescue of an old Chinese man, Papa Chin, who has fallen down a slope. A striking feature of Alvin's story and Mordecai's fiction, as a whole, is its almost playful, tongue-in-cheek tone, even though her general subject is the horror of slavery and colonialism in Jamaica. There is no real malice in Alvin, or he would not have helped Papa Chin: he is a simple prankster. Similarly, in "Corinthians Thirteen Thirteen" the fact that Mr. Cameron can be taken for: "the Vineyard Pen village ram [possibly responsible] for a long line of fatherless children," (p. 128) or that he can make Sister Gertie pregnant and abscond, neither turns him into a villain, nor Jamaica into a sewer of sexual licence. The exhibitionist religiosity that combines with flexible sexual mores in stories in *Pink-Icing* is only one effect of slavery and ethnic mixing in Jamaica's past; and Mr. Cameron and Sister Gertie emerge more as figures of pity or mild ridicule rather than scorn when Sister Gertie launches into him with blind, biblical fervour: "you lecherous pig, you nest of vipers, you...you whited sepulchre." (p. 127)

The secret of Mordecai's success in *Pink-Icing* is her deft deployment of authentic idioms, rhythms and cadences of Jamaican creole speech or patwa to create musical and dramatic effects, beyond the reach of standard English. It is not just oral devices of simple repetition like 'small-small,' (p. 76,) 'at all at all,' (p. 84) 'clear-clear' (p. 84) or the switching of parts of speech as in: "now that somebody 'fall her," (p. 134) but the fulsome eloquence of: "Lef de key inna de cyaar," "Gun still a-watch yu so no bodda make no funny move," and "gwaan keep yu yeye to yuself." (p. 196) It all makes for a seductive tone of deceptively childlike yet shrewdly knowing banter.

"A SINFUL LITTLE PIECE OF CLOTH"

Olive Senior
Arrival of the Snake-Woman and Other Stories, Harlow, Essex, Longman Caribbean Limited, 1989, pp.145. ISBN 0-582-03170-2

Arrival of the Snake-Woman and other Stories is a second collection of fiction (following *Summer Lightning,* 1986) by Jamaican author, Olive Senior, who has so far written about a dozen works of fiction, poetry and non-fiction among which her reference work *Encyclopedia of Jamaican Heritage* shines through like Olympic gold. *Snake-Woman* consists of seven stories of which the title story, "Arrival of the Snake-Woman," and the last "Lily, Lily" account for more than half the collection.

Events in "Snake-Woman" occur probably toward the end of the nineteenth century, since the story's oldest characters recall days of slavery which ended in 1838. The locale, Mount Rose, a remote village in the Jamaican countryside, is miles away from shops or official buildings in the Bay,[St. Ann's Bay] the nearest coastal town. The narrator Ish, a mere boy at the beginning, describes the arrival of Miss Coolie, the first Indian person seen by Mount Rose villagers who, like Ish himself, are descendants of African slaves. The first Indians came to Jamaica as indentured labourers in 1845 and, by 1991, formed only 1.3 % of the island's mainly African population. So Miss Coolie's name alone sets her apart as someone of Indian, indentured stock and culture, an outsider, completely alien to the African or creolised ways of Mount Rose residents. Miss Coolie was first brought from the Bay to Mount Rose by Son Son, a young man who lived with her although he already had three children by two different women. In Mount Rose men and women live together in flexible relationships, while their children grow up in loose, family structures.

Ish's friend Moses explains the stereotypes aroused by Miss Coolie's arrival: "Them [Indians] is the wutlessess set of people, though. The man them is a wicked set of beast, man... But the women them! Whai!" (p. 3) So wicked are Indian men that: "If they have a wife and she just say 'kemps!' – he quick fe chop off her head." (p. 3) Indians are also heathen, as confirmed by the (white) priest Parson Bedlow. Worse still, according to Moses, Miss Coolie wears: "gold bangles all the way up her arms and her ankles, gold earrings in her ears, gold chains around her neck, gold rings on her fingers and – a sure sign of heathenness, a gold ring in her nose." (p. 4) Most telling of all, Miss Coolie's sari is: "a sinful little piece of cloth." (p. 24)

But despite her dismal start as a virtual outcast, Miss Coolie soon becomes more active than anyone around her, "growing garden eggs, Indian kale, strange peas, beans, tulsi and herbs" (p. 9) that are new to other villagers, and starting a small business that develops, over many years, into a large enterprise of dry goods, grocery, bar and butcher shop. Once she learns of Parson Bedlow's school, Miss Coolie even begins attending church to ensure education for her son Biya, who later becomes a lawyer with his office in the Bay. Miss Coolie then encourages Ish to become a doctor which, in time, he does and returns to marry her daughter Najeela.

Ish attributes Miss Coolie's extraordinary success to: "an understanding of the world that the rest of us lacked, a pragmatic drive that allowed her to dispassionately weigh alternatives, make her decisions and act, while we still floundered around in a confused tangle of emotions, family ties, custom and superstition." (p. 43)

"Lily, Lily" surveys a similar social background as in "Snake-Woman" portraying customs dominated by values of race, class and colour. As in "Snake-Woman," too, the dominance of men over women confirms an historical link with slavery in which one function of female slaves was to serve as reproductive machines that replenished the (African) labour force. In "Lily, Lily" the plaintive tone of voices from women different generations registers strong sympathy for a feminist point of view.

In "The view from the Terrace" Henry Barton's peaceful retirement in a big house on a hill is disturbed by appearance of a hut, on the other side, inhabited by what looks like a gang of lively, over-active children. Miss Vie, mother of the children, and Barton's neighbour, is poor and black, while he is a light-coloured, well-to- do gentleman. The hut is suddenly washed away in a storm, and quickly rebuilt; but when Barton hears Miss Vie's full story from his servant Marcus who turns out to be one of several fathers of Miss Vie's children, and actually helps in rebuilding their hut, he (Barton) is struck by the contrast between the sterile propriety of his privileged ethnic, economic and social position, and the life-enhancing vigour and vibrant will-to-live of his neighbours.

In three other stories, using a female, childhood perspective, Senior considers thoughts that are as insightful as those in her adult stories, for example, in "The two Grandmothers" when the unnamed narrator asks her grandmother: "When I hold my hand next to Joyce my skin is not as dark as hers, Grandma Del's or Daddy's even. Is dark really bad, Mummy? "(p. 67)

The foremost skills in Senior's repertoire are her detailed, authoritative comments on birds, plants and flowers, and her perceptive probing of women's psyche which cooperate in "The Tenantry of Birds," for instance, where Nolene and Philip, a university lecturer, are typical brown, middle class Jamaicans observed during a period of radical, black power politics in Jamaica After her unexpected return from a visit to the US, and finding Philip living with a young black student-type woman in her home, Nolene needs all the spiritual resources she can muster to preserve self-respect.

The secret of Senior's remarkable success as a writer of short fiction probably comes out best in Miss Coolie's story of a society so deeply disfigured by divisions of race, colour, class, gender and ethnicity that Miss Coolie's sari, a mere piece of cloth, separates her from her fellow villagers as surely as sin sentences sinners to hell; but such is Senior's studied, narrative poise, that despite the ravage of social/cultural/ethnic division, there are no victims or victimisers in her story, and all in compassion ends, to use Derek Walcott's storied phrase.

"DRIED PIMENTO SEEDS FALLING FROM A BADLY SEWN CROCUS BAG"

Olive Senior
Dancing Lessons, Toronto, Cormorant Books Inc., 2012. pp.369.

Dancing Lessons is the first novel of Olive Senior already well known for her poetry, fiction and non-fiction. Senior studied journalism in Wales, and at the University of Carleton, in Ottawa, before settling in Canada in the 1990s. Earlier, in Jamaica, she edited the prestigious *Journal of Social and Economic Studies* at the University of the West Indies in Mona, and joined the Institute of Jamaica in 1982 to become Editor of the venerable *The Jamaica Journal.* One volume of her stories *Summer Lightning* won the Commonwealth Writer's Prize in 1986. She is also author of *Encyclopedia of Jamaican Heritage,* (2004) as essential a Caribbean text as Richard Allsopp's *Dictionary of Caribbean English Usage.* (1996)

Events in *Dancing Lessons* occur partly in the nursing home, "Ellesmere Lodge," in Jamaica where Gertrude Richards Samphire lives, while her house is repaired from hurricane damage. Fellow residents include characters with names like the Pancake sisters, Miss Loony-Tune and the elderly Mr Bridges with whom Gertrude, the narrator, appears to form a relationship before he suddenly drops dead from a heart attack. Gertrude keeps a diary in which she records her experiences, including, much earlier, her spectacular abduction on horseback by her husband-to-be Charles Leacroft Samphire (Sam). Only later, when she is attacked by Sam's younger brother John while staying with their family, and then saved from serious sexual assault by Mass Ephraim, a servant, does Gertrude get written permission to marry Sam.

We are not given exact dates or times, merely hints that Gertrude was born around the 1940s, marries and has four children – Celia, Shirley, Charles Junior and Lise. We are also led to believe that Gertrude's marriage is typical in tolerating a husband who is seldom around, has frequent affairs with other women, yet supports the family and, in his case at least, proves to be a favourite among his grown up children. When her last child was eight or nine: "he (Sam) left home as usual one day, and he never came back." (p. 58) Strangely, this is both mystifying and normal: "What on earth did Sam have that made us women ready to be such willing slaves?" (p. 64) Nor are Senior's characters poor or unlettered Jamaicans: Sam inherits property that is sold to an American bauxite company for a huge sum; but the family's inevitable decline leaves a clear impression of the narrator's children being gradually sucked into a contemporary culture of drugs, crime, and cheap, celebrity hero-worship.

The plot winds and re-winds depending on suspense to relieve focus on Gertrude's relentless self-examination. Gertrude's reflections on each of her children are interwoven to produce a dramatic, true-to-life tangle of conflicting opinions about family events, and relationships, complicated by details from each member's personal experience, and lapses of memory, mostly the narrator's. Although she scans her children's careers with due parental concern, Gertrude necessarily turns inward on her own: "narrow little life" (p. 91)

She is preoccupied with her own ugliness which, she confesses: "gave me a reason why no one could love me." (p. 17) Lacking self-esteem, she stumbles into a mixture of melancholy feelings foremost among which are self-hatred and self-pity: "The woman with nowhere to go and nothing to do but beat herself against the cage holding a daughter captive. Only to return defeated time and again." (p. 91) Alas, such morbid self-mortification leads nowhere: "If only we could walk backwards together, undoing the miles, unravelling the web, starting all over," (p. 110) and her increasingly bleak options end only in seemingly aimless, anguished agonizing.

When her husband leaves home, not wishing to discuss it with her children, Gertrude produces probably the most withering image in a narrative that can only be the product of practised skills from an author in high maturity: "seeing everything I had invested in life bouncing and scattering like dried pimento grains falling from a badly sewn crocus bag." (p .67) It takes genuine inspiration, surely, to conceive such a telling image of inner failure and fragility so accurately rounded in the physical geography, historical soil and metaphysical culture of Jamaica!

As her major achievement in *Dancing Lessons*, Senior's portrait of Gertrude stands in sharp contrast to Hagar Shipley, the Canadian author Margaret Laurence's heroine in *The Stone Angel*, (1964) in which Hagar defies her relatives' well meaning effort to move her into a retirement home. Hagar fights tooth and nail to preserve every shred of independence or self-respect she has left in old age, for which she emerges as wholly admirable, one of the most loved figures in Canadian literature.

By contrast, it is not threat of confinement in "Ellesmere Lodge" that disorientates Gertrude: she seems to take on an altogether bigger, more treacherous challenge of comprehending the meaning of her life, and her success in this is what determines whether *Dancing Lessons* stands or falls; for the truth is that Gertrude is still left somewhat embattled in the end, and her struggle against life's limitations remains not only unresolved, but nowhere near resolution.

What sustains *Dancing Lessons* is less Gertrude's psychology than the authenticity of aspects of Jamaican culture that Senior deploys, for example, Jamaican speech rendered with deft and effortless expertise that communicates characters' deepest thoughts and feelings, for instance when Millie, a servant, is moved to defend her unmarried freedom and independence, and demands with unanswerable logic: "Why me should stay coop up in a yard like cunno-munno an me nuh have man or pikni to mind?" (p. 61) Standard English has nothing to match such reasoned eloquence from Millie, especially if we imagine the flouncing flamboyance of suggestive body language that goes with it in Jamaica!

"WE'RE ALL JUST PASSING THROUGH"

Colin Channer
Passing Through, New York, Random House, 2004, pp.351.
ISBN 0-345-45334-4

Passing Through, a collection of linked stories, is the fifth volume of fiction by Jamaican-born Colin Channer, who immigrated to the US where he teaches at Wellesley College, plays in a reggae band and, in *Waiting in Vain* and *Satisfying my Soul*, has written novels with titles of songs by the Jamaican reggae, folk hero, Bob Marley. Events in four novellas and three short stories in *Passing Through* occur over a period of about one hundred years on the fictional island of San Carlos which combines features of three Caribbean islands, Jamaica, Trinidad and Cuba. Carlitos have their own language – *sancoche* - and share history with other islanders who wrestle with problems of race, class, colour and gender in former Caribbean, colonial societies with a legacy of African slavery and Indian indenture.

"High Priest of Love," the first novella, introduces a typical, Caribbean colony with characters like white plantation owner St. William Rawle, Lebanese shop owner Khalid Salan, a black priest, and mostly impoverished Blacks, for example, Roselyn who regrets being black: "Is because if anything nobody ain't go take my side because o' color. You see this black here. [pointing to her cheek] It curse." (p .56) Roselyn explains: "This world is a hard world and if you raise your children to be soft you raising them to suffer. You ever see a blacksmith with iron in the furnace how he beat it? Is so you have to beat them [children] to make them take their shape and get hard." (p. 62) Reflecting influence from Rastafarian notions of the elemental rootedness of African civilisation, she also explains the survival strategy of African-Caribbean people to Eddie Blackwell: "You have soft ways. You is a brown man. I could see you have white in you. But you is a black man to the core. You have the white flesh but the black seed." (p. 62) For Roselyn, salvation clearly lies in Africa, or her connection to it.

In the novella "The Girl with the Golden Shoes," the protagonist, fourteen-year-old Estrella Thompson, whose full name is Estrella Roselyn Maria Eugenia Thompson, carries the nickname of "Pepper:" "cause when I cuss my words is very hot." (p .93) Her name and nickname imply boundless vim and vigour in Estrella in a spirired quest for survival. She is no superwoman, for she makes mistakes, for instance, in setting off to get a pair of shoes in Seville, the capital city, when she takes the wrong bus; but she is not deterred. Neither is she scared by sexual escapades when she gets a lift from the bus driver or joins a criollo (a Spanish-speaking Carlito) on a horse.

Estrella ['star' in Spanish] is a modern Cinderella whose simple integrity and childlike persistence place her high up with the stars, for when the wrong bus drops her in a village of unfamiliar *madrasitos* or indentured Indians, she may display curiosity or caution, but never fear: "lemme watch these *madrasitos*, yes. I heard they could thief milk out of your coffee and is only when you drink it you will know." (p. 93) The same spirited independence shines through when her basket is stolen in the market, and she persists with questions and negotiations until she gets it back, or later, as she washes herself in a stream while birds are singing, and her happiness knows no bounds: "it ain't have nobody with more luck than me." (p. 106) By negotiating her way over every hurdle, Estrella exhibits innate optimism and an unshakable will to survive.

"Passing Through," abounds in page upon page of brilliant, erotic writing of a quality rare in West Indian literature. The story takes its title from an epigraph to the whole volume: "We're not here forever. We're all just passing through," which not only admits the ephemeral nature of human existence, but assumes more poignant significance for Africans as victims of Atlantic slavery, and for black people generally in the New World. In Estrella's feisty adventures and escapades, sexuality expresses resistance against both human mortality and transience.

In "Passing Through" Rebecca, wife of St. William Rawle, admits: "we [white women] all want to be the *negrita,* you know, and that is what our husbands want too. But it's the very thing we're supposed not to be...I've never heard of anybody with a mistress who is white. They want a woman with at least a touch of sugar. We're all dull as milk and flour." (p. 233) If this sounds like the fantasy of a white woman created by a male, African-Jamaican author, it is part of Rebecca's comments on charisma, a quality of her politician son: "the proof of his [her son's] charisma is his skill at finding the *negrita* in the most sophisticated girls," (p. 233) and "if a man can talk the drawers off a woman he can talk the vote out of a man." (p. 233) Fantasy plays a legitimate role both in politics and sex. Nowhere else in West Indian literature, not even in the work of Guyanese maestro Edgar Mittelholzer, is sexuality rendered with such wit and wisdom, or the female body worshipped with such relish for both its irresistible aesthetic appeal and fundamental, reproductive role in ensuring human survival. It is a definitive difference between poetry and pornography.

THE BABYLON SHITSTEM NAMED GUN COURT

Marlon James
A Brief History of Seven Killings, New York, Riverhead Books,
pp.688. ISBN 978-1-59448-600-1

A Brief History of Seven Killings, Marlon James's third novel is
the Man Booker prize for fiction, in 2015, the first time the prize
was won by a Jamaican author. On the surface, the subject of the
novel may seem limiting as a mere crime story investigating the
real-life, attempted murder of Jamaican reggae superstar, and
Rastafarian singer, Bob Marley, in 1976, two days before the
"Smile Jamaica Concert" organised by Michael Manley, Prime
Minister and leader of the People's National Party (PNP). One
narrator, Josey Wales, even hints at a comic element when he
addresses one of the would-be assassins as follows: "How you
manage being the first man in history to shoot somebody in the
head and not kill them?" (p. 399)

Seven Killings consists of an elaborate, imaginative,
multifaceted reconstruction of events from seventy-five
narrators who interact through the 1970s to the 1990s, and more
than strongly suggest that their story is not entirely about Bob
Marley (who is called the "Singer" throughout) nor only about
Jamaica, as another narrator Alex Pierce confesses: "I am slowly
realizing that even though the Singer is the centre of the story
that it really isn't his story. Like there is a version of this story
that is not really about him but about the people around him,
the ones who come and go that might actually provide a bigger
picture than me asking him why he smokes ganja." (p. 221)

The bigger picture is the political and economic structure of the Cold War era, internationally, when one half of the world, the West, was dominated by the US with their ideology of: "progress, markets, freedom. That's the free market," (p. 412) while the other half, in the East, was under the influence of the Soviet Union and their ideology of communism. During this period, small nations like Jamaica were compelled to choose between the US, on one side, or a communist nation like East Germany where conditions could not be more regimented: "Things are so bad that a woman will decide to kill her kid rather than let it be born in East Germany. People in East Germany line up for everything... line up for soap. You know what they do with the soap? Sell it for food." (p. 413)

In truth *Seven Killings* is less about the ideological zeal of either super-power, than the inevitable domination of a small nation like Jamaica, by the US with their creed of the free market with its baggage of competition, selfishness and greed going hand in hand with inequality, exploitation, and ugliness.

In attempting to demonstrate ugliness in Jamaica as accurately as possible, James refers to V.S. Naipaul's travel book *The Middle Passage* (1960) by first complimenting the author for his comments on Jamaica: "It amazed me how he [Naipaul] could land in some country, be there for mere days and nail exactly what was wrong with it;" (p. 139) but he criticises Naipaul's claim that West Kingston in the Jamaican capital is so deplorable that: "you can't even take a picture of it, because the beauty of the photographic process lies to you as to just how ugly it really is. James goes on: "even him [Naipaul] have it wrong. The beauty of how him write that sentence still lie to you as to how ugly it is. It so ugly it shouldn't produce no pretty sentence, ever." (p. 452) So it comes down to style, actual words themselves! And it explains the blistering barrage of irreverent expletives and trenchant swearing that form the essential narrative medium of *Seven Killings*, as James attempts to conjure up the most truthful image that he can of raw ugliness in Jamaica - post-colonial poverty, corruption, violence, ganja, gangs, crime, killings etc.

James's linguistic versatility enables him to mix Jamaican creole with standard English (as well as New York speech,) for example, in a scene where Papa-Lo inflicts what he calls "discipline" on a woman: "I walk back to the woman and kick her two time. Then me drag her backside all the way back… The boy bawl out for him mother… me tell a woman to bring a bombocloth of water… me dump the bucket 'pon the woman and she nod and cough and scream… You have half hour to leave yah so, seen? Me see you me kill you, you brother, you mother and you daddy and all you other pickney." (p. 341) Such comprehensively cold and unfeeling cruelty drains whatever dregs of human dignity may be left in James's Jamaican characters, who, in Rastafarian terms, become mere automatons in Babylon, the Western-dominated world they inherit as victims of colonial exploitation and powerlessness.

Commentators have detected influences on James from scenes of crime and violence in films by Quentin Tarantino or novels by James Ellroy whose scenes tend to apply mainly to particular social groups in the US, whereas the malaise in *Seven Killings* infects the whole of Jamaican society, for example, pitched gun battles between national, political parties, Manley's PNP and Edward Seaga's Jamaica Labour Party (JLP). Although it may not be a direct influence, *Seven Killings* seems to draw more on colonial-inspired impulses like those in the novel *The Beautyful Ones are not yet Born* (1968) by the Ghanaian Ayi Kwei Armah whose scatological satire, rather than counting on vituperative language, like *Seven Killings*, excoriates Ghanaian people, institutions and manners for being totally covered in human excrement, by 1966, following Nkrumah's dictatorship as President of Ghana from 1957 to 1966.

"THE WHOLE ISLAND [JAMAICA] IS A MENTAL HOSPITAL"

Alecia McKenzie
Sweetheart, Leeds, Peepal Tree Press Ltd., 2011, pp.134.
ISBN 13: 9781845231774

As winner of the regional Commonwealth Writers prize for
Best First book in 1993 with *Satellite City*, a collection of stories,
Jamaican author Alecia McKenzie followed up with two young
adult novels, and another collection *Stories from the Yard* (2005)
before producing her first novel, *Sweetheart,* whose heroine
Dulcinea Evers, a gifted Jamaican artist, suddenly dies and is
cremated before her story is reported in twelve short narratives,
the first of which comes from Dulci's closest friend Cheryl
aboard an Air Jamaica flight, taking half of Dulci's ashes from
Jamaica to New York, where Dulci lived and worked as a painter.

Sweetheart reconstructs Dulci's biography, from her
schooldays in Jamaica to spectacular success as a painter in
New York, where she changes her name to Cinea Verse, before
her untimely death from cancer at the age of thirty-four. Five
narratives are by Cheryl alone while the remainder come from
Dulci's family, friends and work associates, who conjure up
both a rounded study of the heroine, as well as a general survey
of Jamaican history and culture. Through skilful deployment
of exact features of the personality and voice of each narrator
whether old, young, male, female, American, Jamaican, friend
or foe, the author maintains interest and coherence throughout,
along with suspense if not mystery in almost every episode.

Cheryl's first narrative, for instance, portrays Dulci as an innocent young woman who is exploited by a senior colleague, Calrlton Beckett, in the bank where they work, and where she is physically assaulted by Carlton's wife Dakota wielding a cutlass, and ripping off Dulci's clothes in full view of other employees, before she is rescued by a guard who fires his revolver in the air to restrain Dakota. In his own narrative, Carlton portrays Dulci as promiscuous and unfaithful to him with a life guard, during their love tryst at a tourist hotel. More intriguing is Dakota's later narrative, in which she puts her finger on a central aspect of Dulci's entire life story by earnestly pleading, more in admiring wonder than surly complaint: "What was it you had, Dulcinea Evers?" (p. 50)

This not only adds suspense or mystery, but explains both Dakota's former fury: "Seeing Carlton in his fever of addiction, his willingness to throw away our life together, made me go a bit mad," (p. 50) and her confession after Dulci's funeral: "As I gazed at your [Dulci's] photograph, I felt the most profound shame. I wanted to cry for both of us, for you and me." (p. 51) Dakota's *volte face* is at once poignant and persuasive in confirming the mysterious appeal of Dulci both to friends and enemies.

Other views of Dulci come out of a narrative by Susie, an American who does not hide her dislike of Dulci although, as a professional journalist, she celebrates her (Dulci's) artistic talent. It is a stroke of genius for McKenzie to include an interview between Susie and Dulci in which spontaneous revelations are made, for example, of Susie's suspicion of an "insane aspect" (p. 63) in Dulci's paintings, and of doubt about whether Dulci grew up near a mental hospital. Dulci only laughs out loud and replies: "The whole island [Jamaica] is a mental hospital but don't write that." (p. 63) Similarly, when Susie asks whether it was hard to be taken seriously as a woman artist, Dulci replies: "Nobody takes women seriously. Not even other women." (p. 65)

The spontaneity of Dulci's almost reflex reply adds conviction to the shocking truth of sexism in the art world and beyond. Reacting to Dulci's heartfelt awareness of sexism, Susie refers to her as an "impish child" (p. 65) which only heightens her elusive combination of genius, daring and mystery on which the novel relies for its impact. Susie sums Dulci up as follows: "But you swam in waters that were too uncertain for me, Cinea, and I have a deep fear of drowning." (p. 66)

Other narratives, for example, by Dulci's father Desmond Evers, fill in details of rivalry and infighting in Dulci's family and her closeness to Cheryl, while, through oral history, comments by Cheryl's Aunt Mavis document the fundamental influence of African slavery and Maroon resistance on Jamaican culture, for instance, its legacy of African spirituality or obeah: "But people need their superstitions, don't they, Dulcinea? They need to believe in things that they can't see, and to not believe, at times, what their own eyes tell them." (p. 82)

Dulci's life as Cinea in New York is best described by Josh Scarbinsky, an American art teacher and critic who marries Cinea to facilitate visa requirements for her to remain in the US. Scarbinsky's comments betray a bemused mixture of professional admiration, and over-reaction to genuine, exotic love when he confesses to Cinea: "Your real talent was making people lose all sense of pride, of self, turning us into slaves." (p. 57) More than anyone else, it is perhaps Josh Scarbinsky who most frankly acknowledges Cinea's genius, and its uncanny power in eliciting idealisation from viewers. He admits being moved by the "wild and wicked energy" of her paintings, and their "bold lines and vibrating colours" which remind him of a select group of painters Frida Kahlo (1907-1954), Ioan Miro (1893-1983) and Amrita Shergill (1913-1941).

Kahlo was a Mexican painter whose work celebrates Mexico's indigenous traditions, Miro, Spanish, was attracted by dualities and contradictions, and Shergill was a part-Indian, part-Hungarian artist influenced by the poverty and despair of India. If these clues do not fully explain Dulci/Cinea's elusiveness, we might turn to Cervantes' s *The Adventures of Don Quixote of La Mancha,* probably the most memorable of all novels, in which an ageing aristocrat Don Quixote idealises an ordinary peasant woman Dulcinea into a figure of romance or "Sweetheart," as Dulci is often called.

THE PUREST, SWEETEST WORDS OF A BORN POET

Lorna Goodison
From Harvey River: A Memoir of my Mother and her People,
Toronto, McClelland & Stewart, Ltd., 2007, pp.279,
ISBN 978-0-7710-3383-4.

For some people "13" is an unlucky number. Not for Lorna
Goodison, the Jamaican author, whose thirteenth book *From
Harvey River: A Memoir of my Mother and her People* follows
four volumes of fiction and eight of poetry that have propelled
her not only to head the pack of current Caribbean women
poets, but abreast of male front-runners, Derek Walcott and
Kamau Brathwaite, who first ran into print decades before her;
but literature is neither a race nor lottery, and *From Harvey
River* is best savoured for its special aroma of Jamaican history,
people and culture.

As a memoir, *From Harvey River* mixes biography with
fiction, history and other forms of writing to tell a story of the
author's family on her mother's side, the Harveys who, in 1840,
gave their name to Harvey River, a village in the rural Jamaican
parish of Hanover. The Harveys come from English, Irish and
Scottish stock that includes a famous English ancestor, William
who, in 1578, was credited with being the first to describe the
circulation of blood in reliable detail; but although the family's
story is narrated by the author herself, as the volume's title
suggests, it is really about her mother Doris who was born in
Harvey River, in 1910, one of eight children of David Harvey

and Margaret Wilson. As the author writes, it was after she "dreamed" her mother and was granted a "visitation" to her in heaven, that she was entrusted with the sacred duty of passing on her mother's family story to us.

Harvey River is divided into three parts and numerous untitled and unnumbered chapters which flow into each other with the natural continuity of speech, to jointly contrive a bewitching vision of the community of Harvey River that includes three brothers and four sisters of the author's mother. If it takes a novelist's inspiration to re-create a rich variety of true-to-life pen portraits of her uncles and aunts, it surely calls for encyclopaedic knowledge of Jamaican history and culture to transmit the day-to-day life of their community with such charm, conviction and completeness.

Like other Caribbean societies, Jamaica inherits a creole culture formed out of the physical and cultural mixing of people mainly from the British Isles, Africa and Asia: "It was amazing how all the mixing of bloods produced people who looked like Indians and Gypsies." (p. 27) In colonial times, African slave culture was regarded as deadly poison as it seeped irresistibly into every nook and cranny of Jamaican life; and long after slavery ended (1834), during the lifetime of Goodison's uncles and aunts, in the first half of the nineteenth century, Jamaica was still governed by: "British colonial laws that valued the smallest piece of property over the life of any ex-slave." (p. 38)

This is the heart of the matter: that life in Harvey River, Jamaica, or the Caribbean, for that matter, consists of remnants, bits and pieces, leftovers mostly from the actions and experience of others whether from Britain, Africa, Asia or wherever. Social transactions in *Harvey River* consist largely of people mixing memories and matching fragments in a frenzied struggle to mould something whole and recognisably their own. So bible verses are traded side by side with African folk beliefs or practices, English, either language or literature, is communicated through creole speech; and the modernity of motor cars and travel to America, as special events, are lumped unceremoniously into an everyday saga of coping with common macca thorns and chigoes.

We behold the spirited vivacity of this emerging culture when the author's father, Marcus, changes his lowly chauffeur 's job to open a garage business, only to receive a torrid tongue - lashing from none other than his own mother after the business fails: "You pass you place, Marcus ...You see me, I know my place...High seat kill Miss Thomas' puss! Nayga people must know dem place...Is that Hanover woman you go married to who encourage you inna that damn foolishness." (p. 151) The author's mixture of the dehumanising legacy of slavery with the sustaining, inter-locking solidarity and humanity of mother, son and wife is couched in rich creole idioms and prodigal gifts of poetry that plumb bottomless depths of passion, pity and pathos.

Whether it is her frank admission of Jamaica's colonial history, or determined documentation of her mixed blood family's struggle in the squalor of a Kingston slum, Goodison's reactions convey compassion for routine injustices, along with a distinctly female flavour coming as much from her heart as her brain; for Ripeness is all, as we salivate over mouth-watering descriptions of food, for example: "big country breakfasts or 'morning dinners' of roasted yams and breadfruit, bammies made from grated cassava, fried plantains, fried eggs, stewed liver, kidneys, and light, and escoveitched fish washed down with quarts of coffee and chocolate tea;" (p. 36) and Jamaican relish of local food implies, if not triumph, at least a will to cope with horrors of their colonial past!

Two beams of light guide us through the mixed gloom of *Harvey River*: the author's even-handed, confessional integrity in revealing truth, and her trademark, womanist sense of compassion. It is one thing to learn that the vision in her memoir is handed directly down from heaven by the author's mother Doris Harvey; quite another to discover that: "She [Doris Harvey] dipped her finger in sugar when I [Lorna] was born and rubbed it under my tongue to give me the gift of words;" (p. 27) and create a heavenly vision, through the purest, sweetest words of a born poet.

"AMERICAN MEANS WHITE.
EVERYBODY ELSE HAS TO HYPHENATE"

Paula Williams Madison
Finding Samuel Lowe: China, Jamaica Harlem, Amistad,
HarperCollinsPublishers, New York, 2015, pp.275.
ISBN 978-0 -06-233163-2

Finding Samuel Lowe: China, Jamaica, Harlem is the first
book of Paula Williams Madison, who was born in 1952, in
Harlem, New York, attended Vassar College and at the age
of sixty, after a distinguished corporate career in television
journalism, decided to write a biography of her Chinese
grandfather, Samuel Lowe, (1889-1967) whom she had never
seen. Through dogged research and tireless reconstruction,
relying mainly on oral resources and memories of family
members and friends, spread over decades in China, Jamaica
and the US, Madison produces not only professionally re-
created biographies of her grandfather and other family
members, but also newly-discovered details of African-
Chinese-Jamaican history.

As Toni Morrison, the African-American, Nobel prize-
winning author correctly writes in an epigraph to *Finding*:
"In this country [the US] American means white. Everybody
else has to hyphenate," which suggests, in Madison's case, that
she is best defined as African-Chinese-Jamaican-American.
That Madison succeeds in eliciting a coherent narrative that
deciphers her intricately mixed identity, out of faded and

fragmentary resources, nearly fifty years after her grandfather's death, is nothing less than astounding!

In 1838, after African slaves in British Caribbean plantation colonies were finally freed, British owners brought labourers mostly from India, but also from China, under contract for three or five year periods of indenture, to carry out work previously done by African slaves on sugar plantations. In 1905, as a teenaged labourer, Madison's grandfather, Samuel Lowe migrated from China to Jamaica where he remained for ten years before returning home; then he repeated this pattern of migration four more times till his final return to China in 1933.

Samuel followed a prevailing pattern of Chinese indentured immigrants: "to go to Jamaica and become wealthy, and be able to return to buy farms, land and build houses back in China." (pp. 184-185) For Chinese immigrants to the Caribbean the idea was to quickly fulfil their terms of indenture, before launching into business careers, usually through retail shop-keeping, as Samuel himself did, by opening a shop in Mocho, in rural Jamaica, and another in the larger, coastal town of St. Ann's Bay. Samuel's shops helped to establish what later became an iconic Caribbean totem, the "Chiney shop," more accurately described as a convenience or general store that stocked every conceivable item from groceries, pots, pans and crockery, to patent medicines, hardware and furniture.

By 1915, Samuel's shops were flourishing and he was affluent enough, through arrangements made in China, to marry a Chinese bride, Swee Yin Ho. Nothing confirms Samuel's spectacular commercial success more than the announcement of his wedding in the "Daily Gleaner" Jamaica's leading newspaper. Before he married Swee Yin Ho, however, Samuel had two children from liaisons with local, Jamaican women, Albertha Beryl Campbell, mother of Nell Vera Lowe Williams who became mother of the author, and Emma

Allison who became the mother of a daughter, Adassa, and son Gilbert. As Samuel's first born son, Gilbert never received the prestige due to him, nor, like his half sister Nell Vera, did he ever visit China. Gilbert didn't even know he had a half sister in Jamaica. These are only some of the fractures or gaps of indenture discovered in *Finding*, along with crowded examples of dispersal, and ethnic and cultural mixing that intensify inherent feelings of separation, homelessness and transience in indentured immigrants.

These feelings appear in family members, coming from different branches and generations, and moving from one country to the other, making a strict, chronological record of their lives virtually impossible. It is probably why Madison devises a technique, no doubt based on her expertise as a journalist, to foreground specific subjects, themes or characters, not necessarily in chronological order and, by energetic cross reference, link them together into a richly variegated and suspenseful narrative, mainly from the point of view of her own search for her grandfather's life story, and its influence on her character.

Nell Vera, the author's mother, for instance, may be seen as a tragic figure, abandoned or neglected by her father, Samuel, and underestimated if not abused by her husband Elrich Mortimer Williams, yet resilient, plucky, and capable of dauntless physical courage, unyielding will, and fierce loyalty and love for her children. No wonder Nell Vera is described as a "fight to death" (p. 69) person in a "Nell and Goliath story." (p. 93) In one incident, in New York, when the author's brother Elrich purloins sneakers belonging to one of his friends, whose well built father and four brothers later turn up threateningly at the narrator's apartment, Nell Vera calmly picks up a meat cleaver and, in a hostile confrontation, successfully faces down the father by grabbing the front of his shirt and delicately placing the cleaver on his jugular vein.

What is surprising in all this is the author's literary skill in matching characters to their own group, for instance, the Hakka people, as a persecuted minority from whom most Caribbean Chinese are drawn, or victims of the Cultural Revolution, in China, when Mao Tse Tung held sway in the 1960s. Equally surprising, in spite of dislocation and hardship, twin perils of the indenture system, is Madison's success in endowing her family history with positive effects and a personal touch, for instance, when she describes her uncle Chow Woo who: "never became less Chinese – just as I will never become less Black or less American – but in fathering children with Jamaican women, in living in Jamaica and developing businesses there, he consolidated realms that would never have naturally touched each other. Just as I have." (pp. 228-229)

"SEX CAN MAKE A MAN OR BREAK HIM"

Lionel Hutchinson
One Touch of Nature, London, Collins, 1971, pp.318.

Largely forgotten today, Lionel Hutchinson's second novel *One Touch of Nature,* which follows his *Man From the People* (1969), considers the unusual fate of descendants of white, mainly Irish indentured servants or slaves who were transhipped in the seventeenth century to Barbados where, today, their descendants are known as Red-Legs. (Some Red-Legs later moved to St. Vincent, Grenada and Bequia, but most remained in Barbados.) Like "red" which is also applied to coloured or mixed blood (African/European) people in the Caribbean, the term "Red-Legs" springs from the ruddy complexion of external features, face, arms or legs, of white, manual workers exposed to the fierce Caribbean sun, during long hours of outdoor labour. After African slaves were freed in the English-speaking Caribbean in 1838, Red-Legs were unwilling to work alongside freed Africans, and declined into an economically depressed community sometimes called "Poor Whites."

"Red-Legs," we are told in *One Touch*, could be "as pure-white, or as blue-eyed as your ancestors who sold themselves into slavery in Barbados, three hundred years ago, or as those who came out as indentured servants, and took to the hills after white slavery was abolished on the island." (p. 34) Although most West Indian Whites were privileged descendants of plantation owners, administrators or professionals, pure-white Red Legs were different: "if you [pure -Whites] didn't learn to hustle a living with a fishing boat, or to farm the spot of land on which you lived, then it was the parish workhouse for you." (p. 34)

The fate of Red-Legs is summed up in the epigraph of *One Touch*, a line taken from Book VI of "The Light of Asia," Sir Edwin Arnold's epic poem about the Buddha's life and teaching: "Pity and need/make all flesh kin," implying that need of basic necessities such as food, clothes and shelter, or absence of these necessities through poverty reflects an essential sameness in people everywhere. The epigraph notes conditions in colonial Barbados where, paradoxically, the inhumanity of slavery exposed the common humanity of its victims, Red-Leg as well as slave: "It was a long time now since pity and need had made both Red-Leg and Negro kin." (pp. 45-46)

One Touch dramatises family and social events connected with one Red-Leg couple, Philip Otto and Salome, whose daughters Harriet and Judy, dominate the novel. Harriet's most frequent thoughts centre on sex, men, love and marriage which may not be surprising since she is an attractive, young, single, independent, working woman: what is surprising is the controlling role of sex in the social attitudes and activities of her family, friends, and most of all, herself.

Women in Hutchison's novel do not feel disadvantaged by what may appear as hedonistic sexual practices since, for them sex is a business. By the 1950s, for example, more than a century after the end of slavery, when Red-Leg families had left the countryside to become shop assistants in Bridgetown, capital city of Barbados, social divisiveness by colour still prevailed: "Red-Legs got jobs as shop assistants even if they couldn't read or write because it was better for white tourists." (p. 35) Nothing can beat Red-Leg preoccupation with sex. So consuming are their anxieties over sex, or their options among sexual partners, that Judy's lover Clive concludes: "We like to think we're not slaves to sex, but it doesn't always work that way. Sex can make a man or break him." (p. 159)

As a central figure in this dour portrait of gender relations in 1950s Barbados, Harriet at first appears to hold herself aloof from the free-for-all, sexual extravaganza around her. But she soon abandons herself to a spate of affairs that culminate in her brutal rape by three American sailors, the final straw denying her a "last escape" from "the living death [chastity] in which she previously existed." (p. 313) Then, in a surprising dénouement, while she is recovering in hospital, she accepts a marriage proposal from Robert, a former lover. Although Harriet does not love Robert, she hopes love will come later: "There was no proof that Adam loved Eve the moment he laid eyes on her." (p. 307) What Harriet and *One Touch* suggest is that practical, seemingly scandalous, liberal or hedonistic, sexual relations in post-slavery Caribbean society - for convenience rather than love - are probably as religious or as bible-based as any other.

Sexual hedonism highlights the role of women, in particular: in *One Touch* wives cheerfully tolerate affairs of their husbands. Cynthia, for example, accepts Judy's affair with her [Cynthia's] husband Clive: "she [Cynthia] didn't even make a fuss; for as long as he [Clive] remained a good father to her two children, so long as the children woke up each morning and saw him in the house, then he was entitled to all the fun he could get." (p. 136) No doubt this has to do with the legacy of a slave society in which white slave owners habitually took advantage of female slaves as a matter of practical negotiation, and concubinage in tandem with marriage was common.

If Cynthia is happy with her flexible marriage, Judy is content with casual affairs: "Life is all such a big stinking gamble. I ain't want to be safe and sorry too. My role is to accept, and I've never been sad about it." (p. 87) Similarly, when Harriet hints to her friend Jane Ratesy that her [Jane's] lover Paddy is taking advantage of her, Jane's retort is quick: "I just ain't care what Paddy do to me, ain't care how many whores supporting him, so long as I can see him sometimes." (p. 84) As for Molly who lived off seducing men in exchange for money, but did not consider herself a whore: "it was merely that the strong women of the land were prepared to honour sex as first a pleasure and then a business." (p. 109)

"PEOPLE SO BR'EK THEY CAN'T BE BR'EK NO MORE"

Cecil Foster
Independence, Toronto, Harper Collins Publishers Ltd., 1991.
ISBN 978-1-44341-505-7

Independence is the fifth novel of Cecil Foster who, in 1978, migrated from his native Barbados to Canada where he worked as a radio commentator, completed his Ph.D., and taught at Guelph University, before becoming Professor of African and African/American Studies at the University of Buffalo. Foster is also author of seven non-fiction works including two volumes on race, colour and multiculturalism.

Permanent English settlers first arrived in Barbados in 1627, and the island remained a British colony until 1966 when it became an independent nation. In *Independence,* through the eyes of a fourteen-year-old Bajan schoolboy narrator, Christopher Lucas, Foster re-creates the atmosphere and feelings surrounding independence in Barbados. The novel describes everyday scenes and routine, domestic events of simple villagers, focussing on the narrator and his two chief relationships, firstly with his grandmother Margaret Lucas, and with Stephanie (Stephie) who lives next door with her grandmother, Eudene King.

As neighbours of similar age, with the same school and circle of friends, what most connects Christopher and Stephie is a tenuous link to their respective mothers, Christopher to Thelma, daughter of Margaret Lucas, and Stephie to

Esmeralda, Eudene King's daughter. Thelma and Esmerelda migrated "over - 'n'-away" (Britain) where they expect to prosper and become rich enough to pay for their respective children to join them in Britain. Like a sad, haunting refrain, the elusive expectation of Christopher and Stephie being "sent for" is repeated throughout the novel, ensuring that we do not miss either the dehumanising notion of people being "sent" like mail, or the fundamental dependency of families like Christopher's, Stephie's, and those of other Bajans and West Indians, on metropolitan anglohone nations like as Britain, Canada and the US.

Foster dexterously insinuates his grand theme of dependency into the life-blood, muscles and sinews of his narrative through the return of a Bajan, Wendell Lashley, from Canada where he was enlisted for eleven years in an agricultural labour program for temporary overseas workers. Lashley's earnings have brought him riches that his fellow villagers would die for: he is able, for instance, to run electricity into his home and, most enviably, purchase a television set. In one deft narrative stroke that links dependency with the lives and fortunes of the novel's two central characters, Christopher and Stephie, Lashley uses gifts from his new, foreign-acquired affluence to seduce Stephie who becomes pregnant.

Not only does Stephie's unexpected pregnancy suspend development of her budding romance with Christopher: it temporarily stalls her promise as an athlete, while Christopher establishes himself as a budding cricketer and star batsman. Her pregnancy shakes Stephie's family to its foundations, and inspires probably the most memorable scene in the novel when Dorothy Inniss, older sister of Stephie's mother, rudely confronts Stephie's grandmother Eudene King over her alleged complicity, indirectly, in aiding and abetting Stephie's pregnancy: "you [Eudene King] got she [Stephie] tekking man every night and day God send, and as if she is some big, able cut-open cow." (p. 192) Dorothy's bitter and outlandish exchange continues: "Everybody saying that you [Eudene] as a grand mother, who should know better, how you done sell out the poor girl [Stephie] so that you could get a few new boards on a house and some galvanize on yuh roof. That yuh up and sell she off. And for a paint job." (p. 195)" To protect Stephie from further contamination, Dorothy then takes Stephie to live in her own home.

Dorothy's crude outburst evokes the suffering of African slaves whose labour sustained British plantations in Barbados during colonialism, for it articulates disturbing implications of slave attitudes and practices that still persist, for example, in the eager acceptance by people in independent Barbados, of selling themselves (through their labour) to employers in richer countries. But Dorothy's outlook comes from a more independent, younger generation, unlike her mother and Grandmother Lucas, whose more traditional, colonial outlook is abundantly scattered through lengthy discussions about Bajan society and people.

In trying to soften the effects of Dorothy's wicked tongue-lashing on Eudene King, her bosom friend and confidante, Grandma Lucas consoles her about Lashley's role as godfather (rather than husband) to Stephie, and about Eudene's alleged complicity in the undoing of her own granddaughter: "Nough young people around here does have to rely on a godfather. That is the ways of this island since Adam was a lad. So you can't blame yourself for that... you did only mean good for everybody." (p. 205)

By dramatising Bajan views and circumstances through affairs of the Lucas and King families, Foster captures a positive aspect of the mood in Barbados during independence in 1966, when Christopher and Stephie agree that the future of the West Indies lies in their performance in music and cricket. But in spite of the promise of independence seen in an announcement of free secondary education for all school-age children, a hot meals program, free school books, reduced travel cost on government buses, free health care for the young and elderly, Christopher feels differently after listening to a conversation between his grandmother and a friend: "Everybody seems so hopeless, those that are here on the island, and those that flee overseas. Nobody expects much from tomorrow or any other day." (p. 302) This outlook corresponds with an earlier, brilliantly perceptive pronouncement by Christopher's grandmother, which sounds all the more devastating in the superbly eloquent idiom of demotic, Bajan speech: "People so br'ek they can't be br'ek no more." (p. 170) [People feel so broken, they can't be broken anymore.]

RANTING INCOHERENTLY …
AGAINST LIFELONG INJUSTICE

Cecil Foster
Island Wings: A Memoir, Toronto, Harper-Collins Publishers
Ltd., 1998, pp. 313. ISBN 0-00-255736-3

Since migrating from his native Barbados to Canada in
1979, and launching himself as broadcaster, journalist and
academic, Cecil Foster has produced ten books, including
five novels and perhaps, most impressively, *Island Wings: A
Memoir* which both fills in autobiographical, raw material
for at least two of his novels *No Man in the House* (1991) and
Independence, (2014), and meditates on the effect of colonial
history and manners both on Barbados in general, and the
author and his family. After nearly three and a half centuries as
a British colony, Barbados gained independence in 1966, with a
population of fewer than 300,000, consisting mostly of people
descended from African slaves, another small, mixed/blood
group, part African, part European, and a smaller number of
Whites who inherited economic and social dominance from
former European rulers.

Foster's memoir opens in the 1950s with news that his
parents, dismayed by lack of opportunity in Barbados,
migrate to London, the British capital, then a promised land of
opportunity, culture, work, and wealth for black West Indians.
The economic plight of Barbadians, at the time, may be gauged
from a statistic claiming that, a few decades earlier, one third

of the population of the island, "a little rock in the Atlantic Ocean," (p. 153) had migrated to seek work in construction of the Panama canal.

The plan is for Foster and his older brothers, Stephen and Errol, to remain briefly with their maternal grandmother in Barbados, while his parents are in London, "living in the lap of luxury," (p. 5) and supplying money regularly for their children's upkeep, until they can afford to bring all three of their sons to London. But: "The plane that we [the author and his brothers] imagined swooping down over Barbados and taking us to our home across the Atlantic never arrived." (p. 65) Foster's brusque tone is an essential aspect of the author's matter-of-fact style in a narrative whose finest quality is its realistic facing up to harsh truth.

What little money does come, at first, quickly dries up, while direct contact with Foster's parents gradually fades away. Cecil admits: "Children like us grew up eagerly awaiting the arrival of the next barrel or hamper laden with food and clothes sent by strangers, called parents, from some foreign country." (p. 69) Failure to receive help from London sets the scene for an epic struggle waged by Cecil and his brothers, supervised by their aged grandmother, to secure food, clothes, and shelter and keep body and soul together in colonial Barbados. Their story is documented in *Island Wings* without special pleading, pity or protest: whether it is through kitchen gardening, selling baked goods, buying and selling fruit, rearing domestic animals, or using tar from the public road to patch their leaking roof, somehow, driven by the joint effort of unflinching supervision from their grandmother or other relatives, and their own unrelenting ambition and unwavering bond of family solidarity, Cecil and his brothers prevail and prosper.

While, in time, both Stephen and Errol finish school and find work, (Errol migrates to Canada) Cecil relies on education as his lodestar, first completing studies at Christ Church Boys'

Elementary School, then Barbados Community College, before he attends Harrison College, pinnacle of a somewhat snobbish, class-ridden education system in colonial Barbados. After Harrison College, Cecil starts teaching at St. Leonard's Comprehensive School where he comes to dislike the profession because: "Teachers were expected to beat the students…I saw teachers my own age… adeptly wheeling long straps and canes, and later bragging about their skills in this regard." (p. 219) Instead, Cecil discovers an aptitude for journalism, and joins the Caribbean News Agency, (CANA) a branch of Reuters in London.

Like the first two-thirds of *Island Wings* which succeeds partly because of the narrator's and his brothers' personal triumph over adversity, the attraction in the book's final section lies in the narrator's startling re-connection with family in England, not only his parents but English-born brothers and sisters he had never before seen. As a reporter, despite his sensational reports on public figures, for instance, Maurice Bishop and his failed revolution and murder in Grenada, or political intrigue in Tom Adams's government in Barbados, what really hits home is the narrator's discovery that connection with his parents and Barbados was broken partly by his mother's potentially fatal illness with meningitis, and consequent hardship for the family in London.

Probably the hardest blow is the divorce of his parents, followed by deliberate seclusion of his father, Freddie, from the rest of his family and the world. For Freddie who was once a talented musician and member of the British army, someone to whom Cecil believes he owes his own artistic gifts, to lock himself away in lonely isolation, ranting incoherently and vainly against lifelong injustices inflicted on him by an elusive culprit, British colonialism, is to indict evils of empire as pitifully, painfully and pointlessly as Kurtz through the seething anger of his whispered cry: "The horror! The horror!" in Conrad's *Heart of Darkness*.

"DEY TINK DAT BECAUSE DEY WHITE, DEY BETTER DEN WE."

Thomas Armstrong
Of Water and Rock, Montreal, DC Books, 2010, pp.330.
ISBN 978-1-897190-60-9.

Of Water and Rock is partly the result of a visit which Armstrong, a (white) Canadian, paid to Barbados in 1979. Not only did the visit lead him to marry a (black) Bajan in 1980, it inspired Armstrong to write a story "Flying in God's Face" which appeared in a Bajan journal and became, "the seed from which this novel [*Of Water and Rock*] grew." Defying all expectation, the novel went on to win the National Independence Festival of Creative Arts' (NIFCA) Best Book award in Barbados in 2009, and launched Armstrong on a literary career he had never dreamt of during earlier days as a software developer in Toronto.

Barbados provides a perfect context for distinctly Gothic undertones in Armstrong's story of a young Canadian narrator, Edward Hamblin, who arrives alone on the island, in 1969, to assume a legacy from his father's aunt Sarah. Edward never met his great aunt who lived and died in Barbados, and he knows just as little about his father who was born in Barbados, but left home when he [Edward] was very young. All Edward knows, from his black Bajan lawyer Chesterfield Cumberbatch, is that he now inherits Hamblin Hall cottage in Barbados.

Soon after his arrival at Hamblin Hall, Edward meets black neighbours such as Sissy Brathwaite, an old woman struggling to eke a living out of her own land, his servant Undine who had previously worked for his great aunt Sarah, and Richard Clermont, alias "Doc", who starts life as a brilliant scholar, only to decline into solitude and an eccentric, prophetic pose of talking to trees and searching caves in vain for black coral. When Edward meets other (white) neighbours, the Collymores, James and his two grown-up daughters Judith and Mary, he is bowled over by the difference between Canada and the society he has come to: one that until 1966 was a British colony remembered mostly for its history of white-owned sugar plantations maintained by the labour of African slaves.

Edward encounters Gothic elements in the form of his neighbours' evasive answers to simple inquiries about everyday matters, and their concealment of secrets suggesting sinister or mysterious dealings on an island that, till then, Edward had paradoxically regarded purely as a holiday paradise, not only of water and rock, but of resplendent sunshine, limitless, blue sea, and white, sand beaches. In truth, the paradox is not as strange as it seems: it echoes Jean Rhys's comparison of the Caribbean island in her novel *Wide Sargasso Sea* to the pristine purity of the Garden of Eden before corruption by primal human sin in the Bible. Sissy's nephew RJ catches the spirit of Rhys's comparison when he informs Edward: "People like Auntie [Sissy] learn tuh take abuse and say nuthin. An people like dem Collymores ain't change ever since... Dey tink dat because dey white, dey better den we. Dey abuse our women an nobody ain't ever held tuh account;" (p. 134) RJ puts his finger on the primal Bajan or Caribbean sin of slavery, and its shameful history of grossly abusive relationships between white master and black slave.

Abuse is built into the structure itself of Bajan society with its sharp contrast between a largely compliant, black, working class, and dominant, white, landed families like the Collymores. At a typical white soirée, for instance, held at the Collymore residence, where Edward meets the family of Rupert

Weatherby, the British High Commissioner to Barbados, the difference is driven home between his own neutral Canadian views, and the openly racist attitudes both of his hosts and their visitors. Worse still, in a later scene, where Sissy sells sugar cakes at her market stall, Mary Collymore chaperones a white child Liliane who gratefully accepts a sugar cake generously offered by Sissy, only for Mary to rudely knock the sugar cake out of Liliane's hand, and hotly rebuke Sissy: "How dare you? ... You dirty woman. Who knows where your hands have been?" (p. 126) Mary also turns indignantly on Liliane: "don't ever take anything from these people." (p. 126)

The curse of race is at the heart of Edward's search for his great aunt's lost diary, and subsequent revelations about mysterious connections between his great aunt, his father, the Collymores, Sissy and Barbados and its people. Armstrong displays superb technical expertise in his first novel by plunging his narrator into an exotic voyage of discovery, and guiding him through, stage by suspenseful stage, until older characters like Sissy Brathwaite and James Collymore are dead, old sores are tended if not completely healed, and a much chastened Edward can look forward to a future of living with Judith Collymore.

As a Canadian outsider, Armstrong also displays versatility for catching the verve and vibrancy of Bajan speech. RJ's observation above could not convey the true horror of Bajan history without the directness, raw idiom and lilting rhythm of local speech patterns. There is similar rawness and combativeness in Doc's response to schoolboy taunts over his eccentric mannerisms: "Uh gin tuh pelt wunnuh wit dis here rockstone, yuh black savages;" (p. 115) In one fell swoop, the pungent Caribbean idiom of Doc's vain threats captures the post-lapsarian Garden of Eden of Jean Rhys, with its dereliction of George Lamming's vision in *In the Castle of my Skin*, (1953) and the "passion and wrong" of Caribbean history, in Derek Walcott's purple phrase.

"YOU JUST NEED A MAN TO COME HOME TO LOVE YOU REGARDLESS"

Cherie Jones
The Burning Bush Women, Leeds, Peepal Tree Press Ltd., 2004. ISBN 1900715 58 9

The Burning Bush Women by Cherie Jones, who was trained as a lawyer in Barbados and Trinidad, and lived in Barbados, is divided into two sections: "Homes" consisting of nine stories with local, Caribbean events, and "Aways" containing seven stories about life in the Caribbean diaspora. Several stories employ magic realism with elements of magic and mystery that enhance effects rather than make them cryptic or puzzling. Kamau Brathwaite's term "mathemagicals" gets to the heart of the volume by recognising the author's perceptive exploration of the inner lives of black Caribbean women as wives, mothers, and daughters.

In "A Day of Deliverance" in "Homes" the narrator Ethelene Elvira Ransom is in a relationship rather than conventional marriage for, in these stories, parents are recognised largely by their biological function as "baby father" or "baby mother" rather than as parents bound by some religious, legal or other sanction to children and family. The male role in such relationships is largely financial and irregular, while females shoulder a more constant, caring and unequal burden. The plight of women in such relationships is summed up by Ethelene: "I ain't really want to kill Carson [her "husband"].

Maybe just hurt him a little bit." (p. 69) Ethelene is forty-nine years old and Carson who works on a farm in Canada, returns: "maybe three times a year, flashing gold from tooth to toe nail." (p. 69) Ethelene's problem is that Carson gets "mad, mad, mad" when she asks if he spends money on: "that woman I hear you have up there." (p. 69) Ethelene's impulse for revenge is muted, ambivalent: "sometimes, well, sometimes you just need a man to come home to love you regardless," (p. 69) which admits her toleration if not acceptance of unfairness as a woman entrapped by her gender.

Although there are some middle class women in Jones's stories, most are working class like Ethelene who describes her work as a maid: "You ever had to clean a house from top to bottom that wasn't yours...to make things for other people dinner that you could never afford for your family? You ever had to wait around in a kitchen till other people finish the dinner you make for them...you ever had to take the bus when it raining bad and you does get sick easy...and Mr Vincent [her employer] not even saying 'let me drop you to your house Ethelene.'"(p. 72) Eventually, Ethelene stabs Carson on one of his rare visits home; but he does not press charges, and she contemplates taking a course which could help her earn more money: "to tell Carson to keep his lazy behind in Canada if he wants to."(p. 76)

In addition to gender problems of humiliation at work, and lack of independence at home, Ethelene suffers from exploitation through values based on race and colour, as we see from her daughter Nora: "She [Nora] ain't really mine – her mother is some white German woman Carson take up with one time that make his baby and left it...Nora is the colour of milky tea and she have big cat eyes." (p. 73) Combined with her sexuality, Nora's colour becomes a potent weapon: "And my Nora had some men. Black men. White men. Businessmen. Politicians. The only kind of man Nora never had was a poor man," (p. 73) and she finally goes off with her lover, a pilot, to train as an air hostess.

In "Aways," the fate of middle class women is not much brighter: in "Doll," the female narrator describes her lesbian friend Jane who: "has one son ...from a man who is not present other than financially, and so does not complicate their lives, and one pretty daughter from a fleeting union before she met me." (p. 130). Several stories address more aggressive attitudes for example, "Blind" whose young narrator is sternly upbraided by her mother Miss Marie: "Don't you be trying no stupidness with me, gal. I will fix your ass proper. Ain't tekking no foolishness from you." (p. 107)

Such aggression may conceal inner feelings of hurt and pain, as revealed in "Future Imperfect" where the female narrator is surprised: "That a husband might never come. Or that the father of my son would be married and painfully absent from our lives. That was not the way I had imagined it." (p. 126) If this narrator's disappointed expectation is anything to go by, the surface quality of toughness, fortitude, even aggression, in stories, in *Burning Bush Women* mask immovable sadness deep inside.

UNITY OUT OF CARIBBEAN DIVERSITY

Jasbir Jain & Supriya Agarwal, Eds
Writers of the Caribbean Diaspora: shifting homelands, travelling identities, New Delhi, Sterling Publishers Private Limited, 2008, pp. 288, ISBN 97 8-81-207-3610-8.

Writers of the Caribbean Diaspora: shifting homelands, travelling identities consists of twenty essays on Anglophone Caribbean literature, mainly by female Indian scholars, two of whom have edited the volume. Although the essays take in Caribbean writers who live abroad, the volume casts a wider net that includes George Lamming who lived abroad briefly before returning to his native Barbados, and deceased writers like Seepersad Naipaul (who never lived abroad), Samuel Selvon, Shiva Naipaul and Jean Rhys. Most of the writers considered are Indian-Caribbean since the volume appears to have originated from a seminar on Indian-Caribbean writing. African-Caribbean writers such as Caryl Phillips, Paule Marshall, Austin Clarke and Jamaica Kincaid were later added to give the volume a more (ethnically) representative Caribbean look.

The volume opens with pieces by two Indian-Guyanese cousins, Cyril Dabydeen who reflects on his personal experience in "Shaping the Environment: Sugar Plantation or Life After," and David Dabydeen who comments on "Teaching West Indian Literature in Britain." *Writers* then settles down to articles exclusively by Indian critics, except for a short comment on V.S. Naipaul by Cyril Dabydeen, and an interview with the Indian-Trinidadian author Ramabai Espinet by Elaine Savory.

One doesn't have to get too far into the volume before being struck by the sophistication of its writing and avid enthusiasm for feminist or critical theory gleaned not only from internationally known Indian authors like Homi Bhabha or Gayatri Spivak, but from Europeans such as Derrida, Lacan and Foucault, and black theorists like Henry Louis Gates Jr. and Frantz Fanon. Even more striking is an instinctive identification with common themes in West Indian literature, for instance in "Rites of Passage: George Lamming's 'In the Castle of my Skin,'" in which Nidhi Singh finds apt expression for the feudalistic, social structure of colonial Barbados by comparing Lamming's Barbadian peasants to: "the animals by the end of George Orwell's *Animal Farm*." (p. 139) Only someone steeped in the devilish workings of colonial victimisation would recognise the "manipulation and exploitation" (p. 139) of communist totalitarianism as historic building blocks of British Caribbean colonial society.

Essays on novels by Selvon show equally revealing insight into Caribbean ethnicity. In her discussion of Selvon's *Those who eat the Cascadura*, M. Rosary Royar writes: "The European, the African and the Indian races commingle in the soil of Trinidad only to practice their separateness;" (p. 145) and in an essay on Selvon's *An Island is a World*, Charu Mathur observes that the author's characters: "are caught in a bewildering web of relations in a semi-plural, multicultural world." (p. 174) The lure of creolisation, as acknowledged at least by Mathur, adds to the complexity of Caribbean ethnicity. What is again impressive is the genuine engagement of both critics with this ethnic dilemma. False, escapist or perfunctory solutions are shunned when Mathur claims that Selvon's characters:"do not nurture any sentimental notion of their island as being a happy melting pot which can teach the world how to celebrate life," (p. 174) a clear-eyed opinion that shows genuine understanding of an endemic ethnic problem that still bedevils Caribbean society, especially in Guyana and Trinidad & Tobago.

Two short appendices in *Writers,* "Indenture or Slavery?' and "Indian Colonial Emigration," by the revered Indian leader M. K. Gandhi, illuminate the historical and cultural connection between India and overseas communities of Indians such as those in the Caribbean; for Gandhi's comments come out of heated debates on Indian indentured immigration among Indian leaders during his lifetime, and may help to explain the interest of Indian scholars in West Indian literature. They may also explain why, in her examination of Seepersad Naipaul's stories, Purabi Panwar claims that Hindu sectarian disputes from Northern India had a direct impact on Indian-Trinidadian society.

The interest of Indian scholars in African-Caribbean writers suggests their wider concern with general effects of colonial injustice. Asma Shamail's essay on Paule Marshall's novel *Praisesong for the Widow,* for example, reflects strong awareness of:" the [adverse] consequence of cultural displacement for [Caribbean] people of African descent," (p. 177) and Shamail reflects satisfaction and relief over Marshall's: "imaginative reconstruction of African history and culture to establish an underlying unity that links all people of African descent." (p. 179) Similarly, in her essay on Austin Clarke's novel *The Polished Hoe,* C. Vijayshree recognises that Clarke's heroine Mary: "sees her ancestry linked to Africa through her Great Gran who she often heard mumbling prayers in a strange language, which Mary comes to recognise as an African language." (pp. 254-255)

In their Introduction, the editors of *Writers* announce their aim: "to provide a chronological history of the Caribbean and give representation to writers of different affiliations living now in different host cultures." (p. 6) The chronology is a tall order which may get side-tracked when George Lamming's first novel In the Castle of my Skin (1953), for instance, is discussed after the work of Caryl Phillips (1980s and 90s), or Selvon's novels (1950s and 60s) after Shiva Naipaul's *The Chip Chip Gatherers* (1973); but the editors' assembly of Caribbean writers of African, Indian and European descent, living in Canada, Britain and the US, seems as representative a mix as one can wish for out of a field of such extraordinary ethnic and geographical variety.

Writers of the Caribbean Diaspora: shifting homelands, travelling identities is a brave exercise that makes a valuable contribution to Caribbean literary studies through its incisive and lucid writing, because of its informed theoretical analysis, and most of all because of a sympathetic point of view evidently inspired by a shared (Indian) experience of colonial injustice. It was no doubt this point of view that guided the editors too in their selection of topics and writers, and their organisation of the entire volume. For them to achieve consistency, not to say unity, out of such diversity is remarkable.

BEYOND A SMALL PLACE

Cyril Dabydeen, Ed
Beyond Sangre Grande: Caribbean Writing Today, Toronto,
TSAR Publications, 2011, pp.226 ISBN 978-1 894770-66-8

Beyond Sangre Grande: Caribbean Writing Today consists of
selections of fiction and poetry from writers who are either
Caribbean-born or connected to the Caribbean through
migration or family links; and its editor, a Guyanese-Canadian
author, novelist, poet, and anthologist, has lived in Canada for
more than forty years. "Sangre Grande," literally "great blood"
in Spanish, is a town in North-Eastern Trinidad which, in one
explanation, got its name as a site where much blood was spilt
after a battle between Spanish conquerors and indigenous
Amerindian-Trinidadians. Another version claims that
Spanish surveyors discovered a river with water, the colour
of blood, near to the site. Dabydeen's title also recalls V. S.
Naipaul's plea for writing to: "extend beyond a 'small place"
(p. x) in order to achieve true significance.

Work from the forty-three authors selected in *Sangre
Grande* identifies essential Caribbean topics such as
colonialism, immigration, poverty, race, colour, ethnicity,
homelessness and especially creole speech and language. As
the editor announces in his Introduction: "The choices in this
anthology are aimed at giving the reader some sense of the
[social, cultural, literary] tradition which we have come to
know." (p. xii) But Dabydeen is also keen to promote a view of

the contemporary Caribbean: "without an obvious or artificial generational divide," (p. xii) where the: "overriding criterion of selection is aesthetic quality." (p. xiii)

Classic Caribbean writers are not neglected, for example, Kamau Brathwaite's verbal and other technical gymnastics in "How Europe under developed AFRICA," Derek Walcott's vibrant mixing of cultures in "The Sadhu of Couva," Austin Clarke's celebration of the cultural dynamics and dilemmas of migration in "If the Bough Breaks," and Selvon's genius for self-parody in "Ralphie at the Races" are all represented, as well as Willie Chen's hilarious low-life romp in "The Stickfighter, Olive Senior's sensitive study of polarities of colour/class, town/ country in "The Two Grandmothers," Zee Edgell's compelling documentation of colonial brutality in "My Uncle Theophilus, and Elizabeth Nunez's subtle evocation of the growing complexity of "home" for diasporic Caribbean people in "The Illusion of Home."There are also poems from Opal Palmer Adisa, Edward Baugh, Madeline Coopsammy, Fred D'Aguiar, Ramabai Espinet, Claire Harris and many others. Suffice to say that Dabydeen includes some of the best known Caribbean authors of our time.

In one of the best poems in the volume, "Two Love Poems," we relish the sure touch of Mark McWatt who catches, with penetrating particularity, something as elusive and ineffable as the sensation of love. Both poems argue for the primacy of the actual experience of love over, for instance, mere professions of it in literature. In the first poem, McWatt's persona is a writer like himself who laments: "the sorrow of channelling all of your desire / into such dry tombs fashioned from paper," (p. 151) and in the second poem, the persona speaks of his soul rediscovering: "that surprising peace / beyond the contrivance of composition." (p. 152) Pure experience is all, uncluttered by human meddling or artifice.

Similarly, in Pamela Mordecai's story "Cold Comfort" about job hunting by a newly-arrived Jamaican immigrant, in a presumably North American city, the unnamed narrator takes short breaths as she tells her story, to silently express her deepest thoughts to an absent grandmother. The narrator is looking for a job as cook or waitress, but does not like the cold, North American weather: "Drilling me joints like the lectric hammer the roadworks people-them use to bruck up asphalt and cement when them fixing leaking pipe and thing."(p. 153) Neither does she like other aspects of her inhospitable, new environment: "These people navel string cut pon one thing - money."(p. 157) Mordecai's mordant humour is hilarious yet deeply sympathetic toward her heroine who is buffeted by historical forces she does not even begin to understand. When a prospective employer asks about her knowledge of *nouvelle cuisine*, for instance, she replies: "Know about who cousin, sir? Nouvel cousin? Me don't know nobody name 'Newvel' and for sure me don't know him cousin." (p. 155)

The vision of the contemporary Caribbean in *Sangre Grande* is an updated one of people originally from old continents of the world, Africa, Asia, Europe, thrown together either on the edge or on islands off the edge of a new continent, and journeying onward to places further afield where fresh challenges await them. Their unshakeable will to live is seen not only as a Caribbean phenomenon, but one found in people all over the world.

The excerpt from Marina Budhos's novel *Tell us We're Home* is typical. Mrs. Lal, an Indian-Trinidadian immigrant, lives in the US working as housekeeper for well-to-do American families. When she first arrived, Mrs Lal: "signed up with a home aide agency putting aside fifty dollars a week to send to her own mother in Trinidad." (p. 16) As she works, she advises her daughter Jaya: "Don't you be like those American kids. So spoiled. Wasteful. Designer clothes and doing drugs and bad things;" (p. 15) and when, at the end, her employer falls ill, and Mrs. Lal again counsels Jaya: "we don't have time to be cowards in this life. Not the life that was handed to us, a widow mother and a daughter. We got to be strong," (p. 20) her creed is one for all immigrants, not only those from a small place like the Caribbean.

UNRELIEVED DOOM AND GLOOM

Eric Walrond
Tropic Death, Toronto, Collier-Macmillan Ltd., 1972, pp.192.
(First published in 1926.)

Tropic Death, a collection of ten stories by Eric Walrond (1898-1966), appeared in 1926 as the first and only full length work of an author who was born in Guyana, but moved with his (Guyanese) father and (Barbadian) mother to Barbados where he first attended school. Walrond continued school in the Canal Zone, Panama, where he later worked as a journalist. In 1918, he moved to New York, studied at City College and Columbia University, and was deeply influenced by Marcus Garvey's Universal Negro Improvement Association. Preoccupied with the "plight of the Negro," he established himself as a prolific writer on racial issues for a wide variety of magazines in the 1920s, and when *Tropic Death* g published to great acclaim, he reached a pinnacle of fame that brought him recognition as a member of the Harlem Renaissance.

"Tropic Death," title both of Walrond's collection and its final story, implies that life for his characters, chiefly black or brown workers in Caribbean, colonial territories, in the early decades of the last century, consisted mostly of unremitting toil to keep body and soul together. Toxic, colonial issues of class and colour also ensured that Walrond's characters lived on the edge of poverty, sickness and starvation, never far away from death. "Drought," the first story, paints a stark picture of

Sissie running: "a house on a dry-rot herring bone, a pint of stale, yellowless corn meal, a few spuds," and "thumping the children around for eating scraps, of food cooked by hands other than hers." (p. 26) Such was their hunger that one child, Beryl, dies from eating marl or dust from crushed stone.

In "Panama Gold" fire spreads from a canefield to burn down Poyah's shop while he is still inside, and in "The Yellow One" where a mestizo Cuban helps a mixed blood woman La Madurita during their voyage by boat from Honduras to Jamaica, a fight erupts between a Negro and another light-skinned Cuban, and La Madurita's death in the ensuing crush is casually dismissed by the author's clinical comment: "In the scuffle the woman [La Madurita] collapsed, fell under the feet of the milling crew." (p. 66)

In "Wharf Rats" too the chief characters, a St. Lucian family in Panama, face overwhelming odds. Possibility of a blossoming love affair promises to relieve tension over their struggle for survival, but when a son of the family, Philip later dives into the sea for coins thrown by tourists from a ship, he is devoured by a shark. Again, Waldron's terse comment betrays stoic acknowledgment of the adversity that, evidently, appears all that his characters can expect out of life: "it [the shark] bore down upon him with the speed of a hurricane. Within adequate reach it turned, showed its gleaming belly, seizing its prey." (p. 84) Nothing could be more under-stated or coldly matter-of-fact.

Similar satirical wit takes a grim turn in "The Palm Porch" where Miss Buckner's sombre combination of false respectability and evil cynicism prevail when one of the clients in her brothel, a drunken English vice-consul, proves embarrassing, and is later found dead (no doubt following orders from Miss Buckner,) and quickly removed from her premises. This fictional world of unrelieved doom and gloom also appears in "Subjection" where Ballet objects to the cruel treatment of a fellow worker by their supervisor, a white American marine at the Panama Canal site, while other workers who know what is good for themselves keep very quiet. As expected, Ballet is later shot, execution style, by the marine and, in typically laconic fashion, all that we learn from the Canal Record is that: "the Department ... kept the number of casualties in the recent native labor uprising down to one." (p. 112)

Walrond's terse and tough-minded portrayal of the grim fate of African-Caribbeans in the Caribbean and the US, at the turn of the twentieth century, fifty years before the Civil Rights movement, and a full century before the election of a black American president, is unvarnished truth seen, perhaps most starkly, in the title story when Sarah Bright and her son arrive in Panama from Barbados, looking for her husband, only to find him in the depths of deprivation facing a slow, horrible death from leprosy.

Hints of obeah are most prominent in three stories: in "The Black Pin" two feuding black female neighbours discover how obeah can be re-directed to achieve revenge-justice; in the grotesque ending of "The White Snake" the only story set in Guyana, a woman's baby becomes "the fresh dead body of a bloaty milk-fed snake the sheen of a moon in May; " (p. 143) while in "The Vampire Bat," following his arrogant dismissal of obeah as blind superstition, a white West Indian soldier, Bellon Prout, freshly returned home from service in the Boer war, is killed by a vampire bat.

The resounding literary success of *Tropic Death* is due mainly to brilliantly precise writing. Walrond uses simple words with exact meanings, and intersperses songs, rhymes, hymns, legends and folktales which, along with phonetic creole speech, make for a lively narrative that catches the full richness of Caribbean oral traditions. One example of the author's expertise is his original creolising of the convention of the heroic or epic simile from classical poetry in "The Black Pin" where he evokes the full extent of Zink Diggs's devastation of her neighbour's property: "No rock engine, smoothing a mountain road, no scythe let loose on a field of ripened wheat, no herd of black cane cutters exposed to a crop, no saw, buzzing and zimming, could have outdone Zink Diggs's slaying and thrashing and beheading every bit of growing green," (p. 124) all this, directly in front of the victim, Diggs's hapless neighbour April, who can only stand by, open-mouthed and helpless, disbelieving and defeated. That a writer of Walrond's calibre was silent for the entire second half of his life when his talent was in its prime, remains, probably, the greatest tragedy in Guyanese or West Indian literature!

DIVIDE AND CONQUER

Barry L. Sukhram
Divide and Conquer: The Split in the People's Progressive Party of British Guiana and the Cold War, Hertford, Hansib Publications Limited, 2013. pp.114.
ISBN 978-1 – 906910-67-5.

Barry Sukhram's *Divide and Conquer: The Split in the People's Progressive Party of British Guiana and the Cold War* discusses the PPP's split and refers to works by many commentators, for example, Leo Despres, Peter Newman, Roy Glasgow, Reynold Burrowes and Dr. Cheddi Jagan himself who was leader of the People's Progressive Party (PPP) from its formation in 1950 to his death in 1997. There are also useful Appendices, especially Appendix E which consists of an abridged and extremely rare version of Dr. Jagan's fateful speech to the Congress of his party in 1956, which foreshadows Guyana's political future like the apple in the garden of Eden that predestines human separation from God. Analysis then follows of dismissal of the PPP government by Sir Alfred Savage, the Governor, in October, 1953, the first step leading to the party split in 1955.

The author, Guyanese-born Barry Sukhram, has lived in the U.K. since 1960, and is an activist in the Caribbean community, in London, where he is Vice-Chair of the Jeff Crawford Foundation that supports black youths. Sukhram conceals neither his activism nor his political sympathies, as we can see from the joint dedication of his book to his family and to the: "late and much lamented Marxist President of Guyana Dr. Cheddi Jagan."

Governor Savage's dissolution of the PPP Government which went hand in hand with his suspension of the Constitution is considered together with the split within the PPP to: "explore whether there was any linkage between these events and the Cold War and how they affected the local, Guyanese struggle for self-government from the Colonial Power." (p. 13) The major reason for dissolution and suspension was the alleged threat of a communist coup in B.G. feared by the British Conservative Government, led by Sir Winston Churchill. According to the Governor's official statement, the suspension was necessary: "to prevent communist subversion of the Government and a dangerous crisis both in public order and economic affairs." (p. 32) There were many other lesser charges as well, for example, fomenting strikes for political ends, attempting to oust established trade unions by legislative action, and planning to secularise Church schools and re-write textbooks to give them a political bias.

Sukhram methodically rebuts each charge with cool, convincing evidence. In the case of the main charge about communism he quotes aims from the PPP manifesto, for example: "the encouragement of foreign capital; the development of agricultural machinery stations to aid small farmers; an educational system to suit the local environment and to prevent children becoming "displaced snobs"; the protection of civil liberties, including the right of access to all kinds of political literature."(p. 30) To prove there was nothing subversive in these aims Sukhram quotes the British socialist journal the *New Statesman* which claimed that, in terms of its welfare proposal, the PPP programme had been recommended by the British Government's own Venn Commission in its recommendations for changes in British Guiana in 1949.

As for "a communist plot" or "communist subversion" such talk did not cut any ice even in British Conservative journals such as *The Spectator* and *The Economist*. *The Spectator* claimed, for instance: "Though Dr. Jagan emerges as beyond all doubt a potential Guy Fawkes his gunpowder and his plot are still missing. It is one thing to encourage a strike and to incite a mob; but it may still be another to plan a Communist coup." (p.38) But local anti-communist hysteria was influenced by colonial mimicry especially among urban middle class, mostly African Guyanese. Sukhram mentions a statement by W.O.R. Kendall, an African-Guyanese member of the New Democratic Party in the House of Assembly: "I say now on behalf of all right-thinking responsible persons in this country that the quicker this Constitution is taken away from us the better it will be. "(p. 40) This just kowtows to superior British power by playing right into the hands of a jingoistic British Prime Minister who, through the classic tactic of dividing and ruling, foists a charge of communist subversion on a tiny and utterly powerless, British, Caribbean, colonial outpost. The real tragedy was that toy pistols used by the PPP provoked a response of real guns and armaments from one of the oldest, most powerful, European empires in the world.

Yet it was not simply a case of evil imperialists versus innocent, weak natives. So far as the split is concerned, the PPP itself was partly to blame. The party: "was composed of different classes, interests, Marxists, socialists, workers, farmers; in short it embraced more than one political ideology." (p. 27) Some professional members: "disapproved of the cruder forms of communism adopted by other members." (p. 28) Opportunism was rife: "The career of Dr. Latchmansingh suggests he entered politics for reasons of personal advancement rather than for any desire to be of service." (p. 28) Sukhram stresses that, from the beginning: "there were disintegrative forces at work" ...in the party, and that: "All forces, both local and overseas, were, in varying, unspecified degrees, responsible" (p. 62) [for the dissolution/suspension.] He concludes: "The tragedy of British

Guiana in 1953 is that the PPP was not a Marxist party but one that behaved as if it was." (p. 69) If the party was Marxist, not to say communist: "it would not have confused electoral strength with political power nor substituted revolutionary zeal and rhetoric for careful analysis."

Perhaps the best feature of *Divide and Conquer* is its conciseness. One third of the already short text is devoted to appendices with only about seventy-five pages of commentary by the author. Although Sukhram names neither victims nor villains individually, no reader will miss his message that the PPP's attempt to win Guyana freedom from colonial rule through "a total transfer of power," (p. 29) in 1953, was inspired by a mixture of idealism and naiveté that could not succeed because of inherent divisiveness in Guyanese society, with its motley assemblage of people and different languages and cultures, transported from old continents to the Caribbean, where they were mixed together willy-nilly, and suppressed and exploited over four centuries.

"LIFE ON EARTH IS THE NIGHT, AND THE DAYTIME IS ELSEWHERE."

Sharon Maas
The Small Fortune of Dorothea Q, U.K. Ickenham, Bookouture, 2015, pp.480. ISBN: 978-1- 909490-58-1

The Small Fortune of Dorothea Q follows a blockbuster tradition set by previous novels of Sharon Maas, for example, *Of Marriageable Age,* (2000) *Peacocks Dancing,* (2002) and *The Speech of Angels.* (2003) The title "Small Fortune" refers to the unique value of the "B.G. One cent Magenta" stamp produced when Guyana was still British Guiana or B.G. (until independence in 1966) and a shipment of new stamps from Britain failed to reach the colony. The "Magenta" was part of a replacement batch of stamps printed locally and, in order to prevent forgeries, hand-signed by postal clerks one of whom was the author's great-great grandfather.

Activities of Maas's chief characters in *Small Fortune,* all members of the (fictional) Quint family, are observed over three generations, and across continents, in Guyana and Britain (London.) Maas's narrative technique is challenging: not only does she employ three narrators, the matriarch Dorothea Quint, her daughter Rika, and Rika's daughter Inky, but each narrator speaks from a different perspective of place (either B.G. or London) and time, from the 1930s and 1950s (Dorothea), the 1960s (Rika), and the 1990s (Inky). There is risk of confusion, for instance, when we have to abruptly connect events from Inky's narrative, in the 1990s, to those from Dorothea in the 1930s and 1950s, or from Rika in the 1960s to Inky in the 1990s; but through extraordinary skill, if not genius, Maas ensures that these connections come through with flying colours of coherence and smoothness, in almost every case.

The technique pays rich dividends in creating suspense, and ensuring that chronology is neither sacrificed nor diminished. Events in *Small Fortune* properly begin in the 1930s, in Georgetown, where values of race, colour and class prevail in Dorothea's family and friends, members of a coloured, brown or mixed blood (chiefly African/ European) group that claims status as the colony's urban middle class through employment in business, the civil service, professions and clergy. In the 1950s, however, an era of decolonisation beckons with election of a mass-based party, the Peoples Progressive Party (PPP) which threatens to transform B.G.'s feudalistic, colonial, social structure. But the new government is quickly quashed by British rulers, with the aid of troops, introducing a new era of change, with Guyanese becoming dispersed through migration to richer countries like Britain and the US. Although perhaps driven by personal as well as political motives, Dorothea and her family are part of this migration.

In *Small Fortune*, Dorothea Quint (née van Dam) has four children: twin sons, Norbert and Neville, who migrate, to England and the US respectively; a daughter Rika who leaves for London, in the 1960s, in secret and mysterious circumstances; and Rika's sister, Marion, who cares for her ageing mother, Dorothea, in the family home, in Georgetown, while her brothers and sister are abroad. It is the combined effect of Dorothea's secret hoarding of the one cent Magenta stamp, over decades, and Rika's self-enforced silence about her early life in B.G., during long years in London, that spark travel and tribulation, thrilling suspense, and a clawing climax in *Small Fortune*.

Since it is not fair to give away the climax of the novel to prospective readers, suffice to say that suspense is first sniffed by Inky soon after her grandmother Dorothea moves in to live with her and Rika in London, in the 1990s. For Inky was born in London, and at the age of eighteen, knows nothing of Guyana or her relatives there: all she senses is a "capsule of venom" (p. 241) in Rika and a "knot of discord" (p. 241) between Rika and her grandmother, known as "ol Meanie" because of her stubborn, erratic, cantankerous ways. Inky correctly detects the suppressed tension between her Mum and grandmother that later inevitably explodes.

What Inky does not know is the colonial family history that produces tension: Dorothea was Minister of Women's Progress in the short-lived PPP government of B.G. in 1953, and later achieved fame as a crusading advocate and champion of women's rights; Rika, on the other hand, a girl of merely sixteen when she left B.G. for London, was "a misfit, an outsider bumbling as ever," (p. 132) who read "unusual texts by the Christian Mystics, and the Sufis and the great sages of India, Shankara and Ramakrishna and Ramana Maharshi; "(p. 131) Rika's closest friend was Rajan an Indian-Guyanese whose mother worked as a maid in the Quint household.

Although full details of the novel's dénouement are not revealed here, we can surely imagine the revolutionary impact of Rika's relationship with the son of her family's maid on Guyana's deep-seated, feudalistic, colonial ethics: a potential for uncertainty, dispersal or migration that stems from a shifting, deeply disturbing sense of home. Dorothea sums up this impact in a deceptively simple question: "if you don't know where you come from how you going know where you going?" (p. 335)

As a South Londoner, Inky agonises over the effect of migration on her mother, whether it is caused by her relatives' greed for the small fortune of the Magenta stamp, or their dispersal into homelessness from Guyana: "she [Rika] had left *her territory* at only sixteen! ... Was the texture of Guyana merged into her consciousness as South London was in mine? Did she deny that sense of home... and if so, was she somehow damaged, stunted, broken? Who was she? ... Maybe deep down inside she missed that sense of home. And family. Who were all these people Gran [Dorothea] constantly talked about?" (pp. 237-238) More troubling still, Inky senses a paradoxical effect of homelessness on herself: "I grew nostalgic for a family, a home I'd never known." (p. 239)

"I HAD COLLAPSED…AS A LITTLE GIRL AND STOOD UP A WOMAN"

Sharon Maas
The Secret Life of Winnie Cox, Ickenham, UK, Bookouture, 2015, pp.413. ISBN: 978 - 1 -910751 - 51 - 0

The Secret Life of Winnie Cox is a prequel to Sharon Maas's fifth novel *The Small Fortune of Dorothea Quint* (2015) in which Dorothea appears as an eccentric grandmother playing a pivotal role in action that not only lasts from the 1930s to the 1990s, but jumps back and forth between London/ England and Georgetown/Guyana. By contrast, events in *Winnie Cox* are anchored mostly on one fictional sugar plantation" Promised Land," in Berbice, Guyana, during the decade immediately preceding World War One. In her "Letter from Sharon", at the end of *Winnie Cox*, the author also announces her novel as "the first of a trilogy" that will continue Winnie's story.

Winnie Cox offers the most complete description, in fiction, both of domestic life and politics on a Guyanese plantation, although we should not forget the author's reminder in "Acknowledgements" that: "I also had to rely on imagination and I admit to taking poetic licence." (p. 417) While other novels such as Edgar MIttelholzer's *Children of* Kaywana, (1952) about a slave rebellion against Dutch masters in 1763, or A.R.F. Webber's *Those that be in Bondage: A Tale of Indian Indentures and Sunlit Western Waters,* (1917) about Plantation "Never Out," offer vivid descriptions of fictional, Guyanese plantations, the story told by the eponymous narrator in *Winnie Cox* is more comprehensive, beginning in England with the marriage of the narrator's Austrian mother, Johanna, to her English father, Archibald Cox, son of Lord Cox of Camberley, and following the career of the narrator through her early childhood and teenage years on Plantation "Promised Land."

As so called Sugar Princesses, Winnie and her sister Yoyo (Johanna) are completely insulated from the exploitation and injustice that choke plantation workers with low wages, and the life of animals in mud floor logies. There is no denying the stark difference between white plantation employers or staff, and their coolie (Indian) workers. Only once, through a rare lapse in attention from their stern, English governess, Miss Wright, are Winnie and her sister able to witness, from the privileged safety and comfort of their plantation house, their father whipping and kicking a young coolie. The effect of such brutality on Winnie could not be more traumatic: "Something had shifted within me: a stone curtain of naivete had rolled away; a veil of sentimentality had lifted. I had collapsed on the bed as a little girl, and stood up a woman." (p. 63) In a second incident Winnie visits the logie of Nanny, her retired coolie, nurse maid, with equally traumatic results: "And Nanny! Living out her life in such foulness! The memory of Nanny burst into my consciousness with the immediacy of a bomb blast." (p. 84)

But as we may discern merely from the title of Maas's novel, the horror of plantation conditions proves to be mainly a backdrop, or external *mise-en-scène* for machinations of Winnie's inner life when, still as a teenager, she falls headlong in love with an African-Guyanese postman George Quint. The outrage of a romantic relationship between a pampered Sugar Princess and a lowly, black postman on a colonial Caribbean, sugar plantation, a few years after the end of the Victorian era, is beyond belief, and prompts an enthralling display of cunning manoeuvres that test Winnie's wit and guile, through episodes of suspense and thrills, as she pursues George who suddenly returns to Georgetown from Plantation "Promised Land" where he was only temporarily stationed. Not for nothing does the novel's title stress secrecy since what follows is a stimulating mixture of brazen adventure, and cat-and-mouse deception, spiced with the sheer ardour and excitement of young lovers' intent on subverting efforts to frustrate them!

In a deft display of technical mastery, plantation abuse is seen as part of the general injustice of colonial rule that inspires a wider feeling of shared resistance among Guyanese, hinting at genesis of a national, anti-colonial, political movement of which George is a member. The hint becomes even stronger when we realise that George is a close friend and ally of Bhim, an Indian political activist representing the rights of workers on Plantation "Promised Land." For Maas to devise a plot that ties these political strands together into one anti-colonial bundle that includes the intimate, personal affair of Winnie and George, itself a daring assault on perverse, racist colonial values, is a stroke of genius! That Bhim is shot and killed by Winnie's father, the Honorable Archibald Cox, a white expatriate plantation owner, is the final link to the novel's climax, potent with mixed feelings about the fate of Winnie's father, the future of her family, and values of justice and exploitation, liberty and captivity, right and wrong.

Even if there is a touch of anachronism about the plausible strength of Guyanese nationality that really existed in the first decade of the twentieth century, or about the revolutionary doings of political activists like George Quint and Bhim who resemble actual Guyanese political leaders from the 1940s and 50s - Dr. Cheddi Jagan and Forbes Burnham - *Winnie Cox* undoubtedly catches an atmosphere of incipient nationalism in twentieth century Guyana, before full independence was achieved in 1966.

In her planned trilogy of novels beginning with *Winnie Cox*, Sharon Maas will have achieved a fictionalised version of twentieth century Guyanese politics similar to Edgar Mittelholzer whose three Kaywana novels, survey Guyanese politics from slavery/serfdom in the 17th century to internal self-government in the 1950s. But Mittelholzer's Kaywana novels are long on politics and short on romantic relationships, just as Jane Austen's fiction is long on romance and short on political/military affairs, at a time when England was locked in a dire struggle for survival in the Napoleonic wars. If it does nothing else, *Winnie Cox* is supremely successful in blending the turbulence of political revolution with the torture of romance between two couples, Winnie and George, and Archibald Cox and his wife Johanna.

AN IRON-WILLED CHINESE MATRIARCH

Janice Lowe Shinebourne
The Last Ship, Peepal Tree Press Ltd., 2015, pp. 151
ISBN13: 0781845232467

Of five works of fiction, so far, *The Last Ship* is the fourth novel by Jan Shinebourne (née Lowe) who is of mixed ancestry, her father being Chinese, and her mother partly Chinese and Indian. If her previous novels and stories consider topics both about Chinese in Guyana, or in the Guyanese diaspora, the special achievement of *The Last Ship* is its exploration, more intensely than before, of the social, cultural, and psychological implications of mixed Chinese ethnicity, in Guyana, during the first half of the twentieth century.

In 1838, after the final emancipation of African slaves whose labour had maintained European-owned plantations in Guyana for two and a half centuries, African indentured workers were brought in from nearby Caribbean territories, Portuguese from Madeira, and Chinese from Hong Kong; but by far the largest numbers came from India. *The Last Ship* focuses on the fortunes of its chief female character, Clarice Chung, whose family arrived in Guyana on *The Admiral,* the last ship with indentured Chinese workers, in 1879. After the end of indenture, in 1917, Indians became the largest ethnic group, and the overwhelming majority of workers on Guyanese sugar plantations, while Madeiran Portuguese and Hong Kong Chinese quickly fulfilled their indenture contracts, before turning to business or professional careers chiefly in Georgetown, Guyana's capital city.

In *The Last Ship*, Clarice Chung's family are exceptional, as descendants of indentured Chinese, still continuing to live in Canefield, a fictional plantation where, as owners of the plantation shop, they still share commercial credentials with more affluent, business or professional relatives in Georgetown. Wealth and class form central threads in *The Last Ship*: Shinebourne strikes original gold through perceptive analysis of feudal structures and habits, and historic values of race, class and colour that blight all ethnic groups conditioned by a history of slavery/indenture in the Caribbean. Such analysis already exists in Caribbean fiction about Africans (Blacks) or Indians, even about the Portuguese, for example, in fiction by the Trinidadian novelist Alfred Mendes; but not about Chinese in Guyana.

Although Clarice Chung dies about half way through the action in *The Last Ship*, she survives, as a brooding presence: "Thus did Clarice continue to live like a ghost in the minds of the family she had left behind." (p. 83) Clarice is portrayed as an: "iron-willed matriarch," and her grand-daughter, Joan, hears from her aunts, Clarice's daughters-in-law, that: "Clarice was a terrible snob who had too high an opinion of herself and her clan." (p. 103) Joan is told that Clarice had thrown hot food on one daughter-in-law and threatened to kill her. Also: "She [Clarice] was a cruel and vicious woman who rejected them [her daughters-in-law] for not being fully Chinese." (pp. 103-4) Joan concludes that Clarice was "a manipulative bully," (p. 143) an opinion that carries weight since it is Joan who, many years later, makes the long, atavistic journey to Hong Kong, where she learns the awful, disillusioning truth about "precious", Chinese heirlooms that Clarice (and others) had brought and zealously preserved in Guyana.

Throughout her life in Guyana, Clarice is consumed with concern over the purity of her Chinese ancestry, measured by such artefacts as the heirlooms brought from China, and the wealth and social prestige of her businessman uncle, Arnold Chung, who lives in splendour, in Georgetown, alongside his children who have studied in England and, as Clarice proudly announces: "All turn doctor and lawyer." (p. 21) When Susan Leo approaches Clarice, proposing a marriage match between her two daughters, Mary and Lily, with Clarice's two sons, Frederick and Harold, Clarice agrees despite overweening disdain of Susan for consorting with a coolie (Indian) man. Clarice cannot resist telling Susan to her face: "Me and me family was last real Chinee come he' [Guyana] 'pon the last ship that bring Chinee people. We come here fresh, fresh, pure Chinee, we was not like all you Hakka Chinee that come here long time and get chil'ren with black an' coolie people, eat black and coolie food an' forget China." (p. 21)

Mouth-watering references to Chinese food prove that food is closely linked to purity of race and class in *The Last Ship*. Clarice's mother counsels her family about the academic success of their Georgetown relatives being linked to Chinese food: "Chinese food would keep them Chinese, keep their aristocratic blood and brains pure, make them better than anyone else."(p. 44) But elsewhere Clarice fears the creeping menace of creolisation or cultural indigenisation when she makes the hardnosed confession that coming to Guyana meant: "I had to stop being a Chinee...I had to stop talkin' like a Chinee, we had to stop eatin 'Chinese food...because this is a coolie place we livin' in. Coolie an' black." (p. 67)

This choice between sentimental preference and hard fact, imagination and reality, or ancestral ties and freedom sets the scene for an all too human drama at the heart of the novel. For, at the end of *The Last Ship*, through Joan's reflections, we see what is really left of the Chinese in Guyana: "lonely old women waiting to die, and smoking, drinking and eating themselves to death, gambling away their diminished fortunes," (p. 144) while, in Hong Kong, Joan discovers the trap of fantasy and delusion into which some Caribbean Chinese had fallen: like most Chinese in the Caribbean, Guyanese Chinese, including Clarice's family, are Hakka, not aristocratic descendants of Emperor Chengzong. Nor were Clarice's fake heirlooms fit for anything better than being dumped in the sea, or Arnold Chung's false "scroll of the yellow emperor "worth more than the ashes to which they are finally reduced by Joan. In *The Last Ship*, in spare, simple, yet poignant writing, strongly reminiscent of her third novel, *Chinese Women,* Shinebourne continues her inspired exorcism of demons from a troubled, Guyanese-Chinese past!

"AFTER WE ARE INDEPENDENT WE'LL STILL BE DEPENDENT"

Zee Edgell
Beka Lamb, London, Heinemann Educational Books Limited, 1982, pp.171 ISBN 0 435 98400 4

Beka Lamb, the first novel from Belize to achieve international attention, is by Zee Edgell who, after two further novels and numerous short stories, remains the best known Belizean author of fiction. British settlements first appeared in Belize in 1836 and 1862, after which the territory became the Crown Colony of British Honduras. The main ethnic groups are Creoles (kriols) or descendants of British colonists and their African slaves, and mestizos, descendants of the Spanish and Maya, while British Honduras, renamed "Belize" in 1973, claims both a Caribbean identity, by virtue of its common history with English-speaking Caribbean islands like Jamaica or Barbados, and a Central American identity through its geographical location surrounded by a Spanish-speaking, Central American nation like Guatemala. This ethnic, geographical and linguistic complexity has been crucial to Belize's political development especially after Guatemala lay claim to part of its territory after 1973.

Mainly through descriptions of people and places, and careful documentation of both historical and contemporary events, *Beka Lamb* furnishes a full fictional record of the history and society of Belize just before independence in 1981. Using the deceptively simple perspective of a third person narrator, Edgell assembles an assortment of episodes, mainly through flashback, in the life of her eponymously named, fourteen-year-old heroine, Beka Lamb, a creole girl who, with her family and friends, are seen against the background of a Central American British colony, during its political struggles in the late 1970s. If all this looks like a mere jumble of flashbacks, it turns out, almost magically, as a map of chronological stages in Beka's personal growth and cautious, political steps of Belize towards independence.

While she lives at home in Belize City with her father Bill Lamb, her mother Lilla, and Granny Ivy, Bill's mother, Beka and her best friend Toycie Qualo attend St. Cecilia's, a Roman Catholic Convent School established seventy-five years earlier by the Sisters of Charity, an American order, based in Rhode Island. Like Beka, Toycie also lives with her grandmother Miss Eila, illustrating matriarchal patterns of social organisation that have much in common with other British Caribbean creole societies. While Toycie and Beka are inseparable, Toycie is seventeen years old, more mature, and a very successful student who becomes pregnant by her boyfriend Emilio, and is expelled from school.

Beka, on the other hand, has psychological hang-ups, including an addiction to petty stealing, which hamper her scholastic performance resulting in her failure to pass from First to Second Form. As punishment, Beka's father cuts down a bougainvillea vine she had planted, and Beka transforms herself, repeats First Form and, by the end of the novel, passes to Second Form. On the other hand, depressed after her pregnancy, Toycie is sent to the Belize Mental Asylum which is euphemistically known as the "Sea Breeze Hotel" where, tragically, she is killed by a falling tree during a hurricane.

The tragedy of Toycie's career is matched by Beka's confession that, as a Belizean, she is subject to feelings of inferiority, failure or dependency. Nor does it help to hear from her Granny Ivy: "But nothin' lasts here [in Belize] ... 'Tings bruk down.' (p. 16) As someone over the age of sixty, Granny Ivy speaks with confidence based on long experience: "we creoles have a habit of watching for other people's lives to break down, then we laugh... If we cried every time somebody's life fall apart, this country would be called the one true valley of tears." (p. 42) Strange how close Granny Ivy's thoughts about West Indians closely match those of Moses at the very end of Samuel Selvon's novel *The Lonely Londoners*: "As if the boys laughing, but they only laughing because they fraid to cry."

Beka admits this nagging, Belizean acceptance of colonial dependency to Sister Gabriela, one of her teachers who encourages her not to withdraw from an essay contest on the work of the Sisters of Charity in Belize: "Sometimes I feel bruk down just like my own country, Sister. I start all right but then I can't seem to continue. Something gets in the way and then I drift for the longest while..." (p. 115) Dependency seems permanent when Beka quotes her father saying that: "he feels that even after we [Belizeans] are independent, we'll still be dependent." (p. 116)

Beka's dependency is rooted in her formative experience in a British colony structurally fragmented by inherited divisions of wealth, class, colour, ethnicity and language. Bitter arguments erupt in the novel, for instance, between Granny Ivy who supports the People's Independence Party (fictional name for George Price's "People's United Party" PUP) and her son Bill Lamb who shares British suspicions that the PUP may not only be communist, but may yield to Guatemala's claims over Belizean territory. Despite his British sympathies, Bill realises that the British colonial administration fostered ethnic, class and colour divisions in Belize, for example, by creating a civil service staffed mostly by creoles, while businessmen tended to be white or mestizo.

Division goes hand in hand with exploitation. "What do you do after you suck the juice out of sugar cane?" (p. 153) Granny Ivy rhetorically asks Beka. "You spit out the trash." It illustrates Edgell's perceptive intuitions and illuminating artistic insight in *Beka Lamb* to predict virtually the exact post-colonial history of many former British colonies, or at least one of their most common concerns voiced by Bill Lamb: "Hatred of British colonialism unites us now. There are so many races here now I wonder what will keep us together once they [the British] leave." (p. 96)

WEST INDIAN HEART OF DARKNESS

Ian McDonald
River Dancer New Poems, Great Britain, Hansib Publications
Limited., 2015, pp. 109. ISBN 978-1-910553-26-8

River Dancer New Poems is the sixth collection by an author
who, besides writing poems, has worked as a newspaper
columnist, edited the literary journal *Kyk-Over- Al,* produced
a novel, supervised the Guyanese sugar industry for a lifetime,
distinguished himself in international tennis, and won
recognition as Fellow of the Royal Society of Literature, not to
mention being awarded an Honorary Doctor of Literature by
the University of the West Indies. At the age of eighty-two, in
many poems in *River Dancer,* McDonald's persona now feels
burdened by urgent concern over his age that brings gnawing
awareness of the inexorable passage of time, and inevitability
of death. Mc Donald's persona wonders why we should endure
bad experiences or even good ones, that may include great
beauty, joy, happiness or love, if it is all destined to disappear.

In *The Comfort of all Things* (2012) McDonald considers
themes of physical decline within an Epicurean framework
of birth, transience, and regeneration; but since they lack due
sense of pain or urgent questing, these themes may appear
too confidently rational, lacking in natural emotion. By
contrast, poems in *River Dancer* cannot be more natural:
old age is creeping up on the persona in "Going Away," and
his imminent departure from home for a mere few months

sparks uncertainty about his safe return: "will I return in my eighties nothing is certain" Similarly, "Twentieth Anniversary" registers an heightened sense of mortality when the persona finds his wife crying, and foresees possible threat: "I cannot bear the thought/ there will come a day." (p. 29)

In "Jacob" a poem revelling in the spirited energy and avid enthusiasm of his three-year-old grandson, the persona cannot resist tempering the child's innocent thirst for life with his own fear of ageing: "it will not be long before you want to learn/ what is fear and pain and cruelty and age/ why death will be the hardest one of all. (p.34) In "Father" another family poem, this time celebrating a loving relationship with his own, ageing father, the persona cherishes their unbroken bond, but ends the poem by clutching limply at something out of reach, implying inevitable loss in their relationship: "we [the persona and his father] watched together/ where far far far far out the green and blue/ fades to grey and then to nothingness," (p. 69)

So far quotations reflect a simple, direct diction, without basic punctuation such as capital letters in *River Dancer*, except for obvious names, or commas and full stops, while lines of varying length run on and on, creating an impression of spontaneity or informality. In his Introduction, Professor Kenneth Ramchand praises the poet's technical mastery and, technically, McDonald is clearly at the top of his game, especially as a nature poet. It is not for nothing that he selects an epigraph for *River Dancer* from *The Prelude* by Wordsworth, England's greatest nature poet.

As an Edenic landscape, the Caribbean, particularly the Guyana forest, still retains value and beauty as one of the world's last resources of flora, fauna and greenhouse gases. In "White Orchids at Night" when the persona is taken by a seasoned bushman into the heart of the forest in Essequibo, at dead of night, he beholds: "candles without flame but purely bright/arrayed in timeless halls of splendour" (p. 54), and In

"Rite of Passage," during an adventure with childhood friends in Trinidad, the persona witnesses: "the trees dripping the slush of black mud/ huge crapauds hopping in the muddy pools…/ red bajack ants in angry hunting streams" (p. 74) in a heaving and tumultuous display of primordial energy, life, and movement.

But there is no escape from over-riding concern about ageing and death, for example, in "Moon in Old Age:" "I am an old man/ with pain in the gut / in contact with what may be death" (p. 70) Nor should we forget that the title poem "River Dancer" is a paean, one of several in the volume, to the poet's wife Mary Angela McDonald, to whom the entire volume is dedicated. The persona of "River Dancer" is sustained by a photo of Mary who, during his serious illness, vitally aids his recovery: "every day every single day she was by my side" (p. 105)

As a former student at Queens Royal College, one of the best Caribbean secondary schools, Cambridge University, one of the top British universities, and as poet, journalist, sportsman, captain of industry, and pro-consul of empire, McDonald belongs to a colonial élite in Caribbean society that makes him, in Conradian terms, a veritable emissary of light and learning to benighted Caribbean, creole subjects. "Cane Cutting Gang" offers a glimpse into the unequal, plantation structure that McDonald joined after leaving Cambridge: "destined to run a sugar industry" (p. 96) After workers: "swarmed around" (p. 96) complaining of hard work and late pay, a manager: "chased them back to work" (p. 96)

For all their status, wealth, power and culture, however, personae in several poems, whether out of guilt or charity, earnestly ponder the gross, all-pervading injustice of plantation inequality. In poems such as "Ram" "Prayer in Old Age" "The Potato Farmer" and "Shopping," personae mingle with impoverished, aged and worn out, plantation victims, and in "Carts" the persona's wealth and privilege prompt him to: "want to shout and throw / all my wealth in fury at them" although he realises: "I will do nothing / if I changed my life completely / what good will it do for others." (p. 95) McDonald's persona feels "a sort of death" (p. 95) in falling back on this "age-old justification;" (p. 95) but it is still morally preferable to the Kurtzian, spiritual corruption he would encourage from plantation acolytes, always eager to finagle, flatter and follow his master's voice.

"THE ROT REMAINS WITH US, THE MEN ARE GONE"

Derek Walcott
White Egrets, New York, Straus, Farrar and Giroux, 2011, pp.88

Born in St. Lucia, in 1930, poet, painter, playwright and essayist Derek Walcott, who won the Nobel prize for literature in 1992, has spent a lifetime excoriating evils of empire, for example, in poems like "Ruins of a Great House" where the persona speaks of "the abuse/ of ignorance by Bible and by sword," or yet again of "The rot [which] remains with us, the men are gone," until, at last, he yields, if not to forgiveness, a feeling of almost contented nostalgia. The evil of colonial oppression can never be healed, nor its abuse atoned for; but now, in *White Egrets*, in a poem aptly named "The Lost Empire," it is contemplated without rancour: "And then there was no more Empire all of a sudden / Its victories were air, its dominions dirt: / Burma, Canada, Egypt, Africa, India, the Sudan." (p. 36)

Walcott brings himself to recall, with something like admiring wonder, the panoply and pomp of passing, imperial glory: "there is no greater theme / than this chasm-deep surrendering of power / the whited eyes and robes of surrendering hordes, / red tunics, and the great names Sind, Turkistan, Cawnpore," (p. 36) and if we hear a hint of nostalgia, or sense a tone of sadness in the stately beat of effortless iambic pentameter, it registers the poet's calm acceptance of historical fact, without approval or regret.

In his title poem "White Egrets," the birds remind Walcott's persona that: "The perpetual ideal is astonishment," (p. 8) as they shoot into heaven: "circling above praise or blame" with "high indifference." (p. 8) Walcott no doubt remembers the 1970s, when activists divided the province of Caribbean poetry between him and their alleged champion Edward Kamau Brathwaite, and denounced him (Walcott) as an Uncle Tom for circling above praise or blame with high indifference, because he acknowledged the mixture of multiculturalism emanating out of imperial history, instead of adopting a more militant, black stance of asserting African values as prime in the Caribbean. Not that Brathwaite sanctioned Afro-centricity either, then or now.

The egret is a species of heron or long-legged, long-necked bird found both in coastal swamp areas or open country. (In Guyana and some parts of the Caribbean, it is also called the gaulding or a variation of this word.) The centrepiece of Walcott's volume is his eight-stanza title poem, focusing on his principal theme, at the age of eighty-three: the inevitability of death, and expectation of: "that peace / beyond desires and beyond regrets, / at which I may arrive eventually." (p. 6) In the mind of the persona, We do not miss the pun on "egrets" and "regrets" when the persona accepts that the birds, with all their colour and elegance, will outlive him: "They [the egrets] shall / be there after my shadow passes with all its sins / into a green thicket of oblivion."(pp. 6/7) Walcott worries not only over his approach to the thicket, but over the disappearance of previous lovers or friends: "Some friends, the few I have left, /are dying, but the egrets stalk through the rain / as if nothing mortal can affect them" (p. 9) while mortality stalks his persona's every move.

Many poems in *White Egrets* are simply given a number as title, and "46" conducts the celebrated literary vendetta between Walcott and V.S. Naipaul that has now been going on for a decade or more. Although hugely entertaining, mischief between our two most famous writers from the Anglophone Caribbean, in a bare knuckle contest is unseemly, to say the least. Walcott's persona follows up the opening line of "46" with: "Here's what that bastard [Naipaul] calls 'the emptiness'" with the description of a lush Caribbean scene, and suggests that Naipaul's image of emptiness is taken from Joseph Conrad by: "a vicious talent [Naipaul] that severs / itself from every attachment, a bitterness whose / poison is praised for its virulence." (p. 78) The persona believes that Walcott's verse, which Naipaul regards as part of the emptiness, is: "a genuine benediction as his [Naipaul's writing] is a genuine curse." (p. 78) (Who would believe that, at one time, Walcott praised Naipaul for writing the best sentence in the English language!) The only hint of abatement comes in intimation of Walcott's own mortality: "I reflect quietly on how soon I will be going," (p. 64) and his persona confesses that he wants: "to accept my enemy's [Naipaul's] atrabilious spite, / to paint and write well in what could be my last year." (p. 64)

Physical decline, mortality and transience are everywhere, as in "Barcelona" where the persona admits: "I could never join in the parade; I can't walk fast/ Such is time's ordinance. Lungs that rattle, eyes / that run." (p. 82) Yet, in "The Acacia Trees" the persona summons enough gumption to bristle at the injustice of: "doomed acres/ where yet another luxury hotel will be built / with ordinary people fenced out," (p. 11), and realise that: "these new plantations / by the sea" are no more than: "a slavery without chains, with no blood spilt." (p. 11) But there is consolation: "Happier / than any man now is the one who sits drinking / wine with his lifelong companion under the winking / stars and the steady arc lamp at the end of the pier."(p. 85)

INDEX